To Be a Man Is Not a One-Day Job

To Be a Man Is Not a One-Day Job

Masculinity, Money, and Intimacy in Nigeria

DANIEL JORDAN SMITH

The University of Chicago Press   Chicago and London

The University of Chicago Press, Chicago 60637
The University of Chicago Press, Ltd., London
© 2017 by The University of Chicago
Published 2017
Printed in the United States of America

26 25 24 23 22 21 20 19 18 17   1 2 3 4 5

ISBN-13: 978-0-226-49151-6 (cloth)
ISBN-13: 978-0-226-49165-3 (paper)
ISBN-13: 978-0-226-49179-0 (e-book)
DOI: 10.7208/chicago/9780226491790.001.0001

Library of Congress Cataloging-in-Publication Data

Names: Smith, Daniel Jordan, 1961– author.
Title: To be a man is not a one-day job : masculinity, money, and
    intimacy in Nigeria / Daniel Jordan Smith.
Description: Chicago : The University of Chicago Press, 2017. |
    Includes bibliographical references and index.
Identifiers: LCCN 2017017536 | ISBN 9780226491516 (cloth :
    alk. paper) | ISBN 9780226491653 (pbk. : alk. paper) |
    ISBN 9780226491790 (e-book)
Subjects: LCSH: Men—Nigeria—Social conditions. | Masculinity—
    Economic aspects—Nigeria. | Money—Social aspects—Nigeria. |
    Igbo (African people)—Social life and customs.
Classification: LCC HQ1090.7.N6 S65 2017 | DDC 305.3109669—dc23
LC record available at https://lccn.loc.gov/2017017536

♾ This paper meets the requirements of ANSI/NISO Z39.48-1992
(Permanence of Paper).

To Aunt Liz, Uncle Henry, Aunt Judy, and all the Jordan clan

Contents

Introduction

Beginning in the 1980s, nearly every Sunday morning, twenty to twenty-five men gathered at Owerri Sports Club to play tennis. By early afternoon, when the sun was high in the sky and the heat too oppressive for an enjoyable game, the focus shifted from sports to beer and boisterous conversation. Most of these same men also gathered many weekday evenings after work, sometimes to play tennis, but always for a night of drinking and masculine banter. The club had over two hundred members but the regular presence of a core group of about fifty assured that at least a couple dozen men congregated every day. The club was a quintessentially Nigerian space of male intimacy. Many of the men had been meeting there several times a week for years. They shared with each other their lives and thoughts—about work and family, religion and politics, community and country. I joined the club in 1989, not long after I first arrived to work on a public health project in Owerri, the capital of Imo State. I originally joined because I love to play tennis, but I soon found myself enmeshed in the full spectrum of social activities that being a member could involve.

One typical Sunday I joined about twenty men under the shade of a tree as we began the regular rituals associated with the transition from tennis to beer and the lively conversation that inevitably accompanied it. On Sundays, the members always asked the same man to mark the official beginning of drinking. They seemed never to tire of the way he pretended that the first bottles of beer were candlesticks that needed to be blessed as if the men were in church. Indeed, everyone jovially referred to this man as "our Bishop" to acknowledge the shared fun of the mock religiosity of the proceedings. Nearly all, if not all, of these men were Christians who believed in God. Some even went to church before coming to the club. The playful performance was not meant to disparage Christianity or challenge the existence or importance of God. Instead, it was a conscious celebration by the men of being at the club rather than in church or at home with their wives and children, places where aspects of their masculinity that they enjoyed at the club were held in check or even challenged. In the playful ritual to open their Sunday drinking, the men asserted the importance of their status as men and the privileges that came with it.

Owerri Sports Club was a place where an elite segment of the city's adult male population had created a masculine community in which some of the most valued qualities of being men were celebrated and rewarded. It was not just sport and drink, though they thoroughly enjoyed both. At the club, men found a space where they could converse about and congratulate each other for their successes—in business and politics, in providing for their families, and very often in their extramarital sexual behavior (which was one example of an arena of male privilege they could celebrate at the club, but not at home or at church). These were successful men. Yet even as the club seemed to be place where men basked in successful masculinity, it was also a domain where they spoke frequently and candidly about the challenges and contradictions of manhood.

One evening, early in my first year as a member of the club, a man named Uche (all people's names are pseudonyms) was recounting the recent ordeal of burying his father, emphasizing the exorbitant amount of money he spent to provide a befitting funeral. "Befitting" was an English term that was particularly common, resonant, and meaningful among the majority of Igbo-speaking people in southeastern Nigeria, who regularly switched between and mixed English and their vernacular. Men were preoccupied, indeed even obsessed, with making sure that they provided for and performed befitting rituals of the life course, such as child naming ceremonies, weddings, and funerals; that they built a house befitting their status (especially a proper building in their natal community, even if they almost never lived there); that their children be given befitting educations and their wives be provided befittingly fashionable clothing for church and the many other public occasions that animate Nigerian social life.

Uche bemoaned the escalating expectations society put on people to spend lavishly on burials—expenses that included not only huge amounts of food and drink, but also the hiring of electric generators, sound systems, performers, and tents and chairs; all carefully, if implicitly, calculated and evaluated based on whether the expenditures befit a family's, and especially a man's, status. One of the many expenses Uche had borne was hosting the club at the funeral. We showed up about fifty in number and it was expected that Uche would make sure we could eat and drink until we could take no more. He did exactly that. We each contributed to an envelope of cash to support the burial, but it did not nearly cover even just what Uche spent on us. At the same time that Uche was telling a story of lament about the costs of burials, and his mates were chiming in sympathetically with their own analogous experiences, they also rewarded him for the very behavior—and expenditures—that they all seemed to grumble about. Crates of beer were called for to celebrate Uche's successful performance and the men advised and praised Uche, saying: "You are now fully a man because you have successfully buried your father."

In this conversation, and in countless others I heard over the years, the men at the club—like men I interacted with in just about every other male-dominated setting in Nigeria—constantly fretted about the ever-increasing demands for money that were required for a befitting performance of manhood. Yet, seemingly paradoxically, men also constantly reinforced in each other the very behaviors that reproduced the valorization of money. After several rounds of beers, Uche summed up the situation with a common phrase Nigerian men shared among themselves, an expression uttered with both pride and lament: "To be a man is not a one-day job." When Uche spoke these words the other men all agreed, laughing, but also corroborating the ambivalent sentiment about the challenges of manhood.

Every Nigerian man I know recognizes that having money is essential for successful masculinity, subscribing to the widely spoken saying that "money makes a man." The ever-growing predominance of money is, however, also articulated—by men and women alike—as a perversion of important values and cultural traditions. Money is viewed as a temptation that inspires greed, feeds corruption, and undermines virtuous ethics and behavior. Even as money enables access to many of the things Nigerian men most aspire to in modern life, it also symbolizes just about everything they see as wrong with the current situation in Nigeria. For Nigerians, criticizing their country—not only their government, but also society itself—could be said to be a national pastime, and arguably nothing is more central to this critical discourse than the problems created by money. Even the wealthiest of men, who by most measures are the ones benefiting from all of Nigeria's ailments, feel the burdens of money. Indeed, nearly every Nigerian knows the saying—and recognizes some truth in it even when they are not wealthy themselves—that "with big money comes big trouble."

Fully understanding men's obsession with money, its social importance, and the often contradictory sentiments and behaviors it engenders requires not only an appreciation of its centrality in the public performance of masculinity; it also demands examining the relationship between money and intimacy. At the same time that money is integral to how men navigate their public reputations, their social status, and their political influence, it is also elemental in men's most intimate relationships—with their wives and lovers, their children, their kin, and their male friends. Money enables men to provide and care for their families, even as it is equally a primary medium for the performance of power. In Nigerian families—as much as in politics—money creates constant underlying suspicions about motives, sowing distrust in the very relationships that it supports.

The intersection of money and intimacy in men's lives in Nigeria is the focus of this book. Central to my argument is that the aspects of manhood associated with family—being a husband, father, and head of household—interconnect profoundly with other, more public arenas in which masculinity is pivotal to understanding issues of power and political economy. The image that the world has of Nigeria and the image that Nigerians themselves sometimes hold of their society coalesce dramatically around the performance of masculinity. In so many ways, articulations of manhood in Nigeria are profoundly shaped by the specter of a corrupt state and society, and by the imperative that men participate (both in response to external pressures and to satisfy their own sense of pleasure and manhood) in practices of sociality and politics that are frequently perceived to be immoral or ethically questionable (Smith 2007a; Pierce 2016). This produces paradoxes, contradictions, and seeming hypocrisies that are nonetheless, I argue, united by the structurally entrenched underpinning of manhood as a performance intrinsically linked to money.

I use the term intimacy to signal the importance of face-to-face, personal relationships in men's lives. At times, I also employ the word sociality as a synonym. With the appropriate adjectives—for example, face-to-face, interpersonal, and intimate—modifying the word sociality, it would be equally accurate to say that this book is about masculinity, money, and sociality in Nigeria. Although urbanization, capitalism, globalization, and a host of other powerful processes and trends have increased the number of social encounters in Nigeria that one might describe as superficial, impersonal, anonymous, or bureaucratic, it is striking how much of Nigerian economic, political, and social life is still characterized and influenced by the importance of close personal ties—in short, by intimacy. To the extent that modernizing forces threaten the centrality of interpersonal ties, Nigerians are often anxious about such changes and they push back (Smith 2014a). Further, even as processes like urbanization and bureaucratization transform and undermine intimate sociality in some spheres, in others—such as marriage and fatherhood—new expectations for intimacy seem to be taking hold. Whether it is in their personal lives or in their public political lives, men are navigating a changing social landscape. In the chapters that follow I show how a complex geometry of money and intimacy is at the core of the performance of masculinity in Nigeria.

Patriarchy, Politics, and the Performance of Masculinity

Symbolizing masculinity in Nigeria is the image of the "Big Man," a male figure who not only supports and has authority over his household and family, but who also caters for his political clients in the role of a patron (Smith 2001a; Daloz 2003; Diamond 2008; Pierce 2016). As Nigeria's media and the videos produced in the country's Nollywood film industry regularly portray, the expectations and behaviors associated with being a Big Man span a spectrum from the intimate realms of sexuality and domestic relations to huge public performances of wealth and consumption wherein the pageantry of masculinity as power is on display for popular consumption (McCall 2002; Haynes 2006; Okome 2007). Tellingly, Nigerian critiques of real-life Big Men often focus on their failures in the intimate realms of sex, marriage, and family as much as on their complicity in wider social problems such as corruption, political violence, and the exacerbation of inequality (Lindsay and Miescher 2003a, 18–19). Such frivolous stories might seem to protect elite men from more politically threatening criticism, and in some ways this is true. But they also reflect significant interconnections between public and private performances of masculinity, wherein a perceived failure in private executions of manhood can undermine a man's political power and vice versa.

Scholars of Africa have long recognized—and produced superb scholarship to help elucidate—the relationship between kinship and politics, and in particular the meaning and practical political significance of "wealth in people" (Bledsoe 1980; Guyer 1993, 1995a). In the political arena, something akin to the "patriarchal bargain" (Kandiyoti 1988)—the ways in which women become complicit in affording men the privileges and authority of masculinity in exchange for demanding certain social obligations that they must perform—occurs in patron-client relations. In exchange for political support, powerful men must look after their followers. But in the public sphere, as well as in their personal lives, Nigerian men are navigating significant transformations in social relations. Expectations and practices of sociality, including the nature and meaning of male privilege and power, are seemingly up for grabs. These changes in sociality are at the heart of men's anxieties about the challenges of manhood. The rise of money as the thing that makes a man—both in the intimate domains of sexuality, marriage, and fatherhood and in the public arena of patronage and politics—creates a climate of insecurity, even among men who appear to be most successful in this changing political economy.

While the relationship between money and intimacy produces contradictory pressures in men's private and public lives, in each arena it does so in somewhat different ways. In men's personal lives there has been in recent times a rise in the expectations of intimacy. As in many parts of the world, more men and women in Nigeria have come to see love and romance, as well as trust and communication, as elemental to sexual relationships, and especially to courtship and marriage (Hirsch and Wardlow 2006; Smith 2006; Cole and Thomas 2009). In their role as parents, men are increasingly likely to undertake responsibilities and develop relationships with their children that are more intimate than what they experienced with their own fathers (Osotim-ehin 1999; Smith 2014b). Men's primary identity as providers has not changed significantly, but these new forms of intimacy in the domestic sphere alter the nature of men's authority, and arguably offer women and children more leverage in household relations. Simultaneously, the fact that money has become almost the sole measure of men's ability to provide has itself created challenges to masculine authority, as the vast majority of Nigerian men struggle to keep up with their families' seemingly ever-growing demands: for escalating school fees, increasingly expensive necessities, and the ceaseless appeal of conspicuous consumption. As intimacy has become the moral and emotional currency of personal relationships, the reality that money is the hard currency necessary to make these relationships successful constantly impinges on men's closest ties.

In the public sphere men experience related, but in many ways quite different, worries about the relationship between money and intimacy. Similar to domestic life, in the public arena the specter of money with its social importance often looms as an obstacle to men's aspirations and is an object of collective concern. But while expectations of interpersonal intimacy seem to be on the rise in men's personal lives, in Nigeria's political and economic arenas many forces are at play that create less social intimacy, fostering a perception of the diminishing importance of face-to-face social relations and engendering a greater sense of anonymity and alienation. With a changing economy characterized by the spread of capitalism, the growth of wage labor, and dramatic increases in the proportion of the population living in urban places, economic life is often perceived to be conducted less and less on the basis of social relationships and more and more through the medium of money. In practice, of course, the monetization of economic life does not necessarily mean the demise of sociality, even in the economic sphere. Indeed, Nigerians are constantly engaged in activities that "resocialize" relationships in which money has become the medium of exchange. Even some of the country's notorious corruption can be usefully seen in this vein (Smith 2007a; Pierce 2016; Routley 2016). Nevertheless, Nigerians regularly express concern about money's effects on public life, and for men it permeates relationships at the center of the performance of masculinity.

In the political realm, both the distance of the Nigerian state from most ordinary people and global (and local) pressures to create a more accountable bureaucracy push against the importance of personal ties in politics and governance. In Nigeria, many men experience these changes—and the role of money—ambivalently. On the one hand, Nigerians (and international observers) often decry the politics of patronage as corrupt (Gore and Pratten 2003; Adebanwi and Obadare 2011). Elections, government appointments, and the awarding of contracts based on personal ties are seen as problematic. Exploiting political intimacy to obtain and retain money and power is commonly condemned in Nigeria, even as it is still widely practiced (Obadare 2009). On the other hand, men often also bemoan the extent to which money and the politics it has engendered have undermined a degree of integrity that was perceived to have characterized earlier forms of patron-clientelism (Ekeh 1975; Pierce 2016). Politicians are often judged as immoral not because their actions are interpreted as too cronyistic (favoring their kin or clients), but instead because they are seen as driven by greed that undermines their obligations to their followers (Obadare 2016; Pierce 2016).

Over the past twenty-five years I have continued to spend time with elites—the kind of men for whom the performance of patronage is part of expected masculine practice. But I have also spent even more time with a wide range of "ordinary" men: farmers, traders, teachers, drivers, the unemployed, and so on. In the pages that follow, I attend to ways that money and intimacy intersect for men across the socioeconomic spectrum. The performance of social class through consumption; the measure of masculinity via social support to women, children, and kin; the centrality of men's relationships with each other; and the ambivalence and contradictions that all this creates in men's lives; all these are common experiences for men in Nigeria regardless of their social position—and yet the particular ways they experience them help define their place in society, as I will argue.

Nigerian men appear to face an almost impossible set of contradictions when it comes to money and intimacy. On the one hand, in both public and private realms, money is increasingly essential to perform appropriate masculinity. On the other hand, money taints these very behaviors—personal and political—with suspicions about men's motives. The performance of masculinity requires pursuing and embracing forms of intimacy that are threatened by the same money that is necessary to sustain them.

Nigerian Masculinity(ies)

One Sunday afternoon early in 2012, I joined a number of men for a late lunch after a long service I had attended with them at a Pentecostal church in the town of Umuahia. I was conducting a research project focused on the social effects of these hugely popular churches in southeastern Nigeria. To my chagrin, studying Pentecostalism conflicted with my beloved Sunday morning tennis routine, but it also exposed me to a different arena of masculine identity and practice. Indeed, the born-again Christians with whom I had lunch—like many men who join these churches—self-consciously reject and eschew some of the same masculine behaviors celebrated in the tennis club, especially drinking and extramarital sexual relationships. There were, of course, men who bridged both worlds. Some club members belonged to Pentecostal churches and did not drink or have young mistresses. And I heard plenty of stories of men who were born-again Christians who nonetheless cheated on their wives. Such seemingly contradictory behaviors represented just a small spectrum of the diversity and complexity that must be apprehended to understand Nigerian masculinities.

Ever since R. W. Connell (1995) developed a hierarchy of masculinities—hegemonic, complicitous, marginalized, and subordinated—scholars have both mapped men into these categories and debated whether the concept of hegemonic masculinity (the "culturally exalted" form of masculinity in a given context) accurately captures patterns of male beliefs and behavior and men's experiences (Beasley 2008; Groes-Green 2012). In southeastern Nigeria, and arguably in much of sub-Saharan Africa, certain features of a hegemonic masculinity are easily recognizable and widely shared. The fundamental elements of this masculine ideal involve being a husband, father, and head of household. Above all, these roles require men to be providers, responsible for the provision of food, shelter, protection for their families, and—especially in the contemporary era—for their children's education. The notion that the socially accepted primary foundation of African manhood is the demonstrated capacity to provide for one's family has been documented in many African contexts (Morrell 2001a, 2001b; Lindsay and Miescher 2003b; Hunter 2005, 2010). Certainly for Nigeria there is ample scholarship, both historical and contemporary, that has shown that the male position as provider is central to masculine identities and practices (Berry 1985; Cornwall 2002, 2003; Lindsay 2003). Integral to the African and Nigerian ideal of man-the-provider, and indeed to Connell's concept of hegemonic masculinity, is that along with the obligation of being the provider comes the privilege and authority of patriarchy. In Connell's terms, hegemonic masculinities both mask and enable the problematic inequalities of patriarchal structures and social relations. To most Nigerian men they legitimate them.

Of course patriarchy and the extent to which it is justified through the "patriarchal bargain" (Kandiyoti 1988) or the "conjugal bargain" (Whitehead 1981) is not unique to Africa. Indeed, feminist scholars developed these terms analyzing gender in Western contexts. Many of the dynamics around masculinity, money, and intimacy explored in this book have parallels in other societies outside Africa, including in the United States (Coontz 2006; Zelizer 2005). The social construction of gender is elemental to the configuration of power and the fabric of social relations in every society, a reality that is now well established not only in anthropology, but across a range of disciplines that have probed the meanings, practices, and consequences of how societies "do gender" (Di Leonardo 1991; Fenstermaker and West 2002). I do not suggest that masculinity in Nigeria is unique. Indeed, I hope that some of what I will describe and argue about masculinity there will offer interesting comparative evidence to juxtapose Nigeria with other examples, and also provide compelling material to think about masculinity more generally. I argue that the paradoxes of masculinity in Nigeria can be best understood by examining the particular configuration of the relationship between money and intimacy as they intertwine in men's private and public lives, across social classes and a wide spectrum of social positions.

At my lunch with the men from the Pentecostal church that Sunday afternoon, the conversation touched on many aspects of masculinity. With regard to family, the men asserted that a man's position as the head of his household is God's will and evident in the Bible. While nearly all Nigerian men I know—and many women—subscribe to the notion of men's domestic authority, these Pentecostal men criticized the failures of many Nigerians to behave in ways that they said were required in men's roles as husband, father, and head of the family. Specifically, they condemned drinking alcohol, sexual infidelity, and the failure to raise children "in a good Christian way" as the main faults plaguing modern families. They said it was Christian men's responsibility to correct these problems. Several men also noted that weak manhood led to problems in women's behavior, including promiscuity, fiscal irresponsibility, and disobedience. This conversation and many others like it, as well as countless sermons I observed in Pentecostal churches, convinced me that part of Pentecostal Christianity's appeal to men was its potential to reestablish a patriarchal bargain in an era when men's authority as men appears threatened on many fronts.

While Pentecostals tended to invoke the Bible as the foundation for masculine power, many other men believed that male authority—particularly over women and children—was a pillar of "traditional" culture. Sometimes culture was referenced in ethnic or national terms. Men would start stories about masculine authority with "in Igbo culture . . ." or "in Nigeria. . . ." But frequently male privilege was characterized, with pride, as something "African," often explained to me as contrasting with what many believed was the problematic configuration of gender relations in the West. This was perhaps in semiconscious parallel (but also resistance) to the tendency in North American and European media to characterize "African" masculinity in similarly essentializing terms. When I was doing fieldwork in the mid-1990s, during and after the Fourth World Congress on Women in Beijing, many men in Nigeria jokingly referred to efforts of their wives or other women to challenge or change the nature of male authority as "Beijing." The men vowed: "Africa [or Nigeria] is not Beijing." The assertion that masculine authority—and by implication male privilege—is culturally rooted remains common in Nigeria. This view that male authority and privilege are quintessentially "African" has been observed elsewhere (e.g., see Spronk 2012 for Kenya). The material in this book will demonstrate that the claim of an African cultural foundation for masculine authority is not just an effort by men to preserve their privileges, but also a reaction to their perception that a wide spectrum of social change is threatening forms of sociality they value.

A good deal of what Nigerian men find threatening about ongoing social transformation is related to the reconfiguration of gender roles and identities. These changes are connected specifically to women's increasing access to education, their growing participation in the labor force, and the emergent power they have in both domestic and public arenas. While a rich literature shows that West African women in general and Igbo women in particular have long had more economic opportunities, political agency, and domestic authority than is often recognized (van Allen 1972; Amadiume 1987; Oyĕwùmí 1997), it is also undoubtedly the case that recent rises in female education, rapid urbanization, a changing economy, and the circulation of ideas that can be described as feminist have significantly changed the gendered landscape in Nigeria. Further, such changes suggest even more dramatic transformations are possible in the future. Men are by no means entirely opposed to these changes. Indeed, many men welcome female education, women's income-generating power, and their more equal partnership in public and private endeavors. But large numbers of men also feel that important aspects of masculine privilege, authority, and identity are in jeopardy. Assertions that African masculinity must be preserved are common.

Furthermore, the specific contours of the "African" manhood that emerge through such discursive claims are, unsurprisingly to anthropologists, inflected as much by an idealized notion of the past as they are by any kind of "real" heritage. Yet to reduce this to mere historical fantasy or even to a dialectic between imagined forms of the past and the forces and social pressures of the present would, however, still be too reductionistic. Instead, I seek to explore the multiple, overlapping, and competing pressures, desires, moralities, and social imaginaries that animate masculinity in Nigeria. In doing so, I connect the realities of how men navigate masculinity to the complex geometry of money and intimacy, in both their private and public lives and in their relationships with women and other men.

Over the past twenty-five years it has become common to begin any scholarship about masculinity with the claim that men have been understudied, at least explicitly as men (Gutmann 1997). Studies of African masculinity typically suggest that the dearth is even greater and the attention even more recent than in other parts of the world (Lindsay and Miescher 2003a; Ouzgane and Morrell 2005). While I believe this is accurate, I'm not sure it is any longer possible to justify the study of African masculinity on the basis of an absence of previous scholarship. By now there is a considerable body of excellent research on African men, much of which I try to build on in this book (Morrell 1998, 2001a; Simpson 2009; Hunter 2004, 2005, 2010; Wyrod 2008, 2016). But this growth in good work on African men has only reinforced the important reasons to study masculinity. In the next two sections I offer further examples and analysis to explicate the centrality of money and intimacy in contemporary Nigeria, setting the stage for the ensuing chapters that will explore these dynamics across a range of social contexts, life-course positions, and individual men's lives.

Intimacy and Masculinity in Contemporary Nigeria

Chidozie, a barber with a small salon in the peri-urbanizing community of Ubakala on the outskirts of the Abia State capital of Umuahia, explained to me how he sometimes bathed his wife. In Ubakala, where there is no running water, this meant pouring water over her with a cup from a bucket—water he warmed by heating a kettle on a kerosene stove—gently soaping her body, and carefully rinsing her the same way he wet her. In response to a question I had asked him about the ways he showed love for his wife, Chidozie described this practice with fondness. In 2004, I interviewed about two dozen married men in Ubakala and in Owerri, a city about an hour away. The interviews were part of a larger project about marriage and the risk of HIV (Smith 2007b, 2009; Hirsch et al. 2009). Investigating men's sexual and romantic relationships with their wives, but also with their extramarital lovers, was a main focus of the research. I had anticipated many of the narratives men told me about their extramarital relationships, stories in which having outside lovers was seen as a male prerogative, and in which both sexual conquest and the economic wherewithal to afford girlfriends were presented, and widely accepted, as markers of successful manhood. I was more surprised by men's stories of marital intimacy. In private, a significant minority of men described marital intimacy in terms that were markedly different from the dominant patriarchal narratives in men's public discourse.

I interviewed each man in the study at least three times, and in many cases followed up with lots of informal interaction. Among the men who talked about marital intimacy in ways that appeared to contradict the dominant discourse, which focused on extramarital lovers or men's positions as the head of the household, they described not only practices of interpersonal caregiving such as washing a woman's body or clothing, cooking meals, or massaging an aching back, but also their wives' roles as confidants and partners in household decision making. The joint project of building a family and raising children often featured in these men's accounts of their marriages, with men acknowledging their wives' vital role in a shared project. These men described emotional as well as physical intimacy, and in some cases told me about forms of sexual intimacy that illustrated what they perceived to be examples of love in their marital relationships. Most of these men did not reject entirely the dominant patriarchal conception of gender relations. All the men I talked to saw themselves as head of the family. They believed that a man's position as provider was paramount. But some men acknowledged women's contributions more than others, including their monetary contributions. Nonetheless, none imagined it was possible for a marriage to survive a woman's infidelity, while nearly all felt it could survive a man's unfaithfulness. Still, these less "traditional" men—most of whom were in a younger cohort—saw their marriages as "love" marriages; they viewed their wives as equal (or at least more equal) partners.

In retrospect, I should not have been as surprised as I was by these "new men." Literature in the social sciences in general, in anthropology in particular, and in African Studies most relevantly, has pointed to various dimensions—and the causes and consequences—of these transformations of intimacy, including with regard to masculinity. Focusing on Western societies, grand theorists like Michel Foucault (1978) and Anthony Giddens (1992) have placed the transformation of intimacy, particularly in the domain of sexuality, at the center of some of the most significant social changes associated with modern societies. Foucault offers a complex account that perhaps tells an overly pessimistic story about the history of sexuality, in the sense that the very changes often perceived in society as emancipatory are shown to be a new means of human control. Conversely, Giddens perhaps errs in the opposite direction, suggesting radically positive changes in society and gender relations as result of these transformations. Demographically oriented sociologists such as Tim Dyson (2010), Andrew Cherlin (2009, 2010), and Arland Thornton (2005) have persuasively demonstrated that shifts in gender and marital relationships are tied to larger demographic transformations in fertility and household composition, as well as to related processes like urbanization and development. Scholars such as Viviana Zelizer (2005), Stephanie Coontz (2004, 2006), and Jane Collier (1997) have shown in compelling historical and ethnographic depth how changes in intimacy, particularly in marital life, both reflect and contribute to wider transformations in social relations and political economy. Insightful ethnographies by Jennifer Hirsch (2003), Linda-Anne Rebhun (2002), Laura Ahearn (2001), Yunxiang Yan (2003), and others have demonstrated that changes in intimacy are sweeping the Global South in ways that must be central to our understandings of social life, albeit in unique contexts and with local inflections that require as much attention to differences as to similarities. Sometimes explicit and sometimes more implicit in this literature are the ways that changing masculinities are part and parcel of these transformations of intimacy.

In Africa too, a growing body of literature has examined changing intimacy, often focused on sexuality and marriage, and frequently with attention to men and masculinity. Jennifer Cole (2009, 2010), Mark Hunter (2005, 2010), Andrea Cornwall (2002, 2003), and others (Parikh 2007, 2012, 2016; Mojola 2014a, 2014b) have examined the changing meanings and practices of intimacy in Africa for both men and women, with particular attention to the domains of sexuality and love—and to the relationship between love and money. As in many places around the world, scholars of Africa have noted the rise of love not only as a relationship ideal for marriage, but also for sexual relationships more generally. But as Cole has shown in Madagascar (2009) and Hunter in South Africa (2002), the Western ideological conception that opposes love and money fails as a means to understand the degree to which in many African contexts emotional affection (including love) is demonstrated and expressed through material support (including money) (Cole and Thomas 2009).

Cole argues that the scholarly emphasis on the material and instrumental aspect of love in Africa (e.g., Hunter 2002; Leclerc-Madlala 2003) and the social and emotional work it does offers an important corrective to a dichotomized understanding of love and money; however, she points out that there are also ways—and moments—in which her interlocutors in Madagascar embraced ideas such as "pure" and "clean" love (2009, 129): love that has been divested from material interests. Such expressions point to the way in which money and material motives can be seen as sowing distrust and corrupting a moral conception of what love should be. As alluded to above, I heard such sentiments from Nigerian men and women, with women often accusing men of promising love but failing to deliver money (or vice versa), and men suspecting that women pretended love and offered sex when what they really wanted was cash. Like Cole's interlocutors, both men and women in Nigeria express great ambivalence about these transformations of intimacy, at once welcoming possibilities for new and potentially more emotionally fulfilling forms of personal, sexual, and romantic relationships, while also worrying that materialism, money, and desires for consumption mean that relationships (and people) are not always what they appear to be.

The AIDS epidemic spurred a vast literature on sexuality in Africa, the best of which is helpful in developing the project I am pursuing here. Such work shows how social responses to the disease at once reflect and contribute to people's uneasiness about changing meanings and practices of intimacy, including with regard to the complex terrain of trust, morality, and money (Dilger 2003; Harrison 2008; Mojola 2014a). Some of the most insightful scholarship on masculinity in contemporary Africa takes AIDS as a point of departure and shows that understanding the way men navigate intimacy as an aspect of their manhood is central not only to explaining their behavior during the epidemic, but also to understanding the relationship between masculinity and social change more broadly (Setel 1996, 1999; Simpson 2009; Hunter 2010; Wyrod 2011, 2016). What Hunter argues for postapartheid South Africa is true in Africa's AIDS era more generally: intimacy, especially the materiality of everyday sex, "has become a key juncture between production and social reproduction in the current era of chronic unemployment and capital-led globalization" (2010, 4).

As Hunter further demonstrates for South Africa, and others have shown elsewhere (Cornwall 2002, 2003; Simpson 2009), for men it is the continuing importance of their role as providers—for their wives and children, but also for other networks of kin and supporters if they aspire for wider power and prestige—that creates pressures as they navigate the intersecting worlds of production (including all domains in which they might make money) and social reproduction (including all arenas where marriage, fatherhood, and family making are either happening or potentially possible). Cornwall (2003) showed that in contemporary southwestern Nigeria nothing produced more anxiety for men than the specter of becoming (usually in women's words) "useless men": men without jobs or money; men who are unable to satisfy their women in love (or sex); men who fail at both production and social reproduction. The same is true where I work in southeastern Nigeria. While the meanings and practices of "provider love" (Hunter 2010) have evolved with societal transformation and with the rise of new ideals and practices of intimacy, the expectation that competent masculinity depends on its successful performance is as true as ever.

In Nigeria, men's intimate lives with women are a particularly revealing window onto wider social dynamics because, as Cornwall observes: "The reconfiguration of male identities among changing work opportunities, movements across different spaces and places, and an ever-more-complex palate of cultural referents is thrown into sharp relief within heterosexual relationships" (2003, 232). But as Anthony Simpson (2009) points out for the men he studied in Zambia, it is male peers who are often men's most important audience. It is among male peers that the fragility and insecurities of masculinity are frequently most palpable and are felt most acutely (Simpson 2009, 8–9). As exemplified in my opening anecdote from the tennis club, in southeastern Nigeria, the performance of masculinity is at least as much, if not more, for other men as it is for women. In this book, therefore, men's relationships with other men will also constitute a central arena of inquiry and analysis.

The recognition that intimacy is a feature not only of men's relationships with women, but of men's relationships with other men—as kin, as friends, as patrons and clients—leads me to a conceptualization of intimacy that borrows from and coincides with the way that Peter Geschiere (2013) employs the term in his comparative analysis of the relationship between witchcraft, intimacy, and trust in Africa and elsewhere. In Geschiere's hands, intimacy is a feature of many kinds of face-to-face human relationships. The trust it requires is often (perhaps always) imperiled—hence the potency, and seeming universality, of fears about witchcraft. Jealousy, the possibility of betrayal, and the danger of broken trust are a potential feature of every close tie in a Nigerian man's life, not just his relationships with women. As I show in this book, for men in Nigeria, money—how they acquire it, how much they have, and, most importantly, how they spend it—is central to how they create and navigate intimacy across every kind of social relationship.

In the chapters that follow, I parse the intertwining threads that connect the seemingly distinct realms of money and intimacy, personal and political as well as public and private. I analyze this complex geometry across a wide variety of different performances of masculinity in men's everyday lives. The intertwining of money and intimacy in men's lives—as husbands and lovers, as fathers and kinsmen, and as friends and patrons—reflects and must be understood in the context of broader changes in sociality and in Nigeria's political economy. In order to understand these connections it is necessary to say more about the significance of money in Nigeria, and in men's lives in particular.

Money Makes a Man: Social Inequality and Conspicuous Redistribution

When Onyi returned home from another long day peddling shoes at a small stall in the central market in Umuahia, his mother told him as he prepared to take his bath that she wanted to speak to him. He knew what she would say. He wished he had gone out with his friends for beer after closing his shop and that the evening's comradery had kept him out until after she slept. They had had the conversation—or rather he had listened to her haranguing—many times over the past few years. It was past time to marry, she would tell him. A man his age should have a wife, and by now several children. It was no use explaining one more time that he did not have the means to marry, much less to support a family. Onyi's father died a decade ago and he himself had been a poor man. Onyi's senior brother, Okey, the only other son of his parents, could barely take care of his wife and four children in Lagos. In fact, any requests for help from Okey only poked a sore spot for him: he was actually unemployed and it was his wife's job as a civil servant that mostly supported their household. Onyi had long since ceased asking Okey for help. While Okey also wished Onyi to marry, and he too heard constant complaints from their mother about Onyi's bachelorhood, he tried his best to defend his brother. He knew all too well that without money a man couldn't marry.

It is fair to say that in contemporary Nigeria—as Meyer Fortes (1978) noted about all of West Africa many decades ago—marriage and parenthood remain the sin qua non of full personhood. But marrying is expensive. Money is necessary not only to provide for one's wife and children, but also to be able to marry in the first place. Among Igbo people, paying bridewealth is still a required element for a man to marry a woman (Isiugo-Abanihe 1994, 1995). Even while love as a relationship ideal has come to dominate how young people describe marital aspirations, and even as it is increasingly the case that men and women choose their spouses rather than having marriages arranged by their families, marriage is still perceived as a collective project. Bride-wealth is a material and symbolic marker of this social commitment. And bridewealth is considered high in Igboland relative to the rest of Nigeria.

Of course, men even poorer than Onyi manage to marry on a regular basis. His assertion that he could not marry was more an expression of frustration with his failure to achieve his class aspirations—and to attract the kind of wife he thought befit that class position—than an immutable truth. The cost of bridewealth (which is mostly given as commodities, but also as cash) varies by community, but also tends to be calibrated by class and status. The problem for men, of course, is that one is expected to aim high, demonstrating one's future capacity as provider symbolically through what one can afford in bridewealth. In addition, whereas in the past fathers, brothers, and other kin could be expected to contribute most of the costs of bridewealth, now, increasingly, men are expected to come up with much, if not most, of the money themselves.

While bridewealth can cost even the poorest man the equivalent of thousands of dollars, more daunting in many instances are the costs of the wedding itself. Indeed, in southeastern Nigeria today most people aspire to have two wedding ceremonies: a "traditional" wedding and a Christian, or, as Nigerians often say, a "white" wedding. Although a man who wants to marry can expect some assistance from friends and relatives as well as from his wife's friends and relatives, much of the burden is on him. Food, drinks, and entertainment—typically including hiring a generator, tents, music, a photographer, and more—for two weddings, combined with the expected bridewealth payments, create for most people a huge financial challenge. Many men begin marriage in debt, just as their role as provider really begins. And yet the social pressures to spend—to demonstrate that one has money—are irresistible.

The expectations for conspicuous consumption—which, in Nigeria, might better be described as "conspicuous redistribution" in view of how the performance of wealth requires lavishly sharing with and entertaining others—only grow with a man's wealth and status. In this book, I employ the concept of conspicuous redistribution to elucidate the dynamics of social inequality as they unfold at the nexus of masculinity, money, and intimacy. Specifically, I show that men are expected to spend their money in ways that demonstrate their commitment to intimate social relations, whether those ties are with girlfriends and wives, male peers, extended kinship networks, communities of origin, or political clients. In some respects, the redistributive aspect of conspicuous redistribution builds on a longstanding moral economy associated with kinship and patron-clientelism, in which unequal wealth and power are tempered through obligations to share. In this way, men with money preserve and build forms of sociality rooted in model of wealth in people (Guyer 1993, 1995a). Further, even men without great wealth feel pressure to perform spectacles of conspicuous redistribution at weddings and funerals, but also in more everyday instances of sociality and hospitality. The fact that such practices require money to be spent for social purposes helps mitigate some of the tensions created by rising inequality, but not entirely. As I will show, practices of conspicuous redistribution ultimately benefit elite men and can be seen as reinforcing and exacerbating inequality rather than remedying it. Money—as the means by which all conspicuous redistribution is made possible—is widely lamented for its role in undermining morality and increasing inequality, even as people also feel its attraction.

In addition to weddings and burials, another ritual of the life course that perhaps best represents the dynamics of conspicuous redistribution is when a man takes a chieftancy title. When one of my best friends, James, took a title in his natal community, I was able to observe onstage and backstage activities and experiences, both for James and for his multiple audiences. Many Igbo men aspire to become chiefs. Traditionally, taking a title was an honor associated with culturally recognized achievements of masculinity, whether it was, for example, great success as a farmer or a warrior, a reputation for wisdom and integrity, or the ability to mediate disputes. In contemporary Nigeria, taking a title continues to be an important status symbol of masculinity. But, increasingly, chieftancy in Nigeria is associated with money.

James told me that when his *eze* (the traditional ruler in his community whose role includes awarding titles) informed him that he wanted to bestow him with a title he felt honored. But James was taken aback when the eze said that he would need to give him 100,000 naira (then about $1,200) as part of the process, and that James himself would have to foot much of the bill for the ceremony and celebrations. The eze's demand for a payment fit with a widely circulating critique of chieftancy in Nigeria: that honorific titles were now "for sale" and that such practices undermined the traditional meaning and value of chieftancy. Nearly every Nigerian recognizes the critical appellation "naira chiefs," which has become the shorthand way to describe the monetization and commodification of chieftancy.

But James went ahead and took his title. Along the way he grumbled not only about paying his eze, but also about the exorbitant costs of the entertainment, and about the many people who would come only to "eat his money." And yet the chance to show that he had such money, to convert monetary wealth into social prestige, and to demonstrate that his wealth was not the kind that is kept for oneself, but instead is shared and collectively consumed by one's people; this was precisely what James wanted in taking his title. In the event, James basked in the accolades he received from his natal community, from his professional colleagues from town, from his friends, and from his kin. And even though I heard from a few guests some of the typical snide side comments suggesting that James was made a chief because he was rich, it was equally the case that people respected him for spending his money in this way, and that he had indeed successfully converted monetary wealth into social prestige. As a performance of conspicuous redistribution, a chieftancy installation ceremony and the money it requires are thoroughly embedded in social relations. Even in an era when the idea that "money makes a man" is seen as hegemonic and often lamented, masculine aspirations for money remain deeply tied to highly valued social and cultural projects.

Although only a small fraction of men in southeastern Nigeria have the money and clout to become a chief, in many respects nearly every man feels like a naira chief. Masculinity in today's Nigeria is marked by a contradictory dynamic in which spending money beyond one's means—in ways that men recognize and bemoan, in some moments, as detrimental to their interests—is simultaneously zealously pursued and rewarded, perhaps especially among men themselves. Rituals of conspicuous redistribution are indeed efforts to resocialize money, and yet they have the ironic effect of further valorizing money, thereby contributing to suspicions about people's motives and worries about greed. As money has become the primary medium through which men provide for their intimates in contemporary Nigeria, in both private and public life, ethical uncertainties constantly infuse the performance of masculinity. Whether in the love of a woman or in the pursuit of political support, a man must be seen to spend money lavishly. Indeed, in both politics and romance the same multivalent English verb is commonly used to assess a man's spending and his masculinity: has he "performed"? Rather than seeing all this as hypocrisy that men can or should strive to overcome, or as a paradox that can be resolved, it is important to understand that these dynamics are at the core of masculinity and its performance in southeastern Nigeria.

Nigerians' ambivalence about contemporary chieftancy and about the wider effects of money in society resonates with an ample theoretical and ethnographic literature in the anthropology of money. As Bill Maurer notes, in many typical anthropological accounts, "money and the violence of its abstraction erode sociability subtending human existence, and the very idea of society itself" (2006, 19). This and similar accounts build on sociological analyses of money such as those by Marx (2012 [1844]) and Simmel (1990 [1907]), which examine the powerful ways in which money both stands for and enables huge social transitions. Polanyi (2001 [1944]) famously called this "the great transformation": the societal transition from rural to urban; from face-to-face to more anonymous social relations; from gift economies to market capitalism; from *gemeinschaft* to *gesellschaft*. While theories about money like Simmel's recognize that the profound social changes accompanying and enabled by general-purpose money are not simply positive or negative, there is nonetheless a sense that these transformations alter the nature of sociability. From Bohannan (1959) onward, anthropology has provided numerous accounts of the ways in which modern money changed social life around the world, often with money symbolizing negative repercussions (Taussig 1980; Kelly 1992; Meyer 1998).

Although many ethnographic accounts reinforce the master narrative about money and its role in transforming society, anthropology has also been at the forefront of showing how money—even in its more general-purpose, depersonalized modern forms—remains culturally embedded, mobilized for and symbolizing values that have deeply social purposes (Bloch and Parry 1989; Gilbert 2005). For Africa in general and Nigeria in particular, Jane Guyer (1995b, 2004) has led the way in demonstrating that money in all its forms must be understood in its cultural context and that money always serves social purposes beyond the limited sphere of the economy. Barber (1982; 1995), Falola (1995) and others (e.g., Henderson 1972) have shown specifically for Nigeria that social payments such as bridewealth, funeral prestations, and the taking of chieftancy titles serve to transform monetary wealth into social relationships of kinship and alliance—into wealth in people (Guyer 1993, 1995a). Money is connected to social forms of value, even as it risks undermining them. As I will explore in this book, the tension between the imperatives and risks of money reverberates constantly for men in Nigeria.

Money as the means by which men provide for families and follow-ers operates both similarly to and differently from the provision of ma-terial resources more generally. On the one hand, men frequently use money to provide material resources and often do so in ways that are best interpreted as a continuation of—or even an effort to reassert—forms of exchange that align with gifting as a social and moral prac-tice. On the other hand, in part because it is more fungible and easily abstracted from social relations—but also because the means by which men accumulate money in Nigeria are so frequently suspect—money symbolizes anxieties and ethical uncertainties about modern society that manifest themselves palpably in the performance of masculinity.

The Janus-faced character of money in Nigeria is on display in many arenas of social life (Barber 1995). Popular proverbs such as "if you have money every dog and goat will claim to be related to you," "the bottom of wealth is sometimes a dirty thing to behold," and "money does not announce how it is earned, but whereas properly earned money ap-preciates, improperly earned money depreciates" express a shared rec-ognition that aspirations for money, the means of obtaining it, and the uses to which it is put can be morally and socially problematic. The theme of the dastardly relationship between money and witchcraft is a staple of Nigeria's hugely popular Nollywood videos (McCall 2002) and attests to the wide resonance of the idea that the social importance of money is fraught. Certainly the literature on occult economies in Africa more generally suggests that anxieties about money are at the symbolic center of people's ambivalence about modernity (Geschiere 1997; Comaroff and Comaroff 1999; Moore and Sanders 2001; Ash-forth 2005). In the chapters that follow I show that the paradoxes asso-ciated with the performance of masculinity animate and help explain popular preoccupations with money's ethical uncertainties. As I will show in this book, Nigerians—and Nigerian men in particular—share a grand narrative about money's negative effects, even as they embrace and deploy money as essential to the social project of navigating and constructing masculinity.

Studying Men in Southeastern Nigeria

I did not set out to study masculinity in southeastern Nigeria. But as the anecdotes I have already described suggest—and as the more de-tailed ethnography in the ensuing chapters will attest—being a man living, working, and conducting research in Nigeria over more than twenty-five years, I inevitably spent a lot of time in the company of men. The nature of Nigeria's still quite gender-segregated social life channeled my everyday activities in the direction of male-dominated social settings and interactions. At weddings, funerals, and village meetings, for example, men mostly talked to men, and women mostly talked to women. Further, at a number of common venues for social interaction—for example, bars, particular restaurants, and sports clubs—female participation was severely limited. Even in relatively mixed settings, Nigerian men often had a way of dominating conversation.

As I have already alluded to, and as I will delve into in much greater detail later, my own experience with male fraternity was significantly influenced by the fact that I played tennis and joined tennis clubs in both Owerri and Umuahia. My regular interactions with the men at the clubs integrated me into highly masculine social worlds. While the tennis clubs were exceptional in the relatively elite status of the men who were members, they turned out to be revealing—and in many ways very typical—of how the dynamics of money and intimacy cut across almost all men's private and public performances of masculinity, no matter their social class.

In addition to all that I learned about manhood by spending so much time with men—at the tennis clubs, but also in so many other arenas of everyday social life—my formal research projects also frequently touched on masculinity. In my dissertation research in the mid-1990s I was interested in how changes in kinship relations were affecting fertility-related behavior. Based in a semirural, but gradually urbanizing, community in southeastern Nigeria, the study included surveys of students in local secondary schools, students at the state university, and interviews with adult men and women in over two hundred households, as well as almost two years of participant observation. The focus on families and fertility inevitably turned my attention to men's positions not only in their families, but also in more political networks of patronage (Smith 1999, 2001a, 2004a).

My first major post-PhD fieldwork investigated the relationship between youth, rural-to-urban migration, and Nigeria's HIV epidemic, a topic that led me to examine the transition to adulthood among both men and women (Smith 2000, 2003, 2004b). Following migrants from the site of my dissertation research to two large cities of destination, the project included interviews with young men and women about their lives, livelihoods, and ambitions, as well as data about their sexual behavior. I supplemented the interviews with extensive participant observation I conducted over three summers, as well as yearlong work by a young Nigerian research assistant.

Another major AIDS-related project addressed the problem of the marital transmission of HIV. The study included more than twenty intensive case studies of married couples representing a range of ages, socioeconomic positions, and migration experience. The work involved considerable effort to understand men's extramarital sexual activity and first started me thinking about the important connections between men's peer groups, money, and their heterosexual behavior (Smith 2007b; Smith 2014a; Hirsch et al. 2009). Although I did not think of it that way when I was writing it, even my first book, about corruption in Nigeria, was in some ways very much about the performance of masculinity, and particularly the ways that money and intimacy are bound up in men's political-economic lives (Smith 2007a).

In many of my research projects women have figured centrally. I have interviewed scores of women about their lives, and female research assistants have interviewed many more. Further, despite the gender-segregated character of social life in southeastern Nigeria, I have spent a lot of time in the company of women—as work colleagues, neighbors, friends, and in-laws. For most of the twenty-five years I have lived and worked in Nigeria I was married to a Nigerian woman. In addition to always having her perspective, being married to a Nigerian afforded me all kinds of advantages (and occasional disadvantages) when it came to forging good relationships, including with women. Nigerian women's views about Nigerian men have shaped my own thinking, and that is reflected in this book. The fact that gender is a relational identity and social position means that it could not be otherwise. But while women and their perspectives appear in my narrative, this is first and foremost a book about men. I do not know nearly as much about women in southeastern Nigeria as I know about men. In that sense, this is not a balanced account, though I hope that an ethnography that is simultaneously empathetic toward and critical of Nigerian masculinity will be equally as interesting to women as it is to men.

Methodologically, this book draws primarily on participant observation. As will become clear in the ensuing chapters, the venues for my research included a large swath of places that span public and private, as well as economic, political, religious, social, and personal spaces. Most of the cases of individual men I discuss in the book are people I met and got to know through some combination work, research, and everyday social life. In all, since 1989, I have spent almost eight years living in Nigeria. While some of what I present below is drawn from memory, in most instances I also rely on field notes and transcriptions of interviews. In all cases I have used pseudonyms for men (and women) to protect their privacy, and in many examples I have altered some other minor details such as age, location, or occupation. I opted for these further protections when not doing so would make identification too obvious.

Most of the men I describe in this book I got to know in three places. The first is Owerri, the capital of Imo State. I worked there for an American nongovernmental organization (NGO) from 1989 until 1992, and I have continued to do research and maintain friendships there ever since. When I started working there the population was approximately 120,000 people. Now it is probably closer to half a million. The second place is Umuahia, the capital of Abia State, a city about half the size of Owerri. I have conducted research there since 1994, and when I am in Nigeria I live just outside town. The third setting from which I draw my findings is Ubakala, my place of residence and my former wife's natal community. It lies about six miles outside of Umuahia, is made up of eleven villages, and has a population of approximately 30–35,000 people. In the two decades I have conducted research there, it has evolved from a community with a semirural ambience into a bustling, periurbanizing suburb of Umuahia. Most of the men I describe who live or work in places other than Owerri, Umuahia, or Ubakala—places like Lagos, Abuja, or Kano—are people I met through connections that run back through Ubakala.

All of the men in this book are Igbo. Igbos are the third largest language group and—as Nigerians say—tribe in Nigeria. They hail mostly from five southeastern states but live throughout the country. Because the politics of tribe and region are so intense in Nigeria, tribe is not counted (nor is religion) in the country's always-contested censuses (Obono 2003). But by most estimates, Igbos number about thirty million in Nigeria's overall population of approximately 180 million people. Nigerians differ in many ways by region, language group, tribe, and religion (to name just a few major axes of diversity). Igbo people are almost universally Christian. In Nigeria, they are renowned for dominating certain sectors of the economy. Among other Nigerians, Igbos are both respected and resented for their migratory entrepreneurialism. It is often said that Igbos love money too much, though most Nigerians would admit it is a national trait. My account of masculinity, money, and intimacy in Nigeria is no doubt heavily influenced (one might even say biased) by the Igbo experience. Readers who are more familiar with different groups in the country will find some of what I describe or argue about southeastern Nigeria to be inapplicable else-where. But my guess is that they will find much that is common. In the text that follows, I frequently refer to Nigeria and Nigerians rather than every time specifying "southeastern Nigeria" or "Igbo-speaking Nigerians." I adopt this style for easier reading, but also because thirty million Igbos *are* Nigerians and southeastern Nigeria *is* in Nigeria. As long as readers are aware of who and where I am talking about, I see no harm in calling Igbos Nigerians.

Organization of the Chapters

In the chapters that follow, I show—across the life course and in vari-ous domains of men's lives—how the intertwining of money and inti-macy both animates men's personal lives and offers a revealing win-dow into more public arenas of politics and power. For many men, the problems and possibilities attached to money manifest themselves most vividly in changing meanings and practices of intimacy. Simi-larly, men experience the social importance of money as throwing into sharp relief changes in intimacy that they find at once appealing and troubling. I weave together an account in which masculinity, money, and intimacy are shown to be deeply entangled realities. I argue that considering each in relationship to the other is not only an illuminat-ing analytical endeavor, but also a faithful representation of men's lives and an informative reflection of the society in which they live.

Chapter 1 explores the fast-evolving arenas in which boys struggle to become men in Nigeria. Historically, a boy's transition to manhood was marked by well-established phases in the life course, often denoted by public rituals such as the passage from one formally recognized age grade to another, marriage, the establishment of an independent household, the farming of one's own plot(s) of land, participation in community political institutions, and, of course, fatherhood. As noted, marriage and fatherhood remain the sine qua non of Nigerian male adulthood. But many of the other milestones to achieve manhood have shifted dramatically in recent decades. In school, at university, in their efforts to find employment or establish a business, and in their sexual debuts, young males in Nigeria face daunting pressures to make money, measure up to new expectations of intimacy, and prove that they are competent men. For a growing majority of young men, the transition to adulthood occurs through real but often ritually unmarked ad-justments to urban life. Becoming a man in Nigeria now commonly means learning to live in the city. The experiences, meanings, and consequences of these adjustments to schooling and to urban life are examined to understand the transition to manhood in contemporary Nigeria.

Chapter 2 looks at courtship, marriage, and fatherhood, focusing on the ways intimacy is changing in these domains. Although marriage and fatherhood remain the pillars of manhood in Nigeria, the ways that men find their wives, the character of the marriage relationship itself, and the ideals and experiences of fatherhood are shifting dramatically. The rise of romantic love as a relationship ideal for marriage has transformed courtship practices and with it men's behavior. Men must now win women's hearts as well as raise the money for bridewealth. In the same historical moment that bridewealth can include ever-more-expensive commodities and large amounts of cash instead of (or more likely in addition to) cattle and kola nuts, men are also expected to master new practices of intimacy. Fatherhood too is being reconfigured, as men—particularly urban-based men with fewer children and employed wives—take up a greater share of parenting duties that used to fall primarily on women or on the extended family more generally.

Chapter 3 examines the multiple ways men seek to make money, the meanings of money and work, and the ways that different livelihoods both reflect and reproduce increasingly unequal class dynamics. Vivid examples of the lives and livelihood strategies of farmers, poor urban laborers, and small-scale artisans are portrayed and juxtaposed with similar accounts of middleclass civil servants and merchants, elite politicians, and business moguls. Through descriptions of Nigerian men striving to accumulate the money to pay bridewealth, saving toward building a symbolically obligatory house in their ancestral rural villages, struggling to raise school fees, or trying to win elected office, the inextricable links between money and masculinity are investigated and analyzed. While Nigerian men regularly suggest that money is their biggest problem, a close look at their lives shows that they are so obsessed about money because their social projects as men require it.

Chapter 4 explores men's relationships with their male peers as a central arena for the performance and assessment of competent masculinity. Relating appropriately with other men—in school, in the workplace, at social venues and events, in the political arena, and in the myriad spaces connected with family and community—occupies more of men's efforts to be masculine than anything else. Men's concerns with what their fellow men think of them animate and explain a large array of men's behavior. While men's relationships with other

men are undoubtedly important in every society, in Nigeria the relatively gender-segregated character of social life means that men's relationships with each other dominate their daily lives. Drawing on my
decades-long experience with men's tennis clubs in southeastern Nigeria, this chapter explores the importance of men's relationships with
each other, and culminates with a description and analysis of how
even men's decisions, behaviors, and representations of their sexual
relationships with women are deeply influenced by their ties to other
men. The intersection of heterosexuality and homosociality is central
to masculinity and the meanings attached to it.

People in Nigeria commonly perceive everyday life as perilously insecure. Mostly this is a perception related to difficult livelihoods and
frustrated economic aspirations, but it is often crystallized and voiced
in terms of fears about an escalation of crime, especially violent crime,
almost all of which is perpetrated by men. Even as this book challenges
many of the assumptions associated with the assertion that there is a
"crisis of masculinity" in Nigeria, and rejects the idea that the country's social problems reflect some fundamental flaw in men, it is necessary to acknowledge, examine, and understand the various ways in
which masculinity gone awry both results from and in some ways contributes to many of Nigeria's difficulties. While virtually all men face
challenges and experience ambivalence with regard to the expectations
of modern Nigerian manhood, only some men resort to crime or violence. Chapter 5 begins by exploring the problems of domestic violence
and marital rape and then examines the lives of men whose behavior
fuels the popular perception that Nigeria is increasingly dangerous and
insecure. Using examples of a drug smuggler, a scam artist, an "area
boy," and a vigilante, the chapter shows how these men and their behaviors exemplify both the challenges of manhood in contemporary
Nigeria and the misunderstandings produced when social problems are
explained by blaming a presumed crisis of masculinity.

For generations of men in southeastern Nigeria, reaching the status
of elder marked the culmination of successful masculinity. Yet the respect accorded to seniors is a value nearly every older person in present-
day Nigeria sees as declining. At the same time, arranging a befitting
burial for one's parents remains one of the most important obligations
that any man experiences in his life. As noted, many Nigerian men will
say that one is not fully a man until one has buried one's father—not
simply because it marks one's transition to the senior generation, but
because of the social pressures, financial burdens, and emotional work
involved. Chapter 6 examines the experience of older men—elders—in

southeastern Nigeria, focusing especially on the centrality of circular migration for men's actual or anticipated retirement. The chapter also juxtaposes men's worries about disrespect for seniority with the virtual arms race that has evolved around funerals. These end-of-life rituals now include expectations for lavish ceremonies involving extreme amounts of conspicuous consumption and redistribution that often strain families and kin-groups, creating both financial hardship and social disharmony. Presenting a few detailed examples, the chapter argues that both the perception of diminished respect for elders and the escalating expectations around burials exemplify the challenges of social changes in Nigeria for men. The twin aspirations of performing the duties of kinship and exhibiting success in the arenas of wealth, consumption, and social class make men deeply anxious and ambivalent about behaviors they nonetheless feel utterly incapable of avoiding.

The conclusion draws together the book's larger argument about masculinity in Nigeria. First, I look again at what performing masculinity means in practice, particularly as it plays out in the complex geometry of money and intimacy. Then, I offer some final thoughts to refine the concept of conspicuous redistribution, which provides useful analytical leverage throughout. Next, I briefly revisit the contributions of the individual chapters to the overall argument, with an eye to tying the dynamics of money and intimacy not only to masculinity, but also to the nature and consequences of relevant social changes in Nigeria. Finally, the book ends by considering the misconceptions created when Nigeria's—and Africa's—difficulties are reduced to a "crisis of masculinity." Such a perspective misdiagnoses the problem, eliding the deeply social motivations for men's behavior and the fact that almost all men want to be good men, something that, as they continuously point out, is not a one-day job.

ONE

From Boys to Men: Learning to Love Women and Money

Nwankwo arrived at his Aunty Chinwe's flat in Lagos with little more than the clothes on his back. His parents had put him on a bus in Umuahia, the town nearest to their village home, twelve hours earlier. They had arranged that he would live with Chinwe and her family. She and her husband, Nwabueze, would find him a secondary school, pay his fees, provide a uniform, and feed him. In exchange, Nwankwo would be expected to perform many domestic chores for the family. Nwabueze and Chinwe had four children of their own, as well as Nwabueze's elderly mother, living with them in their modest three-bedroom flat. Nwankwo's daily chores in his new urban household included fetching water, sweeping, washing clothes, assisting in cooking, and running multiple errands to nearby vendors or the main local outdoor market. His relationship with his new guardians and their family was part-kin, part-servant—a status common in child-fostering arrangements in contemporary Nigeria, and in many other places in Africa (Isiugo-Abanihe 1985; Bledsoe 1993; Castle 1996; Renata 2009).

Although he missed his parents at first, Nwankwo was enamored with the hustle and bustle of Lagos, a city of over fifteen million people. The mega-city contrasted in many ways with life in his home village, a community of fewer than two thousand. Nwankwo's daily chores were not much different from or more onerous than the work his parents expected of him in the village. But his new arrangement had the added benefit of enrollment in secondary school. He had dropped out of school two years earlier after completing his primary education because his parents could not pay the fees. Further, the food in his aunt's household was generally superior to what his parents could afford; unlike in the village, in Lagos he ate some meat or fish almost every day. Perhaps most appealing, Lagos presented daily enchantments. Nwankwo regularly encountered novel experiences and developed new desires on his way to and from school, moving about the city as part of his round-the-clock errands, and on family excursions to Sunday church or visits to village relatives spread across the vast metropolis. Over time, however, some of the indignities of his quasi-son, quasi-servant status grated on him, especially as he began to compare himself with some of his peers in secondary school. But, overall, he was happy to have come to the city.

I knew Nwankwo because I often stayed with his guardians in Lagos. Nwabueze hails from Ubakala, the community near Umuahia in southeastern Nigeria where, as I have explained, I live when I am doing research. I have been able to observe the family periodically for twenty years and had regular conversations with Nwankwo over four years, after he moved to Lagos. He was not the first person in the household to be fostered there under a kind of kin-servant arrangement. Nwabueze and Chinwe sent the last boy, Oke, back to his mother after they caught him stealing a significant amount of money from their bedroom, a sad event that ended what had appeared to be a mostly happy arrangement of several years. In Oke's tearful admission, he confessed to his aunt and uncle that he'd stolen the money with the hope of buying a pair of Nike basketball sneakers, the kind that popular, wealthier boys in his school had been sporting in the latest fashion statement.

The transition to adulthood for many boys (and girls) in contemporary Nigeria is increasingly an urban process. Nowadays, a majority of young males either grow up in the city or move there at some point before maturity. This chapter explores the fast-evolving arenas in which boys struggle to become men in Nigeria. In school, at university, in their efforts to find employment or establish a business, and even in their sexual debuts, young males in Nigeria face daunting pressures to make money, measure up to new standards of value, and prove that they are competent men. For a growing majority of young men, the transition to adulthood occurs through real but ritually unmarked adjustments to urban life. But even when the transition still happens in

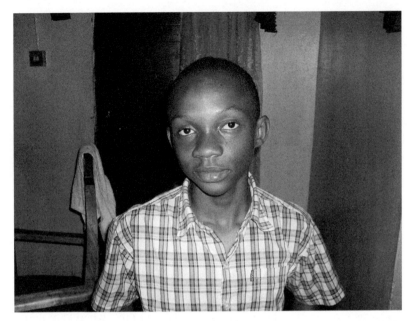

1   For many boys in Nigeria, the transition to manhood includes migration to the city, which accentuates the allure of money.

the village, young men face these new pressures. I analyze the experiences, meanings, and consequences of these adjustments to contemporary life to convey the expectations for masculinity in Nigeria.

I argue that in the transition to adulthood, young men in Nigeria confront and begin to learn to grapple with the paramount importance of money as the means by which intersecting aspirations for manhood and upward mobility are imagined and realized—and also frequently frustrated. Even in adolescence and young adulthood, the intertwining of gender and social class is central to the construction of masculinity. The experience of growing from a boy into a man is marked by powerful peer expectations about consumption, conspicuous redistribution, and the performance of social status associated with them. How much money one has and how one spends it both situate and shape young men's understanding of what it takes to be a successful man.

It should not be surprising that for boys on the path to manhood in Nigeria, in addition to the pivotal importance of male peer group expectations and approval in configuring masculine trajectories, the desires for and interactions with the opposite sex are significant factors (Izugbara 2001, 2004a, 2005, 2008). In contemporary Nigeria, young

men face a changing gendered landscape, in which the rules for interaction between boys and girls are in a period of rapid transformation,
whether in relation to coeducation, gender and the division of labor in
society, premarital sex, courtship, or expectations about social, sexual,
and romantic intimacy. Further, as I try to show not only in this chapter, but also throughout the book, the changing landscape of intimacy
intersects in powerful ways with the centrality of money as the medium through which so much of the social work of human relationships is negotiated. While in some ways the monetization of sociality
and increasing expectations of intimacy in relationships with women
might appear to be antithetical, I show how, in fact, boys learn that
money is a primary means of navigating intimacy.

Making Men in Village Nigeria: Stalled Transitions

Before exploring the transition to manhood that ever-larger numbers
of Nigerian boys experience in cities, it is instructive to provide some
context with regard to the traditional transition to adulthood in village Nigeria. Until Nigeria became so urbanized—now half of the
country's population resides in cities (Mberu 2005; White, Mberu, and
Collinson 2008)—most people grew up in villages. In southeastern Nigeria, where I work, for boys in rural communities the transition to
adulthood historically involved economic, social, cultural, and political milestones and accomplishments. Economically, manhood meant
establishing an independent farm, or perhaps learning an artisanal
skill or a small trade (Henderson and Henderson 1966; Olutayo 1999).
Socially, becoming a man required, above all, marrying and having
children, with marriages commonly arranged by one's family rather
than chosen individually based on love or some other individual ideal
(Ukaegbu 1975; Smith 2001b). Culturally, in addition to ceremonies
associated with marriage and fatherhood, manhood could be marked
by joining a men's secret society, or by passing through different symbolically recognized age grades that signified one's generational status
(Uchendu 1965; Ottenberg 1982, 1988, 1989). These economic, social,
and cultural achievements then conferred the political privileges of
manhood, and specifically the right to speak publicly about and have
influence over a community's collective decisions (Ottenberg 1971;
Henderson 1972; Harneit-Sievers 2006).

Although the transition to manhood still involves economic, social,
cultural, and political accomplishments, a host of social changes—from

globalization, urbanization, and a changing economy to the spread of formal education and the rise of consumption as a primary marker of status—has transformed expectations and practices not only in cities, but also in villages. Few boys aspire to be farmers or to live in their natal villages after they marry. While almost all young men want to marry and have children, most resist the idea of an arranged marriage and many view romantic love as an important criterion for marriage (Smith 2001b, 2006). Age grades and secret societies no longer exist in many villages, and are waning in others. And the most valued forms of political influence are in relation to the state rather than vis-à-vis local community dynamics (Harneit-Sievers 2006; Smith 2007a). Boys and young men want to leave their villages in search of more and better education, employment, the amenities of modern urban life, and the kinds of spouses and children they imagine to be possible in the city, but not in the village (Mberu 2005). Indeed, for many young men in Nigeria, villages are perceived as emblematic of a transition to manhood that is threatened, stalled, and even impossible, a situation common in other settings experiencing similar social and demographic transitions (Singerman 2011; Dhillon and Yousef 2009; Sommers 2012; Honwana 2012, 2013).

Emeka saw his transition to manhood stalled by being stuck in his village, Amibo, on the outskirts of Umuahia. His experience was representative of many young men whose lives I have observed and whose complaints I have heard over the past twenty-five years. Emeka is the third son in a family of six children. His father was a farmer who supplemented his small agricultural income by sometimes doing masonry work on local construction projects. His mother also farmed and had a little stall in the local market where she sold children's clothing, mostly used clothes that she would purchase in bulk on occasional trips to Lagos. His parents' multiple—but meager—sources of income are typical of village households in southeastern Nigeria, where farming alone does not provide sufficient income, especially as nearly everyone aspires to educate his or her children and to be able to buy a wide range of modern commodities that are increasingly seen as essential for contemporary life.

Emeka attended one of the local primary schools and enrolled for two years in secondary school until his father died and his mother and older siblings could not afford to pay his fees. One of his older brothers and one older sister finished secondary school. The brother got a civil service job in Abuja, Nigeria's capital, and the sister is married to a small businessman in Port Harcourt, the largest city in Nigeria's oil-producing region, about a two-hour drive from Amibo. At my last visit to Nigeria, all of Emeka's siblings, save his youngest sister, had migrated away from the village. He and his youngest sister lived in the family's village compound along with their mother. Emeka helps his mother farm the family's plots of land, occasionally assists her at her stall in the market, and regularly goes to Umuahia, about five miles away, in search of employment. He has pleaded with his eldest brother to help him find work in Abuja, made a trip to his sister's in Port Harcourt that lasted almost two months without finding a job, and approached various kinsmen from his village about help to go back to school or to find him an apprenticeship to learn a trade. But none of this has yielded success. As a result, Emeka regularly voices frustration that his transition to manhood has been stalled in the village.

In one of several conversations we had about his life and his aspirations he said:

Nothing is moving here [in Amibo]. There are no jobs. No money. Without money it is impossible to be a man. I cannot marry. I cannot train my children. In this our place a man does not have a mouth to speak if he has no money, if he cannot marry, if he cannot feed his family. I have been looking for work in Umuahia, but without a proper education all doors are closed. I want to transfer to Lagos or Abuja. There are more opportunities in those places. At least something is moving. But even to find work in the city I need money. Without money I am stuck in the village.

Amibo and the other villages in southeastern Nigeria appear to be slowly emptying of young men, most of them migrating to urban areas in search of education, employment, or other opportunities to earn income. But even as ever more young people migrate to cities (young women are moving too [Adepoju 2003; Mberu 2005]), many are left behind, living rural lives that do not allow them to achieve their modern aspirations.

In southeastern Nigeria, the frustrations of stalled transitions to manhood in rural areas are exacerbated by the fact that for successful rural-to-urban migrants, the periodic return to one's village of origin remains a paramount practice in the performance of masculinity. Migrants come home not only to fulfill their kinship obligations, but also to show off their success. Further, for the vast majority of longtime urban residents, marriages are still undertaken in connection to place of origin. Migrants' weddings (and funerals) are ubiquitous weekend activities in virtually every rural community. Rural people are constantly confronted by the displays of spending that determine how impressive any ceremony is perceived to be. Village-based men who have not yet married see wealthier migrant men perform lavish weddings, which can accentuate their sense of failure (Masquelier 2004, 2005). For young men stuck in the village the aggravations of approaching manhood without money are perhaps most palpable when their migrant peers visit home.

Of course even for men who manage to migrate to cities, making enough money and being able to marry can be serious sources of anxiety. I will return later to examine in much greater detail how and why the intersection of money and marriage occupies such a central place in the ways men navigate expectations about masculinity in contemporary Nigeria. Suffice it to say here that many young men in rural communities share a perception that the transition to the kind of modern manhood they desire is nearly impossible when stuck in village communities, above all because money has become the essential means to prove one's value as a man.

School and the Stuff of Becoming a Man

If a boy manages to start early enough and stay on track long enough, the most established path to modern manhood in Nigeria is formal education. The expectation that money (and the capacity for conspicuous consumption and redistribution that it enables) is the most important marker of manhood is produced and reinforced throughout society, including in school. At first glance, schools do not look like places where consumption-based social status is established and displayed. Students in Nigerian secondary schools appear remarkably homogeneous. Uniforms are required. Everyone in the same school dresses identically. Similar haircuts are mandated. Behavior is strictly monitored. But this seeming uniformity is misleading. A naïve observer might not notice the dramatic statements about status these kids manage to display in the few areas where variation is permissible.

Like most boys his age, when Nwankwo, the fostered child of my friends in Lagos, is at his secondary school he pays as much attention to these markers of status as to his lessons. Among his fellow students, some lads stand out for their sneakers, their backpacks, their watches, and, these days, their mobile phones. The boys with more things—and by implication more money—are frequently more popular among their male peers, and perhaps even more importantly, among the girls. Boys

2 Despite required uniforms, social status among schoolboys is marked by fine-grained assessments of consumption.

learn early that their success as men is measured in the things they can buy, display, and share.

In school, footwear is a primary domain of distinction. Everyone is required to wear shoes, but the type and quality vary from often-repaired cheap rubber sandals to imported Nikes bearing names such as LeBron James, Michael Jordan, and Kobe Bryant—sneakers that cost more than some families earn in a month. When it comes to commodities associated with social status, Nigerians recognize and evaluate multiple gradations of quality. Things are generally divided into four categories, more or less in ascending order of prestige: local, China, *tokunbo*/Belgian, and original. Boys learn these categories early and carry them into adulthood.

While the relative prestige of the three lower categories can occasionally shift for reasons I will explain in detail below, with regard to schoolboys' sneakers and just about every other imaginable consumer good, "original" carries the highest status. Typically, original means made in Europe, Japan, or North America, though given that so many products meant for Western consumption are now made in China (or elsewhere in the Global South), Nigerians increasingly recognize that original means "produced for Western markets" rather than "made in the West." In schoolboys' conversations, debates rage about whether a particular product is China or original. One of the only ways to be relatively sure that something is original is to demonstrate that it was, in fact, purchased in Europe or North America.

The price differences between originals and the other three categories of quality/origin reflect the highly valued status of originals. For example, a pair of original Nike sneakers could easily cost more than the equivalent of $100, while various options from the categories of local, tokunbo, or China might cost $10 or less. For boys' sneakers, as for many commodities, the relative ranking of local, tokunbo, and China can shift. Local is generally the most inferior category because Nigerian products have a reputation of being shoddily made to save costs and increase profits, with no regard for the consumer. Skepticism about locally made products reflects a larger cynicism about the extent of fraud and deception in society; the often-expressed sentiment is that Nigerian manufacturers could make better products, but they don't because they are greedy. For shoes, the nomenclature for local is often "Aba," which is the name of a commercial city in southeastern Nigeria that is home to the country's largest shoemaking industry (mostly small-scale firms) (Meagher 2010). Aba-made shoes typically carry labels like "made in Italy" and are reputed to come unglued quickly in Nigeria's rainy season. To me, Aba-made shoes often appeared superior to many China-made shoes. While some Nigerians have recognized this and take pride in locally made products, among most secondary schoolboys "local" is still a derogatory label, typically the lowest on the totem pole of consumption-based status.

"Tokunbo" and "Belgian" are synonyms for used products imported from abroad. While both labels were originally associated with imported used cars—vehicles shipped from Belgium once constituting a significant fraction of these imports and hence the name—nowadays all imported used commodities are known as tokunbo or (now less commonly) Belgian. Tokunbo products include everything from cars and refrigerators to shoes and clothes. While the super elite in Nigeria rarely purchase tokunbo products, the vast majority of Nigerians, including many people firmly in the middle class, routinely buy tokunbo. For the urban working poor and many rural Nigerians, tokunbo goods constitute a lifeline to commodities that would otherwise be inaccessible. In some instances, tokunbo products can rise to second in the hierarchy of commodities. For example, for Nwankwo and his secondary schoolmates, a fine pair of tokunbo Nike sneakers that appears little used is much more prestigious than any pair of China or Aba shoes. However, a ratty pair of tokunbo shoes falls to the lowest-level status.

"China" products, including sneakers and shoes worn by students, are the subjects of extensive discourse in contemporary Nigeria. On the one hand, the fact that China produces a huge range of products at prices much more affordable than Western goods has made many commodities available to ordinary Nigerians that were not within reach in the past. Indeed, I have heard many Nigerians express appreciation for affordable Chinese goods. On the other hand, China has become shorthand for "imitation" or "inferior." To describe someone's possession as China is to dismiss it, sometimes even with the insinuation that the person is faking a prestige-through-consumption status they haven't actually earned.

Over the years, Nigerian students have typically been quick to point out the shortcomings of my own consumption choices. I remember a few of years after mobile phones first began to be widely available in Nigeria (in the early 2000s) I was talking with a group of secondary schoolboys in the home of one of my friends, who was the mother of two of them. My mobile phone rang and I removed it from my backpack to take the call. When I finished the call the young men asked to examine my phone. Compared with the much smaller versions that had by then become available in Nigeria—including popular Nokia phones with LCD screens or flip designs—my bulky, bright blue, no-frills Motorola looked anachronistic. As they passed it around, the young men smirked. When I looked at my friend's son as if to say "What?" he finally laughed and said in Pidgin English: "Mr. Dan, this phone, e no fit you-o." He meant that I did not have a phone befitting my social status. The boys thought it was something of a disgrace, but they also realized that as a foreigner I could get away with having a phone none of them would be caught dead with. And this was at a time when cell phone ownership was much less common than now. The latest estimate is that nearly 140 million cell phones are in use in Nigeria, and many secondary students have them (Nigerian Telecommunications Commission 2016). These days, I carry a much smaller, sleeker Nokia, but now people wonder why in the world I don't have a smart phone. My social class and masculine status feel less at stake in these constant judgments about the quality of one's possessions than is the case for young Nigerian men, mostly because in Nigeria my status is so closely connected to my race and nationality. But the fact that they make fun of me (and I am sure sometimes openly mock me behind my back) is additional evidence of how strongly the possession of particular commodities counts in establishing the class-based aspects of one's masculinity.

Of course there is nothing peculiarly Nigerian about these connections between money, consumption, and gendered social status. Indeed, such trends suggest Nigeria's further integration in the global capitalist economy (Majekodunmi and Adejuwon 2012). Nonetheless, to Nigerian boys on the path to manhood, these material markers of status and success are experienced as a never-ending acceleration of expectations for money. Manhood is increasingly measured in monetary and material terms. But as I will show, when these material desires are examined more closely, the centrality of social relations becomes clear. This is evident not only in the ways men (and boys) use their money and display their things, but also in the ambivalence they express when obsessions with money seem to subvert important shared values regarding sociality.

"Proposing Love"

For schoolboys on the path to becoming men in Nigeria, girls loom large. Whether it is in still-common same-sex secondary schools that separate boys and girls for the day (often in nearly adjacent school compounds), thereby augmenting desire through artificially created distance, or in the increasingly popular coeducational secondary schools where boys and girls sit side by side throughout the day, the expansion of secondary education in contemporary Nigeria has played a central role in reconfiguring the dynamics of gender and intimacy. New ideas about gender equality, growing desires for and acceptance of premarital sexual experiences, and changing expectations about the role of intimacy in sexual relations have created novel and shifting landscapes in which boys learn one of the most central elements of manhood: how to succeed in the eyes of women.

With their adolescent populations, secondary schools around the world are places where ideas and practices of gender, sexuality, and intimacy are cultivated and cemented (Coe 2005; Parikh 2005; Stambach 2013). The intersection of love and money is certainly not unique to Nigerian youth. But for young men coming of age in Nigeria, the tangled connections between sex, gender, and social class—between access to wealth and success in the romantic realm—are perhaps especially explicit. Whereas in many places one senses that society works to shroud the influence of money in sexual and romantic relations, in Nigeria, even secondary school students are acutely aware of and remarkably direct about the importance of money in these relationships. And yet the rise of love as a relationship ideal has complicated the economic-erotic landscape. Love and money are inextricably—and in a quintessentially Nigerian way, starkly—intertwined; nevertheless, the importance of money for sex and love sits uneasily with changing norms about gender and intimacy, creating suspicions of deception. Even as money is very much the currency of sex and love, the specter of money—with its connotations of selfishness and greed—makes managing relationships a tricky business. Love both requires money and is simultaneously threatened by it. Boys in secondary school begin to map and navigate this terrain as they seek and establish their first relationships with girls.

The idea of romantic love as an appealing and justifiable reason for a premarital sexual relationship is certainly not new in Nigeria. For at least a few generations, the notion that love can be the basis for sex and marriage has been taking hold (Obiechina 1973; Mann 1985). But certainly the rise of formal schooling, and particularly the huge increases in the number and proportion of girls who enter secondary school, has changed both the dynamics of gender inequality and the landscape of premarital sex. Increasingly, as I have written about elsewhere (Smith 2000), premarital sex is seen as a marker of being modern for both young men and young women. And yet it remains morally suspect, especially for young women because gender double standards remain quite powerful. It is in this complex social-moral landscape that boys (and girls) in secondary school learn about and traverse the often-contradictory dynamics of love and money.

Schooling and literacy have spawned an important narrative genre in secondary school sex and romance: the love letter (Ahearn 2001; Parikh 2016). Love letters seem like overdetermined symbols of modernity, indexing both educational attainment and a contemporary sensibility. They sit squarely, if precariously, at the boundary between secrecy and publicity. Many Nigerian youths pass love letters furtively to hide their sexual and romantic attractions, intentions, and actions from parents, teachers, friends, and even other lovers. Yet written down they also serve as potentially public declarations and documentation, which can be revealed in ways that are either desired or dreaded (and sometimes both). Love letters were a popular genre in secondary schools during two long stints of fieldwork I conducted in southeastern Nigeria from 1995 until 1997 and again in 2004. By the time of my last long-term fieldwork in 2012, cell phone texts began to replace love letters as the means of romantic communication among students. While scholars have begun to explore the ways cell phone usage intersects with young people's sexual behavior (Melvin 2013), I did not have access to such messages during my research. As I will explain further below, I did see many young people's love letters.

In both the mid-1990s and in 2004 I lived in proximity to a lot of young men and women in secondary school. In the 1990s, as part of my dissertation project about changes in family and fertility in southeastern Nigeria, I was explicitly interested in what young people thought about sex, romance, marriage, and having children, and I did a survey of nearly 800 students in nineteen secondary schools in and around the city of Umuahia. I also interviewed many young men and women in depth, including many of my neighbors, whom I got to know quite well. In 2004, I was focused more on married adults and infidelity and its relationship to HIV, but I continued to talk to young people about sex, love, and marriage (and, often without realizing it, about money).

While I had interesting conversations with both young men and young women—indeed many young women were quite candid regarding topics about which I thought they would be more secretive—not surprisingly, it was boys and young men who seemed more at ease opening up to me. Many of them were willing to share love letters that they were writing or had received from girls they were interested in (or in relationships with) in school. Although the relatively few love letters I was shown cannot be characterized as a random or representative sample, I do think that what I saw, and the ways that young men (and to a lesser extent young women) talked about them with me, reflected important aspects in the changing arena of gender, sex, and romance among Nigerian youth, and particularly the complex dynamics of love and money that already preoccupied my young interlocutors.

Many of the love letters boys showed me were the first they planned to send to particular girls they were interested in. It was common for the letters to have a title or main topic in capital letters or underlined, below the date but above the opening salutation. More than once this title or topic contained the words "proposing love." In the hands of these boys, the meaning of proposing love ran the full spectrum from declaring deep romantic feelings to simply asking if a girl was willing to have sexual intercourse. But most often, the ambiguity (and implied interconnection) between love and sex was evident in boys' language. Girls were free to emphasize whichever appealed to them more, but most of the boys hoped (whether they felt romantically inclined or not) that their entreaties would result in something sexual. Young men's motives ran the spectrum from boys who were genuinely smitten—convinced they could not live without the love of the girl they were writing—to boys who hoped that a disingenuous declaration of love might make it easier to get sex. And of course what boys said to girls, what they said to their male friends, and what they said to me might differ a little or a lot. Rather than one being "true" and the others "lies," each might (and often did) contain kernels of truth.

A selection from a letter written by Obioma, a male SSII (second-to-last year of secondary school) student to Ekeoma, a female SSI (third-to-last year) student is typical of the somewhat common tendency to obscure the distinction between love and sex in boys' letters to girls.

October 20
Proposing Love With You

Dear Ekeoma,
Please do not be offended. I see you at school everyday but you may not know me. Or maybe you do, but you are shy to say hello. I have been admiring you for long. My heart desires you. I want to propose love between us. I hope we can meet somewhere to share that love. If you agree to love me please write back.
Expecting your reply.

Sincerely,
Obioma

Many of the letters I was shown were much more flowery. Some boys emphasized love in clearly romantic terms, without any necessary implication that their letters also proposed sex. A smaller number of boys expressed sexual attraction and the desire for sexual relations much more directly, even with no pretense of love. But much more common, like Obioma's letter above, was a language of love that could be interpreted in both romantic and sexual terms, revealing what boys thought girls wanted to hear, what they themselves felt, or both. For their part, girls' replies were typically coyer (though not always). To the extent that they embraced boys' entreaties, they commonly chose to emphasize love more than sex, at least in part because gender double standards made it inappropriate for girls to easily or explicitly express sexual desires. Of course sex between boys and girls in secondary school occurred fairly frequently. In the survey I conducted in 1996, which was among SSII students, about 36 percent reported that they had had sexual intercourse, including 48 percent of boys and 28 percent of girls. Given that premarital sex is generally socially rewarded among boys, but more ambivalently judged among girls, it isn't surprising that boys were more likely than girls to report having had sexual intercourse.

Even in secondary school, where most boys and girls had little access to money, it featured in negotiations around love and sex. Boys would often bolster their advances by presenting gifts or offering to take a girl somewhere nice to eat. And girls would frequently request gifts. Boys simultaneously wanted money to impress girls and envied their peers who had it. But they also frequently condemned girls for being money-hungry. Schoolgirls evaluated boys' seriousness in terms of money and their willingness to engage in interpersonal forms of conspicuous redistribution: if he is willing to spend, he must be serious. And yet money could also trigger worries about insincerity: maybe he is just spending money to get sex. Already in secondary school, both boys' and girls' ambivalence about the love/sex–money nexus revealed itself.

Masculinity and Sexuality on University Campuses

Over the past two decades, access to university education in Nigeria has expanded dramatically. Nigeria now boasts over one hundred universities, as well as another two hundred colleges of education and technical schools, most of which were established in the past two decades. Student enrollment in government-accredited tertiary institutions was estimated to be more than 1.6 million by 2009 and has continued to grow (Shu'ara 2010). While it is still true that the majority of young Nigerians aspiring to attend university do not achieve that dream, the boom in university education has affected not only the individuals who attend these institutions, but also many families and communities and the society as a whole. Further, as I will show in this section, for young men, university campuses are places where the intersection of money and intimacy is powerfully shaped by—but also highly influential in forming—wider societal trends and patterns. Whereas in secondary school boys are just beginning to learn how to navigate the intertwining worlds of money, sex, and romance, and relative poverty and sexual inexperience are expected and at least somewhat accepted, by the time young men reach university campuses, the pressure to have money and women can be intense. The enactment of masculinity on Nigerian university campuses is very much about young men's efforts to navigate the interconnecting worlds of money and sexuality.

My knowledge about life on Nigerian university campuses comes primarily from four sets of experience. First, in the mid-1990s I was a visiting scholar and instructor at Abia State University, where I had a Fulbright fellowship for a year. I spent at least one day on campus each week and got to know many students and faculty quite well. That year I also conducted a survey of 406 undergraduates, with a major focus on their beliefs and practices regarding sexuality. Second, for nearly three decades I have worked in city of Owerri, including three years living there and multiple other months of research when I have watched the city's university-student population grow from a few thousand to well over a hundred thousand. In addition to interacting extensively with dozens of Owerri university students over the years, I have also observed wider social changes that have resulted from Owerri becoming a university town. Third, in Ubakala, I have interviewed many university students returning to their community of origin during holidays, asking them about everything from dormitory life to campus cults. Finally, in both Owerri and Umuahia, I spent time at the university staff clubs where many faculty socialize at lunch and drink in the evenings after work.

In all these experiences the salience of sex and money in campus life was a regular theme. Much could be said about Nigeria's tertiary education system—about the quality of education, about topics such as violence or religion, and of course about what Nigerian campuses are like for women. Here, I touch on those topics only implicitly as they inform my exploration of masculinity. Three aspects of university life help build the larger argument about the ways that the transition to manhood in Nigeria imprints in young men the inextricable connections between money and intimacy. These three aspects are: (1) the importance of consumption—particularly fashionable consumption—in campus life, and especially how it affects young men's success in sex and romance; (2) how young men deal with and feel about the culture of "monetizing" and "sexualizing" grades (terms I will explain below); and (3) the relationship between all-male campus cults and opportunities for sexual relations with university women.

Fashionable Consumption

During a stint of long-term fieldwork in 2012, a young man named Tochukwu worked for me helping with the logistics of both my research and my everyday life. He lived in the same house with me for several months and we had countless conversations about his long-frustrated attempts to enter university. The problem, as he narrated it, was lack of money, as well as insufficient personal connections. Tochukwu's analysis of admission to Nigerian universities paralleled my own observations over many years. While a bit oversimplified, essentially admission happens in three ways. The first way is the official way, by scoring high enough on the national entrance exam (known as JAMB). Each year a cutoff mark for admission is established. In theory, anyone with a good enough score is admitted. Further, the better the score the better the university one can attend. In addition, within individual universities there is a hierarchy of majors or "courses." For example, one needs a much better score to read medicine than to study sociology or French literature. Some fraction of Nigerian students do indeed gain admission through the JAMB process. But the exams are hard and most students do not score well enough to matriculate this way. For many young Nigerians, the challenge is to gain admission despite insufficient scores, or if only eligible to study optometry, for example, to somehow upgrade to read medicine.

The other two ways to gain admission are unofficial and involve either money or social connections, or typically a combination of both. If one has enough money, admission slots are clearly available for purchase outright, though even then one needs to know whom to bribe. But without enough money, most Nigerians try to rely on some kind of personal connection such as a kinship or community tie to a faculty, staff, or administrator. As I have recounted elsewhere, Nigerian academics often feel bombarded and burdened by these frequent requests (Smith 2007a). Nonetheless, a significant fraction of university admissions depend on this kind of social capital, which usually does not entirely circumvent the need to pay bribes, although these ties lessen the amount and assure that the person paid off is the right one.

I found myself using my own social capital to try to help Tochukwu. Through a friend who held a senior position in a university in another state, I arranged that Tochukwu would likely be able to gain admission there. In the end, Tochukwu's senior brother had some sort of similar connection at Abia State University, and it was decided that it would be better for Tochukwu to matriculate nearer to home. In the whole process of admission, the specter of money loomed large. It was not just the exorbitant official fees (then nearly $2,000 per year at Abia State University—a huge amount for most families), but also the unofficial costs. For guys like Tochukwu those unofficial costs included living up to peer-enforced fashion standards, such as the kinds of clothes and shoes to wear and the type of cell phone to carry.

I remember going shopping with Tochukwu in the weeks before his matriculation and being amazed by his critical assessment of each type of clothing—which jeans were cool and which were not; which shirts might betray his village origin or relative poverty; which shoes would be both affordable and socially acceptable. All the categories I described in the section on secondary school emerged again—tokunbo, China, local, and original—but the stakes seemed more intense, the costs higher, and the nuances more precise. When I explained to him the kinds of informal fashions and ragged blue jeans that were common on elite campuses in the United States, Tochukwu was aghast. "Ah, Ah," he exclaimed, "how can?!"—a common Nigerian shorthand for "how can that be possible?" Further, Tochukwu's preoccupation with what would be successful with women was more explicit and more pronounced than would be typical for Nigerian secondary school students or American undergraduates. At various inappropriate pieces of clothing he scoffed, "They will laugh at me." Tochukwu wanted to be properly prepared.

On Nigerian university campuses, one of the most striking observations to be made is how well everyone is dressed. Students look incredibly fashionable. Though I was no doubt blind to many of the nuances that students themselves could more easily detect, to me, the vast majority of students looked great. In contrast, the few times I entered crowded dormitory rooms it was jarring to see that behind the façade of fashion was relative squalor. For most students the stuff they displayed in public covered the fact that they actually had very little. Even though almost everyone shared this larger reality of economic struggle, pulling off a successful performance of fashionable consumption in public was a social imperative on campus, both mirroring and girding similar trends in wider Nigerian society.

For young men in university, looking fashionable, but not looking like one is trying too hard, is a big part of what determines success in relations with coeds. Young men know that young women talk a lot about how men look, including how they dress. While fashionable clothing helps to attract university girls, in any kind of actual relationship, cash is necessary—for food and drinks and to finance the chance to get away from campus for privacy. The primacy of money looms large in university students' narratives about sex and romance. The dominant discourse among men is that women are money-hungry and that most women wouldn't want a man without enough money. Of course there are counternarratives about love and romance, and men without much money sometimes manage to find women who care about them for other reasons. Women hold a similar range of views: one would be a fool to go for a man who has no money, but it also might be possible to find love without money. I certainly do not mean to suggest that sex and romance on Nigerian university campuses are all about money, but by students' own accounts money always intervenes in one way or another. To say that university campuses have an active "sexual economy" is to use language that Nigerian students themselves would clearly recognize.

Chibike, a male student whom I got to know quite well, told me about his troubled romance with a young woman a year below him at university. His account contained many elements I also heard from others about the tension between love and money. He met Olamma when she was a first-year student and he was in second year. He thought she was beautiful and was also impressed that she seemed to study hard. Their relationship first unfolded through meetings in the library. Chibike said that they fell in love and by the end of his third year they even discussed marriage. But along the way there were various troubles. She had told him that one of her professors had pursued her and, while she maintained she was never interested, Chibike felt great jealousy. Worse, one of his fellow male students who was wealthy, had a car, and reportedly was in one of the all-male campus cults once took an interest in her at a party, and while she again assured him that nothing happened, he felt threatened (and even afraid) by this turn of events. Members of campus cults were known to use violence in disputes over women. Chibike was not in a cult and he came from relatively modest means, so the worry was palpable that Olamma would leave him (or be taken) by someone with more money or power.

For a long time Olamma apparently navigated around these overtures. But eventually Chibike noticed that she had a lot of nice new things: clothes, shoes, and perfume, for example. Further, he often did not find her in her dorm room or at the library as he used to. After weeks of suspicion and torment, he finally confronted her and she confessed that she had begun seeing someone else—a young businessman from her community of origin who had lots of money. She broke up with Chibike and explained that this young man had approached her parents about marriage and they were putting pressure on her to give the man a chance. Chibike was crestfallen and he attributed their breakup to his relative lack of money. Among Nigerian university students it is almost impossible to separate money and matters of the heart.

The Sexual Economy: "Monetizing" and "Sexualizing" Grades

As hinted above, the political and sexual economies of Nigerian universities intersect in students' relationships with faculty as well. If they are struggling to pass or do well in a class, students are sometimes prompted by faculty to "monetize" their grades. In other words, some faculty members are known to take bribes in exchange for giving students better grades than they deserve. Both male and female students have this option. Female students also sometimes have the option to "sexualize" their grades; that is, male instructors will elevate a young woman's grade in exchange for sex. Because most faculty are men and because gender norms and gender inequality make such behavior much more socially problematic for married female faculty than for married male faculty, it seemed to be the case that the practice was highly gendered. But I did occasionally hear rumors of male students who managed to sexualize their grades with female instructors. It was impossible for me to know exactly how common these practices were, but stories about them circulated ubiquitously among students and faculty. And it was also evident that students were sometimes the ones to propose these arrangements. At the faculty/staff clubs in Owerri and Umuahia and in other private conversations, many faculty lamented (but some occasionally bragged about) being approached by students to sexualize a grade.

For male students, the threat of female students sexualizing grades with instructors posed particular challenges to their masculinity, mirroring a wider worry and problem that young women were often more attracted to older men with money (and/or power) than to younger men who could offer little but love. In my observations, university women tried to conceal these arrangements from their fellow students, especially from male students, and for obvious reasons, most especially from male students in whom they might be interested, or with whom they might even be having a relationship.

I once heard a male faculty member confide after several beers that the boyfriend of a girl with whom he was sexualizing a grade had threatened him. Male faculty members feared young men in the campus cults, who could be prone to violence. Over the years I heard stories of faculty members who were beaten by campus gangs for having sex with one of "their" girls. At one point a popular faculty member at Alvin Ikoku Teacher's College in Owerri was murdered and among the common theories I heard was that a campus cult member had him assassinated for sleeping with his girlfriend.

Although members of campus cults inspired fear even among faculty, for most young men in university, the power of money in campus sexual economies pervaded social life in less violent ways. In addition to the possibility that lecturers might be preying on one's girlfriend to sexualize a grade, university girls were constantly the objects (and often the willing recipients) of attention from wealthier (and often older) men off campus, commonly referred to as "sugar daddies" (Smith 2002; Luke 2005; Brouard and Crewe 2012). It was common knowledge that many university girls tried to juggle boyfriends. Having a sugar daddy could provide financial help while one kept a campus boyfriend for love (or, in some girls' narratives, better sex). But for most young men that I talked to about these issues, the fact that their girlfriends might love them more than their sugar daddies was little consolation if they discovered such behavior. Inevitably, young men interpreted these episodes in financial terms: they occurred either because of women's insatiable greed for money or their own lamentable lack of cash.

Campus Cults: Money, Power, and Sex

It is difficult to separate a discussion of masculinity as it is manifest in violent campus cults from the larger context of social changes in Nigeria that blur the boundaries between politics and criminality (Gore and Pratten 2003; Adebanwi 2005; Watts 2007; Ellis 2011, 2016). Throughout the twenty-five years I have worked in Nigeria, stories about university cults have been a regular topic in the media, often spurred by violent clashes and unsolved murders in which cult members are implicated but rarely if ever prosecuted (Smah 2001; Ajayi, Ekundayo, and Osalusi 2010). In recent years, scores—and possibly many more—students have been killed in open conflicts between cults or in secret retaliatory assassinations. It is not my intention to examine Nigerian campus cults in detail. Indeed, most of what I know about these cults comes from gossip and rumor, the Nigerian media, and the scholarship of others (with very little of that based on actual participant observation). That firsthand accounts are rare is not surprising. On the Nigerian campuses with which I am most familiar, secrecy is a hallmark of these cults. Trying to learn too much about them could be quite dangerous.

The literature suggests that today's violent campus cults evolved from more prosocial fraternities that were created in the 1950s (Rotimi 2005; Eguavoen 2008; Ellis 2011). In a society where the majority of university graduates struggle to find employment, and where criminal connections and violence have been modus operandi for political elites at least since military rule beginning in the 1960s, it is perhaps not surprising that parallel phenomena would emerge on the country's campuses. My purpose in this section is to show that both the behavior of campus cultists and the wider interpretations and responses to cultism on Nigerian campuses reflect important realities about how university students are socialized to understand the performance of masculinity, and particularly the relationship between money, power, and sex.

Perhaps the most interesting aspect of how university students understand campus cults is the widespread belief that membership in these cults is dominated by children of the elite. I heard it from students and faculty and it is a perception shared widely in Nigerian society, circulating in popular discourse and reproduced in the media. Whether cults were truly filled with children of elites is hard to know for sure, but the fact that many cult members had cars and the cash to be able to procure guns certainly suggests a significant elite presence. Stephen Ellis (2011) hypothesizes that campus cults purposely recruit children of elites to bolster their material and social capital, and that the social connections established in school endure beyond graduation, affecting political and business opportunities later on. From my perspective, regardless of the true level of elite participation and its effects beyond university days, the fact that most Nigerians share the belief that cults are elite ventures is telling. It reinforces wider perceptions that successful masculinity in Nigeria requires money, that money and power are deeply intertwined, and that access to women is highly structured by money and power. It further suggests that many people are deeply discontented about the effects of money on society, and worried about the association of successful masculinity with a nexus of money and power that frequently involves violence to maintain it. In this sense, campus cults and the anxious discourses they engender are emblematic of wider trends in Nigeria.

If money and power are vital—if troubled—markers of masculinity in modern Nigeria, they often play out in the context of competition over women. On Nigerian campuses, cults seem to be most active, most violent, and most feared in relation to such competition. Many male students not in cults told me that they always checked whether a woman who they were interested in pursuing "belonged" to a cult member before making any advances, and I heard stories of guys who lost their girlfriends to cultists. Presumably, for some members of campus cults, greater access to and power over women was part of the appeal. Campus cult members enforced their status not only through the threat of violence to other men, but also through violence against women.

In 2011 five campus cultists allegedly raped an undergraduate female student at Abia State University. One of the perpetrators filmed it on his cell phone and someone posted it on the Internet. It went viral in Nigeria and generated a huge public response on Internet blogs, in the media, and in popular discourse. I followed the case online and when I went to Nigeria in 2012. For many Nigerians, the fact of the rape was evidence of both the persistence of pernicious gender inequality and the tyranny of cults on university campuses. The case led to many more accusations of campus rape and, to a limited extent, the beginnings of a national discourse about sexual violence, particularly in universities. But this did not prevent equally vociferous voices from questioning whether the episode was in fact rape, suggestions that the event had been staged, and so on.

Ultimately, the police arrested some suspects, but the official account of the university and the state government was that while a rape had taken place, it had not, in fact happened on the university campus and it was not perpetrated by students in a campus cult. I did not try and probably would not be able to sort out the truth of the matter, but it seemed obvious that the government and the university had political interests in promoting their version of the story, particularly given that the federal government passed a law in 2004 banning over one hundred known cults on university campuses (Ellis 2011). Both the government and university officials had been working to portray the problem as under control. On the Internet, in the media, and in everyday conversation, there was much debate about what was true. Over and above particular interpretations, the incident had such popular currency because it touched on a widely shared nerve regarding the role of money and power in Nigerian society, particularly as it unfolds in men's access to women.

From Servant to Master: Entrepreneurs and Apprentices in Nigeria's Informal Economy

Although formal education all the way to university is the ambition of the majority of young men and women in southeastern Nigeria, the reality is that many do not achieve that dream. For most who do not finish secondary school, or who finish secondary school but do not go on to university, the primary explanation is lack of money. Stories of stalled—and, all too often, completely terminated—educational trajectories due to lack of money are without a doubt the most common frustration I have heard among young men (and young women) over my twenty-five years of experience in Nigeria. Even for those fortunate enough to finish secondary school, or university, unemployment is a likely reality. Indeed, so bleak has been the problem of unemployment that beginning in the 1990s, large numbers of young men left secondary school not because their families could not afford it, but because the prospects of unemployment and little or no income after investing in education pushed them to pursue other alternatives. Whether because of no money to pay school fees or because completing school seemed to offer little prospect of producing enough money, for many young men the most appealing and available option besides formal education is to learn a trade through apprenticeship (Meagher 2006, 2010; Onokala and Banwo 2015). Possible apprenticeships include learning artisanal skills such as carpentry or tailoring, but among Igbo youths by far the most attractive option is to learn a business—something that would eventually, ideally, result in lots of money.

In the mid-1990s data from southeastern Nigeria suggested that for the first time in the region's history, more girls were attending secondary school than boys. The trend has continued. In the most recent data for Abia State (where Ubakala and Umuahia are located), girls made up 56 percent of enrolled secondary school students (National Bureau of Statistics 2014). While this reflects remarkable progress for women, and many people in the region lauded this achievement, the trend also provoked concern. The data underlined the well-known problem of unemployment and understandably raised concerns about the elusive benefits of expensive and highly sought-after education. In discussions about the new gender imbalance in secondary schools, I frequently heard people say that in an environment where schooling did not result in employment and good monetary returns, people could still "afford" to keep girls in school, but not boys. After all, schooling would make girls more attractive to potential husbands and better mothers to their children, but they could not risk keeping boys in school because boys needed to become men who would make money.

Apprenticeships in business as a route to financial success are, like formal education, fraught with pitfalls and far from a guaranteed. Typically, an apprenticeship involves a boy or a young man (apprenticeships can begin as early as in the teenage years or much later, sometimes extending into a man's thirties) attaching himself to a "master" who is a reasonably successful businessman. Usually the relationship itself is the result of some kind of kinship or community tie; apprentices are often relatives of their masters. At the very least there is almost always some kind of personal tie, usually running back through a community of origin. Although specific arrangements between master and apprentice can vary considerably, the basic model is that the apprentice works with the master for a number of years with little or no pay, but with the master taking care of the apprentice's upkeep. During this period the apprentice learns the business—for example, by overseeing a shop in the master's absence and negotiating with customers, by traveling to and making purchases from wholesale suppliers in more distant places, by assisting with bookkeeping or dealing with bank transactions, and by representing the business at associational meetings, and so on. At the end of the period of apprenticeship (which may last several years), in exchange for the apprentice's labor, the master then provides the capital for the apprentice to start his own business.

Although many Igbo men have achieved economic success in business by starting as an apprentice, these master-apprentice relationships do not always go smoothly. Usually conflicts and disagreements revolve around money. Apprentices chafe at their relative poverty and lack of cash during their training. Masters sometimes accuse their apprentices of mismanaging or stealing money. But most frequently disputes surface around the timing and amount of the capital payment to enable the apprentice to start his own business. In Igboland business sectors are often dominated by people from particular regions, with clusters of communities known for specializing in a particular line, such as pharmaceuticals, motor vehicle spare parts, electronics, and so on (Silverstein 1984; Meagher 2010; Peterson 2014). When one enters the huge semi-outdoor markets common in the cities and towns in the Southeast, one typically encounters stall after stall of the same product line. In this context, in addition to masters and apprentices having divergent interests regarding how much capital is appropriate at an apprentice's "graduation," a former apprentice is also likely to become a direct competitor. Everyday life in southeastern Nigeria's markets is animated by endless stories of master-apprentice conflicts, even as the system endures because, despite the structural differences in their interests, both masters and apprentices can benefit significantly from these arrangements.

One of the most successful examples I followed over the years was Bonafice. Bonafice's parents both died when he was a child and he was raised by one of his uncles and the uncle's wife in Ubakala. Before Bonafice completed secondary school he and his uncle agreed that he would leave school and become an apprentice to a distant relative who had a business selling electrical supplies, mostly various gauges of electrical wire, light fixtures, outlets, etc. Bonafice was an apprentice for nearly a decade, which is not unheard of, but considerably longer than a typical arrangement. In the early years he mostly just sold parts and supplies at one of two retail shops, but in later years he made most of the trips to Lagos to make purchases from wholesalers and he handled much of the business's finances. This was made possible by the twin facts that (1) his master had a number of other successful businesses and could afford the risk of allowing Bonafice to more or less run the electrical parts enterprise and (2) Bonafice proved himself to be extremely competent and trustworthy.

By the end of his apprenticeship Bonafice was pretty much running the business and seemed to draw significant earnings of his own—how much with his master's consent and how much by his own discreet ingenuity I never knew. But I do know that the negotiations around Bonafice's ultimate independence were somewhat disputatious. Partly, his master did not want him to separate at all, but when it became clear that Bonafice was determined to make a go of it on his own, the amount of start-up capital he would receive was the biggest bone of contention. In the end Bonafice received much less than he thought was fair. But along with what he had saved, it was enough to get him started. Perhaps more importantly, because he had been more or less running the business for years, his relationships with suppliers, creditors, and customers were so good that these people gladly worked with him when he established his independent enterprise. By the last time I visited him in 2012, more than five years after he had separated from his master, Bonafice was married with two children, had a nice car, had built a good house on the outskirts of Umuahia, and had a opened a second shop of his own. By every measure he had become a successful man.

It is worth exploring a bit more deeply why Bonafice was so successful, not just in transforming his apprenticeship into a successful independent business, but also in establishing himself as a competent, respected man. Even during the years when he was apprentice, Bonafice used his position to benefit his family and community—he was skilled in the art of conspicuous redistribution. For example, he convinced his master to let his junior siblings sometimes work the retail shops in exchange for small commissions, even though they never became full-fledged apprentices. He also contributed some of his earnings to help his uncle pay his junior siblings' school fees. And everyone in the community knew that Bonafice would give them a fair price if they purchased from Bonafice's master's shop.

Like many kin and community members, I was the beneficiary of Bonafice's goodwill. In the mid-1990s when I was doing dissertation fieldwork, Bonafice's shop had a landline telephone. This was long before the advent of Nigeria's now-ubiquitous cell phones. Bonafice allowed me to receive calls every few weeks from my parents in the United States. It did not cost him any money, but I knew many people in Ubakala to whom he extended the same courtesy. Had his master known how frequently Bonafice allowed the business's phone to be tied up by friends and relatives receiving calls from distant places, he probably would have been upset. But Bonafice was exceptionally generous. So when he succeeded financially most people were happy for him. There was remarkably little of the jealousy that typically accompanies another's good fortune in southeastern Nigeria. Bonafice managed to escape much of the suspicion and mistrust that wealth often brings with it by expertly fulfilling the social obligations of a man with means. It was a dynamic that I saw unfold over and over again, in its breach as often as in its realization. It is partly about sharing versus selfish greed, but it plays out most poignantly in the sometimes-subtle differences between conspicuous consumption and conspicuous redistribution. It is a theme to which I will return as I explore various arenas of men's lives throughout the book.

While enough apprentices succeed to make apprenticeship in business a prospect that many young men desire, the reality is that many such arrangements do not pan out, and even for those who complete the traineeship most struggle to forge a successful independent business. For example, Nwoye had been an apprentice for two years to a man from Orlu who sold pharmaceuticals in the Umuahia market. At the time of his "graduation" he received less capital than he thought was fair to start his own business, but his aged father persuaded him to accept the amount because the family desperately needed Nwoye to be making money to help out with family problems.

When I met him in the Umuahia main market in 2004, Nwoye had been on his own for about a year. He was thirty-one years old, single, and living in a room he rented from another more successful trader. He complained that his business was struggling because he lacked the capital to have a large- and wide-enough stock of drugs to compete with more established traders. As I mentioned above, in Nigeria's markets types of products tend to be clustered in "lines," so when a customer is looking to buy drugs (or shoes, or stationery, or rice, or almost anything at all) the stalls selling them are lined up one after the other. A potential customer walking the pharmaceutical line in the Umuahia market could not fail to notice that other shops had considerably more product than Nwoye's shop. He tried to mitigate this through creating good relationships with customers, by offering reasonable prices and flexible credit. But all that could only go so far in a competitive market. Further, he complained, because he was not from Orlu—the cluster of Igbo communities known for dominating the drug market not just in the Southeast, but throughout Nigeria (Peterson 2014)—he did not have the social ties to get the best deals or favorable credit from large pharmaceutical wholesalers in Onitsha and Lagos.

What stressed Nwoye most, however, was the pressure from his family. There were constant requests from his parents to help with his juniors' school fees. His father was ailing, often visiting a local clinic, and the medical bills added up. But most taxing for Nwoye was the constant harping about getting married. He said:

It's to the point where I don't want to visit home or even call because my mother will always bring up the issue of marriage. When I go to the village she points out women whom she thinks I could wed, and on two occasions even invited them over to greet me without informing me in advance. But how can I marry now without anything? A man needs enough money to marry—not just for the dowry [Nigerians sometimes call bridewealth paid by husbands to their wives' families "dowry"] and the wedding, but to start a family. With what I have now I can't even entertain a girlfriend properly, much less start a family. Until my business starts moving how can I take a wife?

Nwoye's anxiety about the cost of marriage and children is extremely common among young men in Nigeria, not only among apprentices and newly established businessmen, but also for men across all walks of life. The quest for money remains deeply tied to the central pillars of social reproduction—marriage and family making—and the intimate relationships that accompany them.

Conclusion

For boys making the transition to manhood in Nigeria, the all-important power of money becomes apparent at an early age. Whether it is in secondary school, where various forms of conspicuous consumption heavily affect social status; in university, where expectations about fashionable consumption are even more intense; or among those who have failed to complete school and set out to make a living by starting a business or apprenticing in a trade, the imperative of money for the performance of masculinity is constantly reinforced. But even early on in men's lives, the double-edged character of money is starkly evident. It is the thing that makes a good life possible in Nigeria and yet simultaneously the symbol of much that people agree is wrong with contemporary society.

Nowhere is the Janus-faced nature of money for masculinity more apparent than in sexual and romantic relationships with women. Boys learn that money is part of what women want from them, and yet its importance raises questions about the genuineness of intimacy, with both male and female motivations open to suspicion. Further, money as the necessary for means for social reproduction has created profound anxieties among young men about how—and sometimes even whether—a complete transition to manhood will be possible. It is to men's efforts to marry and become fathers that I turn in the next chapter.

Expensive Intimacies: Courtship, Marriage, and Fatherhood

Ikenna thought long and hard after I asked him whether he intended to marry Nkechi. He had been seeing her for over a year and clearly it was a serious relationship. In the ten years I had known him, she was the only woman he had ever brought to my house for a visit. Others I had seen at the club where we played tennis or at some of the bars and restaurants where many of the men I knew entertained their girlfriends. But Nkechi was different. Ikenna sometimes went with her to church. He introduced her to his parents. He told her there were no other girls. He even admitted to me that he was in love. The relationship had every sign that it would lead to marriage. After all, Ikenna was thirty-five years old. He had a decent job as a teacher. And his mother had been telling him for nearly five years that it was high time he married. But when I asked him about marrying Nkechi, he hesitated.

When Ikenna finally responded, it was in an anguished tone. He said:

Nkechi is the woman I want to marry. She doesn't behave like so many of our girls these days, just chasing money here and there. She's educated. She comes from a good family and from a community from which my people have married for generations. She's a good Christian, but not the overzealous born-again type. She is a serious person. And there is love in our hearts. I want to marry her.

But how can I marry her with what I have? I don't even own a car, much less a house. My father is poor and retired in the village. I am the *opara* [eldest son] so I have no seniors to help me. When I think of the list alone ["the list" contains the expected items needed for bridewealth that is provided by the bride's family to the groom and his family] I wonder how I can manage. Never mind the costs of the ceremonies, both a traditional wedding and a white wedding. We would start our married house in debt and then imagine the costs of children—feeding, school fees, and the rest . . .

Ikenna's voice trailed off. He knew, in southeastern Nigeria, that without marrying and having children he would not be considered a full man. More than once, at the tennis club, I'd heard older married men openly dismiss his opinions as those of a "small boy," a slight that had nothing to do with his age, education, intelligence, or occupation, but instead referred entirely to his status as a bachelor without children. But it wasn't only social expectations that made Ikenna want to marry. He wanted it for Nkechi and for himself. He told me many times before that he desired children—not six like his parents had, but at least three or four. Enough to make him feel like he had produced a "complete family," as he once put it. Ikenna was in love. He had a job. He was well past the age where it was appropriate and expected to marry. Yet like so many young men I knew, he found it difficult.

As I have emphasized already, marriage and fatherhood remain the pillars of manhood in southeastern Nigeria (Fortes 1978; Olawoye et al. 2004; Smith 1999, 2004a), but the ways that men find their wives and the character of the conjugal relationship itself are changing. The rise of romantic love as a relationship ideal for marriage has transformed courtship practices and with them men's behavior (Mann 1985; Cornwall 2002; Smith 2006, 2009). Men must now win women's hearts as well as raise the money for bridewealth and lavish ceremonies. In the same historical moment that bridewealth can include ever-more-expensive commodities and large amounts of cash, men are also expected to master new practices of intimacy. Fatherhood too is being reconfigured, as men—particularly urban-based men with fewer children and employed wives—take up a greater share of parenting duties that used to fall primarily on women or on the extended family more generally.

This chapter examines courtship, marriage, and fatherhood as primary spheres for the performance of masculinity. In keeping with the overall theme of the book, I focus on the intertwining of money and intimacy in these domains. During courtship, men must perform economically as well as emotionally. Once betrothed, the heavy double burden of performing both "traditional" and "white" wedding ceremonies reveals the seemingly ceaseless financial responsibilities men feel as they embark on matrimony. At the same time, the social rewards of marrying make it almost impossible to imagine anything else. Fatherhood itself is both more expensive and arguably more demanding than in the past. As in every arena of men's lives, money features prominently in these most important relationships (Constable 2009). Social reproduction, it seems, hinges on having money. Monetary wealth is desired and required; yet it also poses some of the most significant obstacles to men's efforts to meet their most basic obligations as men. Not only is money difficult to acquire in sufficient amounts, its centrality in these intimate relationships regularly challenges and occasionally undermines the emotional connections that are supposed to solidify and protect these bonds. Often, even when men have plenty, money can imperil the very relationships it enables.

Contemporary Courtship: For Love and Money

In the early 1990s, Nnanna met his future wife, Chinyere, in the town of Owerri in southeastern Nigeria, where she attended a teacher's college after completing secondary school in her village community. Nnanna was eight years her senior and when they met he was doing very well as a building contractor—well enough to own a used car, a prized symbol of wealth and success. On their first date he took her to the disco at the Concorde Hotel, at that time the best in town. In addition to being educated, Chinyere was a beautiful young woman and consequently had many suitors. Her courtship with Nnanna lasted almost two years. During that time they often dined out and went dancing together. Among the more memorable events of their courtship were a weekend outing to the Nike Lake resort near Enugu and a trip to Lagos during which they attended a performance by Fela Ransome-Kuti, a famous Nigerian musician. During their courtship, each bought the other Hallmark-like cards on birthdays. They went to many social events together and acknowledged to their peers that they were "a couple." Not long into their courtship, Nnanna and Chinyere began sleeping together. Many months before they decided to marry, they were sexually intimate. Prior to approaching Chinyere's people and his own family about getting married,

Nnanna asked Chinyere. They agreed together to get married and then began the process of including their families.

Like many men I observed as they progressed from youth to manhood, and specifically from bachelorhood to marriage, Nnanna felt the dual pressure to impress Chinyere romantically and financially. He was more fortunate than most because of his relative affluence, but the dilemmas for men are similar regardless of social class. While young men like Nnanna and Ikenna had numerous girlfriends during their bachelor years whom they had no intention of marrying, at a point in time, usually in their late twenties or early thirties, most men began to look out for a woman they might wed. The young men I asked about selecting a spouse offered a number of criteria. Most common among them was that she be educated and hardworking. Many men said they wanted their future wife to be a good Christian. Most men at some point mentioned the importance of being in love, though it was rarely the first thing they said. Quite striking was the regularity with which men used the adjective Ikenna applied to describe Nkechi: that she was "serious." As far as I could discern, all men seemed to mean something similar by this somewhat vague, but, in men's parlance, widely encompassing term. Asked to define "serious" in this context, my interlocutors offered explanations that incorporated several common characteristics, including not being wanton sexually, being responsible about money, being willing to work hard, being committed to family, and being a good Christian (which, in most men's narratives, seemed to be both a prerequisite for and a symbol of this seriousness). But in the Nigeria of today's youth, where men (and many women) seek sexual adventure before marriage, and where everyone's motives vis-à-vis money are constantly suspect, for men to feel confident that they have found such a woman is no small task. Further, navigating the balance between performing the role of suitor through love and through money poses constant challenges.

As has been well demonstrated in the literature on love in Africa, the emotional and material aspects of showing or proving love are not readily divisible (Cornwall 2002; Cole 2004; Cole and Thomas 2009; Mojola 2014a). For men, this means that if you claim to love a woman, you have to be willing to spend to show it. A man who does not spend is, from a woman's perspective, not serious. Women, too, want to find a serious man. The inextricable connection between love and money during courtship in southeastern Nigeria is captured by the widely used expression—usually spoken by or attributed to women—that there is "no romance without finance." Without money, there can be no love.

But this multivalent expression also captures some of what men worry about as they try to identify, and then court, a future wife. For while "no romance without finance" signals the connection between what has been called "provider love" (Hunter 2002, 2010; Bhana and Pattman 2011) and romantic love—a link both men and women in Nigeria generally and implicitly agree is legitimate—the expression can also be used to allude to a much starker reality, namely, that women will only have sex with a man who has money. Even as young Nigerians of both genders participate in a sexual economy where money and sex are deeply intertwined, these circumstances also generate discourses of complaint. Men condemn women for having sex for money; for requiring them to "pay" for sex; and for loving money (and sometimes sex) too much in the first place. Similarly, women condemn men for thinking they should have free sex without offering any (or enough) material support; for assuming that just by having and providing enough money they should be guaranteed sex; and for being really only interested in sex when they profess love. With regard to their money itself, men can be criticized either because they have too little or because they flaunt it when they have too much.

In most premarital sexual relationships, and certainly in courtships that might lead to marriage, women do not usually literally ask for money for sex and men do not offer it that way. Rather it all plays out in subtler, more socially acceptable ways. Sex is often talked about as love (think of the "proposing love" letters that I discussed in chapter 1, which so many secondary school students write) and money is transacted not as cash, but in the form of gifts such as clothes or cosmetics, or by paying for entertainment such as meals, drinks, or a nice hotel room. Still, cash does change hands, though not in the idiom of a direct payment for sex. A young woman may ask for help with school or university fees, or a man may offer money for transportation, or to help her parents in the village. But in moments of more crass conversation, which both men and women sometimes engage in, there can be an explicit acknowledgement that a man is expected to "perform" financially for a woman with whom he is having a sexual relationship.

In premarital relationships in which there is no pretext of marital courtship, the veils that shade the connections between sex and money can be fairly thin. In a courtship that might lead to marriage they must be thicker, and in particular, men in contemporary southeastern Nigeria seeking to marry a woman are expected to show love rather than just a desire for sex. Indeed, while women are definitely looking for a man that they believe will be a good provider, most are also looking for love—and hoping that love will help insure marital fidelity. A man's love for his wife does not necessarily guarantee he will be faithful. Interestingly, however, compared to after marriage, during courtship women seem to have significant leverage to enforce male fidelity and impose their expectations for romance. This is, no doubt, mostly because before marriage a woman can more easily end the relationship. In southeastern Nigeria it is difficult, uncommon, and still quite stigmatized to divorce. The collective interests and social expectations that come with marriage do not bind unmarried women in the same way. During courtship women are more or less free agents. Men know this and they behave accordingly. In my observations, during courtship men were much more likely to do things like buy a card, write a romantic letter, or say "I love you" than after marriage. And while it is difficult to know for sure, a man seriously courting a woman seemed much more likely to be faithful than once married. Even if this is not always the case, there is no question that many men were more concerned about being caught cheating by a woman to whom they were engaged (or trying to become engaged to) than after they were married. I will explain much more about men's extramarital sexual behavior in chapter 4, but suffice it to say here that while all men have to balance provider love and romantic love in their relationships with women, during marriage they could often get away with performing only the former. During courtship they had to get it right on both accounts.

Given the changes that commonly take place in gender dynamics after marriage and the achievement of parenthood, it is worth asking whether Igbo men are as committed as Igbo women to the idea of romantic love as the basis for marriage. While one could argue that men profess love to their desired spouses in order to secure their consent in marriage, and that they enter marriage with a nod and wink, knowing that they will eventually look for outside women, I think the true explanation is more complicated. Certainly young women I spoke to were well aware that men try to manipulate women's affections in order to get sex, and some married women I spoke to who were unhappy with their philandering husbands wondered out loud whether their husbands had ever really loved them. A married woman whom one of my female research assistants interviewed said about men:

When a man wants to marry you he tells you all sorts of lies. "You'll be my true love; I'll be faithful to you," and you decide, "This is the man I will marry!" But as soon as he has paid bridewealth and completed all the ceremonies, the trouble starts. . . .

Once you've had a couple of children he loses interest in you and starts moving about here and there [a euphemism for infidelity].

While I know from countless conversations with Nigerian men that they do indeed manipulate women's affections, using proclamations of love to secure sexual access, it was my impression that men were often genuinely caught up in romance. Certainly most young men openly stated that "being in love" was an important criterion for selecting a spouse. Despite women's fears, I do not think that most men consciously lied about their feelings to secure the acceptance of a marriage proposal. The transformation that occurs in gender dynamics after marriage and parenthood, and the propensity and social acceptability of men's involvement in extramarital sexual relationships, must be understood in other terms. But during courtship, men must do their best to provide both love and money.

Bridewealth, Marriage Ceremonies, and the Performance of Masculinity

One of the biggest changes for today's men compared to earlier generations is the demise of arranged marriages. A man must first convince a woman to marry before anything else. But things have not changed entirely. While young couples now choose each other rather than having their marriages prescribed by kin, inevitably a man must seek the consent of his future wife's family and his own people, especially both sets of parents. Without their cooperation it is not possible to pay bridewealth or complete a traditional wedding ceremony. Men (and women) frequently meet resistance from their families in their choice of spouse. I have written elsewhere about these family and community expectations and how they can conflict and eventually be reconciled with individual preferences (Smith 2001b). Suffice it to say here that, ultimately, any man who intends to marry a woman must approach her people, seek consent, and begin the process of bridewealth payments.

Beginning with the oil boom in Nigeria in the 1970s, the cost of bridewealth in the Southeast escalated dramatically. The items on "the list" expanded to include many modern commodities (some for the woman's kin and some mandated to be provided to the bride herself as part of her transfer to her husband's household). Things like refrigerators began to appear as part of bridewealth payments. One community called Mbaise became infamous for requiring that a man provide a motor scooter for his new wife. When Nigeria's oil economy crashed in the 1980s, it did not seem to diminish the ever-increasing escalation of bridewealth, and the accompanying expectations that a man should be able to provide modern commodities for his wife and family (Masquelier 2004; Constable 2009).

A lot of ink in anthropology has been spilled to demonstrate that bridewealth payments are "social payments"; that is, rather than being a bald economic transaction to "buy" a woman and her reproductive capacity, bridewealth payments are a socially embedded form of reciprocal exchange that creates, symbolizes, and helps maintain an enduring set of social relationships between families and communities, with marriage at the core of these ties (Lévi-Strauss 1969; Goody and Tambiah 1973; Comaroff 1980; Isiugo-Abanihe 1994, 1995). In southeastern Nigeria, even with the seemingly ever-inflating costs and the huge amounts of money that are now required to marry, the social character of bridewealth has endured. Marriage remains a deeply collective endeavor with wide societal interests and investment. Indeed, that is precisely why nearly all men (and women) remain so profoundly committed to marrying despite its burdens. But it is also true that bridewealth costs plenty of money, and—without negating the notion of social payments—men also feel and say that they are paying for a wife. In many instances in which men complain about disputes with their wives, I've heard them say things like, "After all, didn't I pay for her?" Such exclamations do not mean that Igbo men generally think of bridewealth payments as resulting in monetarily based ownership. But at times when it was convenient for voicing their discontents, that seemed to be exactly what some men wanted to imply. Given the imperative of money to make marriage possible at all, perhaps it should not be surprising that socially embedded payments would sometimes be talked about as if they could be reduced to a cash transfer.

In the 1990s many communities began to recognize that exponentially increasing bridewealth demands were making it almost impossible for men to marry. While in the past the details of what was expected in bridewealth payments were the result of collective custom, recent trends exceeded anything communities had consciously agreed to. To try to address the problem, communities generated standard lists meant to restrict and reform bridewealth payments for their area, with the hope that this would encourage families to refrain from the arms-race-like escalation in conspicuous consumption and conspicuous redistribution that seemed to affect not only wedding ceremonies, but also funerals and other collective rituals. At the time, everyone lamented these escalating costs, but no one seemed willing to make unilateral changes because to do so would make one's daughter (or dead parent) seem less valuable than others. Most people welcomed these interventions and they seemed to tamp down bridewealth inflation to some extent. But compliance was voluntary and variable, and if people thought they could or should do better than the community standard, they tried. Further, the new standards were not exactly cheap. Most men would have to save a long time to have enough money, even for the newly narrowed bridewealth lists. In addition, although these collectively created new standards helped curb the bridewealth arms race, they did little to control the rising costs of wedding ceremonies. As many men told me, the expectations and costs of the rituals themselves were often more daunting than bridewealth itself.

In southeastern Nigeria, people clearly distinguish between what they call the "traditional wedding" (the *igba nkwu* ceremony) and a modern "white," or Christian, wedding. The traditional ceremony is obligatory; no one dares neglect or evade it. Not to perform it would mean—in the opinion of parents, other kin, affines, and the wider community—that the couple is not married. The traditional ceremony is for and about the couple's lineages and their communities as much or more than it is for and about the man and woman who are marrying. The series of exchanges that establishes and legitimizes a marriage is talked about in terms of obligations and duties. The traditional wedding ceremony symbolically marks an enduring social alliance (albeit one potentially fraught with antagonisms), and a lifelong series of exchanges (again spoken about as obligations) between the extended families of the husband and the wife. At the center of that alliance is a mutual interest in the children produced in the marriage. In contrast, the white wedding is an ideal; one can be married in the eyes of society without it. Performing a Christian ceremony is more of a luxury and a symbol of wealth, progressiveness, and religiosity. In recent years, however, more and more couples—even those not particularly affluent—opt to do both (Onyima 2015).

But even as traditional wedding ceremonies continue to fulfill social functions in relation to kin and community, these events have become spectacles of conspicuous redistribution. For most men, like Ikenna with whom I opened the chapter, the prospect of paying for a traditional wedding is daunting. Whereas in the past the costs of the ceremony were borne primarily by a man's patrilineal kin, especially his father, increasingly the man who will marry is expected to pay many of the expenses himself. All manner of kin and many friends and associates still contribute to the wedding costs, but mostly in token, symbolic amounts. Occasionally, a wealthier relative will shoulder most of the costs. I even know of some instances where the bride and her family have contributed significantly to costs that should be paid by the man and his family. In rare cases, if her family is much wealthier than his, they might carry the lion's share. But this is the exception rather than the rule, and few men would be happy having people know that a woman had to underwrite his traditional wedding ceremony. Despite these exceptions, and even with the contributions that are generally offered by friends and family, the predominant trend is that individual men are increasingly responsible for financing their weddings. And the costs seem to keep soaring.

I have attended more than a twenty traditional weddings in southeastern Nigeria over the years. While each is, of course, slightly different, they generally follow a similar script, including with regard to what is expected in terms of "entertaining" the guests. Some parts of the so-called traditional wedding do indeed appear quite traditional. For example, the ceremony always opens with the blessing, breaking, and sharing of kola nuts, which is the traditional Igbo ritual of hospitality (Uchendu 1964; Nwagbara 2007). Further, most times the bride and groom eventually share palm wine to mark the actual moment of marriage. But in many ways the igba nkwu ceremony is a performance of modernity, social class, consumption, and conspicuous redistribution. In other words, it is very much about having and spending money.

Chima and Adanna did their traditional wedding in 2012. It was neither the most extravagant nor the most modest I have attended in recent years. It seemed quite typical, in fact. I describe it here to give a sense of the level of conspicuous redistribution that is usual, and the manner and degree to which the groom's masculinity is at stake in performing it properly. The ceremony itself took place in Adanna's natal community, the home of her father's patrilineage, as is normative. But the expenses began long before the ceremony itself. Invitation cards had to be designed and printed. A hall, as well as tents or canopies, needed to be rented to accommodate the guests and protect them from the rain or the blazing hot sun. A generator had to be hired to assure there would be power, given that the national grid provided electricity unreliably, and in recent years, in Adanna's natal village, rarely at all. Electricity would be necessary for the loudspeaker system that would also need to be rented, which would be used by the master of ceremonies. Chima and Adanna had an extroverted friend serve as MC, but frequently the MC must be paid too. Electricity was also required to power the sound system (also hired) with which the DJ (who was paid) would play music for people to dance to at the conclusion of the formal ceremony. Someone also had to be contracted to video the whole event. I have not attended a single wedding in Nigeria that didn't include a videographer, no matter how wretched the couple.

And then there were the souvenirs. Over the past couple of decades it has become increasingly common and expected that guests go away with souvenirs to remember the occasion. Usually the names of the bride and groom, the date, and some romantic cliché are printed or engraved on souvenirs, often with an image of the couple copied from a photograph as well. Chima and Adanna made plastic cups and small umbrellas. The umbrellas were more expensive. They made only fifty to be given to the most important guests. They ordered two hundred plastic cups and hoped they would suffice to go around to the rest. In advance of the Saturday event they also paid for half a dozen large banners, which would be hung in strategic places approaching the venue, announcing the event, the time, and the location.

The expectations to meet or exceed prevailing standards of conspicuous redistribution were palpable. Like many men preparing for their igba nkwu ceremonies, Chima anticipated that the event would attract people who were not invited—villagers who saw the banners or knew about the wedding and came, in Chima's estimation, mainly for the free food and free drinks. He told me: "Many people who we don't know will appear and they will expect to be fed and to drink plenty. There are always such people. We don't want them there, but we can't turn them away." And yet in some ways, the larger the crowd, the more impressed people would be by the performance, especially if there was enough food and drink to satisfy everyone. Like most men anticipating their wedding ceremonies, Chima both yearned for a huge crowd and dreaded it.

In advance of the ceremony many cartons of beer, bottles of wine, and crates of soft drinks would need to be purchased. Chima and Adanna chilled some in a big refrigerator but many had to be served warm. At more extravagant ceremonies I've seen people hire an entire refrigeration truck just to keep the drinks cold. A small army of women from Adanna's and Chima's respective families and communities was drafted to cook huge vats of food for the guests, in this case jallof rice, a common dish at weddings. Prior to cooking, four goats and many chickens were purchased and slaughtered, and of course all the other many ingredients had been procured as well. Plates, spoons, and cups had to be rented or borrowed. As should be apparent by now, the whole thing is a huge, complicated, and wildly expensive affair.

On the day of the ceremony, Chima and Adanna were lucky. It was the beginning of rainy season, but there was not a cloud in the sky. While Chima and Adanna had anticipated at least two hundred guests, easily three hundred showed up at various points, all needing to be fed. Fortunately, they had prepared enough food and the drinks sufficed to serve everyone. But the souvenirs ran out. Further, it seemed that the strategy of umbrellas for more important people and cups for the rest had been a mistake because, of course, everyone wanted an umbrella. I heard many people grumble about receiving only a cup. But such complaints always seem to surface at weddings and funerals. At these events, where the level of conspicuous redistribution is a primary measure of success, everyone is attentive to whether they received their fair share.

These dynamics are almost impossible to manage without some people feeling slighted. On the one hand, "entertainment" at Igbo ceremonies is organized highly hierarchically. There is always a "high table" where the most distinguished people are asked to sit. Venues, food, and drinks are allocated based on status. At Chima's wedding, for example, people were sent to various venues to eat and drink, and the rank in venues was clear for all to see. The most distinguished guests went to the nicest nearby houses; the least important people were served outdoors, under the rented tents. At each venue everyone got jallof rice, but the amount of meat per plate varied considerably; so too did the quality of beer and whether or not there were also bottles of wine available. Everyone expects things to be ordered this way and even those at the bottom of the social ladder would be aghast if these tacitly agreed status hierarchies were violated and the entertainment botched. And yet, on the other hand, these same inequalities produce discontent. The person at the lowest-status venue doesn't expect to be at the high table, but in each grouping there are always people who feel they have been slighted. And in southeastern Nigeria people are not afraid to say so. Once the formal ceremony was over and the entertainment began, Chima spent much of his time moving around to the different places where people were eating and drinking, to greet and thank everyone, but also to offer personal attention that would help mollify any discontents. Multiple times I saw him rush off to get someone another beer or shout for a man to be brought another piece of meat.

But these things are normal at Igbo weddings. Overall, Chima and

3   In southeastern Nigeria, wedding ceremonies are occasions of conspicuous redistribution during which guests must be entertained in a befitting manner.

Adanna's igba nkwu ceremony had been a success. When the couple was officially married after sharing palm wine, people sprayed them with countless crisp, clean naira notes—the type that people often pay a commission to get because they are the most prestigious with which to shower people at social rituals. Indeed, the symbolic importance of "spraying money" at social events is emblematic of the intimate connections between money and sociality that are so powerful in contemporary Nigeria. What could be a more obvious act of conspicuous redistribution than publicly showering someone with cash?

Like so many young couples, Chima and Adanna planned to follow their traditional wedding with a Christian ceremony. Then timing of the white wedding can vary a lot. Sometimes it is organized for the weekend after the igba nkwu ceremony. More often, it takes place many months later. This is to give the couple, especially the man, time to muster the resources required for another expensive event. In some cases couples wait years. Recently, the burgeoning popularity of Pentecostal Christianity seems to have sparked a more general impetus to demonstrate religiosity through performing a church wedding (Onyima 2015). Indeed, over the last two decades I have observed a large number of middle-aged and elderly couples arranging Christian weddings that they never thought of performing when they were married many years ago.

In contrast to the traditional wedding, the Christian ceremony is officiated in a church, often in town, by a single minister or priest who serves to legitimize and sanctify the marriage in the eyes of God. Following a Western model, the bride dresses in a white wedding gown and the groom in a tuxedo or dark suit. Bridesmaids (who are often urban/school friends, as well as relatives) dress in matching outfits and the groom is assisted by his "best man" and perhaps some ushers. The ceremony is followed by a reception at which there are formal toasts, a very ceremonial cutting of a wedding cake, and of course much eating, drinking, and dancing. The message of the Christian ceremony is that the success of the marriage depends above all on the individual couple, and on their relationships with each other and with God. Families are, of course, asked to assist in supporting the marriage, but the ceremony very much reinforces a conjugal, companionate model of marriage, with the couple as partners in a particularly individual kind of project.

By almost all accounts the white wedding is less costly than the igba nkwu ceremony, mostly because it is easier to control the guest list. Whereas more or less anyone can show up at the village venues where traditional rites are performed and he has to be entertained with food and drink, at Christian weddings most guests are specifically invited. But the receptions that follow white weddings also arenas of conspicuous redistribution where a man's wherewithal is on display. And like at the igba nkwu ceremony, markers of social class stand out—from the size of the guest list to the type of venue for the reception, to the quality of food and drink, and so on. If marriage is a major marker of full adulthood for Igbo men, and wooing a woman requires both demonstrating both romantic love and provider love, for most men the most daunting challenge is finding enough money to perform the ceremonies required in a manner befitting the admiration of his various communities and the public.

Money, Intimacy, and Modern Marriage

Patterns of courtship and the growing symbolic importance of Christian wedding ceremonies mark significant changes in Igbo conceptions of what a marriage is. Marriage relationships themselves have also changed. Polygyny, once fairly common, is exceedingly rare among the younger generation. Within monogamous marriages, the strength of the conjugal relationship has grown vis-à-vis other family and community ties. A young man and his wife are far more likely than their parents to share one bedroom, eat together, maintain a single household budget, and live in town away from the compound of the husband's family, which is the traditional place of residence. The quality of a young couple's personal relationship, including the degree of emotional intimacy and sexual compatibility, is more likely to figure in their private assessments of the state of their marriage than was the case with their parents.

Perhaps the most concise way to contrast modern Igbo marriages with the past is to note that young couples see their marriages as a life project in which they as a couple are the primary actors, whereas their parents' marriages were more obviously embedded in the structures of the extended family. People in more modern marriages tend to emphasize the primacy of the individual couple, often in conscious opposition to the constraints imposed by ties to kin and community. For example, a forty-three-year-old teacher reported: "For me and my wife our marriage is our business, whereas in my parents' time everything was scrutinized by the extended family. If they had any little problem everyone might become involved. We try to keep things within the married house. If we have any problem we handle it ourselves and maybe pray over it, but we don't go running to the elders broadcasting our problems here and there."

But it is important not to exaggerate these trends. Even in the most modern marriages, ties to kin and community remain strong, and the projects of marriage and parenthood continue to be embedded in the relationships and values of the extended family system. Indeed, concerns about the collective expectations of wider social networks permeate young men's stories of modern courtship, the resolution of marital disputes, and decisions about childrearing. The fact that modern marriage in southeastern Nigeria remains a resolutely social endeavor creates contradictions for younger couples; they must navigate not only their private individual relationships, but also the outward representation of their marriages to kin and community.

Many young men talked about the quality of their sexual relationships and the ability to communicate about sexual matters as important aspects of their marriages, and as characteristics that distinguish their marriages from their parents' marriages. At the same time that young men and women have aspirations for modern sexualities, they also face enduring social pressures created by discourses that depict modern sexual behavior as immoral. Women in particular face a double bind: they need to satisfy their husbands' modern sexual appetites to help keep them faithful, yet they risk being branded as sexually licentious, and even unfaithful, if they demonstrate too much sexual expertise or pleasure.

One man told me a story of a friend whose civil servant wife had a government post that required her to live apart from him for an extended period of time. When she returned home permanently her husband interpreted her sexual aggressiveness (apparently she initiated a position they had not previously tried together) as evidence that she had been unfaithful. Men also are cautious about introducing new sexual styles during marital sex, for fear that their wives might suspect they had learned and practiced them with other women. One highly educated man who worked for the local government told me a very funny story about a married couple who were both having extramarital affairs in which they were experimenting with many different sexual positions and styles, but had only missionary sex in their matrimonial bed. Each wanted to hide from the other what they really knew and enjoyed. He added that probably many married couples knew much more about sex than they ever showed each other.

These stories illustrate the degree to which intimacy in modern Igbo marriages often requires a certain sexual decorum, in which men and women must appear to subscribe to social values about sexual morality. Ironically, in contemporary Nigeria, concerns about sexual morality may be more powerful than ever because sexual immorality has come to stand for people's discontents about various aspects of social change—a phenomenon most evident in popular responses to the HIV/AIDS epidemic, in which people commonly associate risk with too much sexual liberty (Smith 2003, 2014a). But it would be a misrepresentation to suggest that modern Igbo marriages are largely places of sexual inhibition. While the above stories rightly signal that marital intimacy, and marital sex, is shaped by widely shared, publicly circulating concerns about sexual morality, many young men told me that sexual intimacy, sexual pleasure, and even a degree of sexual experimentation were central and welcome elements in their marriages.

For young men in modern marriages the importance of romantic love and the new forms of conjugal intimacy it entails have not resulted in a diminished significance of provider love. If anything, men feel ever more pressure to provide money. Even as the quality of a couple's personal relationship figures heavily into assessments of the state of their marriage, money featured prominently in just about every narrative I collected from both men and women about their married lives. From men's perspectives (and women's too) the vast majority of marital conflicts involve money. For men, in most cases, the issue is women's unreasonable demands or excessive expenditures. For example, when I asked Udo, a trader who ran a small shop in the Ubakala main market, about sources of conflict with his wife he said: "It is always money. Sometimes she will make purchases that we cannot afford. Other times she will bother me about the children's school fees or something she thinks we need for the house. When I tell her that sales were not good at my shop, she twists her face and that can be the start of a conflict." Women, of course, had different perspectives. In their view, men often appear to be misusing money for selfish masculine purposes such as drinking with other men or pursuing extramarital sexual relationships, rather than paying children's school fees or otherwise providing for family needs. But in both men's and women's accounts of marital discord, finances usually stood center stage, with both genders agreeing implicitly that the performance of masculinity in marriage hinged on money.

For men, the centrality of money was a kind of double-edged sword. On the one hand, in an economy where earning enough income was a perpetually challenge, the lack of sufficient funds assured that competent masculinity was always threatened. No matter how good or kind a man might be to his wife and children, if he could not provide for them he felt his manhood was imperiled. And while some women were quite supportive and forgiving if they thought their husband was really trying, a man without money risked losing face with his wife. On the other hand, the fact that the economic project of provisioning a household and raising children constituted the main measure of manhood in marriage meant that if a man could provide sufficient money for his wife, he felt empowered to violate other aspects of the marital accord with greater impunity. In southeastern Nigeria, men with money felt much more entitled to have extramarital sex, not simply because having girlfriends or lovers cost money, but also because if a man was providing adequately for his wife and children, he typically believed that this empowered him to do whatever he wished with the rest of his wealth. Understanding men's extramarital sex, including how it connects to men's performance of masculinity for other men, is something I take up in chapter 4.

Manhood as Fatherhood

In an era of lower fertility, love marriage, and changing family structures, men in southeastern Nigeria are beginning to adopt new approaches to fatherhood. Men are more involved in the daily lives of their children than in the past. They help more with childcare, exhibit greater intimacy with their children, and generally treat them in a less authoritarian manner than fathers in the past. While many Igbo men participate in and support these changes, ambivalence and contradictions abound. For example, messages from ever-more-popular Pentecostal churches that exhort men to embrace monogamy and fidelity compete with male peer pressure to prove masculinity and economic status by spending money on young mistresses. Further, the emergence of globally influenced ideals of romantic love and marital intimacy— and, to an increasing extent, gender equality—frequently come into conflict with the enduring conviction that a man must be the king of his castle. Pressures to have fewer children and invest in them educationally and emotionally contend with still salient notions of wealth in people and patriarchal authority. Just as they do as husbands, as fathers men constantly navigate the entanglements of money and intimacy and the implications for masculine power.

In anthropology, demography, and other social sciences, the relative dearth of accounts of men's lives and roles in the spheres of family, reproduction, contraception—and, indeed, fatherhood—has been lamented for at least a couple of decades (Connell 1995; Gutmann 1997; Green and Biddlecom 2000; Inhorn et al. 2009). Matthew Gutmann (1996), Nicholas Townsend (2002), and others have drawn attention to the connections between notions and values of fatherhood and those of masculinity. While the vacuum in the study of masculinity in sub-Saharan Africa has begun to be filled (Lindsay and Miescher 2003b; Miescher 2005; Ouzgane and Morrell 2005), relatively little has been written in anthropology about fatherhood in Africa (though for South Africa see Richter and Morrell 2006). Further, I am aware of no anthropological accounts specifically focused on fatherhood in contemporary Nigeria. In the wake of seemingly more spectacular shifts in the lives of women, marked by new patterns in the gendered division of labor and more widely accepted global norms about women's rights, it is easy to overlook the quieter and more uneven shifts in how men navigate their status as fathers.

This section examines changes in men's experience of fatherhood in southeastern Nigeria. As marriages have become more companionate, and as fathers find that the burdens of raising children fall ever more directly on their shoulders, men experience fatherhood as, simultaneously, an essential arena to forge and prove masculinity and a tremendous challenge to their manhood. In the face of changing expectations about marital dynamics and a shifting gendered division of labor, new ideals and practices of fatherhood produce deep anxieties about the weakening of male privilege.

The Pressure to Become a Father

The preeminent Africanist anthropologist Meyer Fortes noted long ago that it is "parenthood that is the primary value associated with the idea of family in West Africa" (1978, 121). "Parenthood," Fortes said, "is regarded as a *sine qua non* for the attainment of the full development of the complete person to which all aspire" (1978, 125). In southeastern Nigeria, even with all the changes in marriage, fertility, and kinship—some of which might lead one to expect that the social importance of parenthood would diminish—Fortes' observation is as true now as ever. Indeed, one might reasonably argue that marriage and parenthood are more valued than ever, in part because they are perceived as ever more difficult and costly to achieve.

Further, in southeastern Nigeria marriage remains the only socially approved arena in which to be a parent. While marriage rates are waning in some parts of Africa, including some dramatic declines in parts of southern Africa (Hosegood, McGrath, and Moultrie 2009; Preston-Whyte 1993), this is not the case in Igbo-speaking Nigeria, where the expectation to marry is almost universal, the overwhelming majority of adults marry, and most children are born to married couples. The two cases below further exemplify how men experience the social pressure to marry as a pressure to become a father, how fatherhood is a marker of competent masculinity, and how at least some men are beginning to question society's expectations, even as they feel compelled to live up to them.

Silas was the third son of his parents, the fourth child in a family of five. His oldest brother disappeared and almost surely died as a child-soldier fighting for Biafra in Nigeria's civil war. Silas's surviving brother and his two sisters—one several years younger than him—were all married more than fifteen years ago. Each has at least three children. Silas's father died more than a decade ago, but to Silas's aging mother's deep disappointment, Silas had passed the age of forty and still was not married. His mother constantly reminded him that he needed to marry, and when he visited Ubakala from Lagos, where he had lived for well over a decade, she often arranged for him to meet young women from around the community whom she hoped he might be persuaded to marry. She also recruited everyone she could—her son and daughters, cousins, neighbors, the pastor in the family's church—to convince Silas he must marry.

Like other men struggling to find enough money to marry, Silas would often say—to me, but also to his mother when she hounded him—"How can I marry when I don't have anything doing?" By this he meant that he did not have steady work or a stable income, so how could he afford a wedding ceremony, much less the costs of a family? Nevertheless, about three years ago Silas finally married. His sisters contributed significantly to the cost of the wedding and his sister-in-law (Silas's brother's wife) was instrumental in finding the bride, who was a relative of hers. I had the impression that Silas may have received a discount in the amount of bridewealth he had to provide because it was a second marriage between these two extended families. Not more than a year after the wedding, Silas and his wife (almost twenty years his junior) had a baby boy. Everyone in Silas's family is extremely happy about the marriage and the child, especially Silas's mother—though she is already hurrying her son and daughter-in-law to have another baby. Silas seems much relieved to have finally procreated. The last time I saw him in 2012, he proudly took me to his son's daycare center so that I could take pictures of him and his son.

While marriage and parenthood remain the most imperative and taken-for-granted dimensions of social adulthood in southeastern Nigeria, and while the main reason most men delay the transition to marriage and fatherhood is a worry about the economic burdens entailed rather than because of reluctance to marry and have children in and of itself, I have recently begun to hear a few unmarried Igbo men question the very institutions of marriage and parenthood. Although such sentiments remain the exception, they suggest that the costs of marriage and fatherhood have grown so great that they have enabled previously unthinkable contemplation about alternatives. At the very least, such feelings are indicative of the anxieties men feel about the most vital aspects of the performance of masculinity.

During my last visit to Nigeria I had a long discussion with a young researcher at a local university in Umuahia. Chiwendu was thirty-six years old, several years past the normative age for men to marry in southeastern Nigeria, but still young enough not to have reached the stigmatized status that Silas experienced before he finally married in his forties. I had noticed Chiwendu spending a lot of time with one particular young woman, and I asked him about the relationship.

He narrated a long story about how they met and how the relationship evolved, culminating in his telling me that he would likely marry her. He lamented how much pressure he was under—not only from his parents, but also seemingly from society at large—to get married. "Everyone is looking at me somehow," he said. "In our society, no one takes you seriously unless you are married and have children. You cannot speak up. Your opinion is dismissed. I am tired of being looked at as small boy." He then explained some obstacles that remained to marrying the young woman—the principal one being that she belonged to a Pentecostal church and that her pastor and her parents wanted her to marry from within the church. Chiwendu was attending her church and taking classes with the pastor that would enable him to be baptized (and "born again"), thereby allowing him to officially join her church and get the pastor's and the woman's parents' permission to marry.

While he was forging ahead with this plan, he expressed some displeasure at several aspects, including that it was the traditional practice in Igboland for the wife to join the husband's church, not vice versa. Chiwendu also had some apprehension about whether he really liked this church, though one of his friends pointed out that men often attend church with their fiancées, only to eschew regular worship once the marriage is official. Chiwendu's family was Anglican, and he knew his father would not like his leaving their church. But his father had pressured him not to marry a woman a couple of years ago because investigations had uncovered that her family had a "spiritual" problem (in my experience this could mean anything from a history of mental illness in the family to rumors of witchcraft). In that case, Chiwendu relented to accommodate his father's wishes. He said his father was now so eager for him to marry that he would probably overlook his misgivings if Chiwendu had to join his girlfriend's church in order to marry her.

Most interestingly, as Chiwendu narrated his experience regarding the social pressure to marry and have children, he said: "If it weren't required to by society I don't need it. What do I need marriage and children for? All that trouble. I'm okay like this. But I have no choice. I will marry and have a couple of kids and that's it." He went on to elaborate further, emphasizing that he had only just begun to save enough money to contemplate buying a car, but that if he had to finance a wedding, a car would have to be postponed indefinitely. Like for many young men I knew, for Chiwendu the money needed to marry was a source of serious anxiety. But unlike most men, he went further and questioned the necessity of marriage and fatherhood in the first place. I suspect Chiwendu's negative attitude about marriage and parenthood was partly a result of the stress from the immediate pressure he was feeling from his family and peers. But it is extremely unusual in southeastern Nigeria for people to voice any dissent regarding the ubiquitous expectation that a full and proper life requires marriage and parenthood. That said, the notion Chiwendu expressed—that there might be any alternative to marrying and having children—is itself evidence of the influence of incipient social changes. And yet the fact that men like Silas and Chiwendu, who married late and who articulated the burdens of marriage and fatherhood, ultimately decided to follow convention attests to just how powerful these norms and institutions remain, even in the face of significant challenges.

Fathers and Child-Rearing

When I arrived for a planned interview with Ugochukwu he was busy in the kitchen warming *akamu*, a soft, semiliquid food made from corn flour. Ugochukwu's older son held Ugochukwu's eighteen-month-old daughter who would consume the pap, jiggling her up and down on his knee to ward off the crying that seemed imminent. Ugochukwu immediately apologized that his task would delay the start of our interview. He then explained that his wife had yet to return from the office and his daughter was hungry. Judging from the confidence with which he tested the consistency of the pap to decide whether it was ready, Ugochukwu had done this before, but he also made it clear that, had his wife been home, this would have been her job. When the akamu was ready, Ugochukwu handed the bowl and spoon to his son to feed his younger sister. But as Ugochukwu moved away, motioning me to the parlor where we would talk, his daughter cried and pushed away the spoon, spilling pap in her brother's lap. Ugochukwu then took his daughter from her brother, carried her and the food to the parlor, and at the same time asked me if it was okay to begin the interview while he fed his daughter. She ate as we spoke, and eventually she fell asleep in her father's lap.

While it is still far more common to see mothers undertake the routine household tasks of parenting—cooking, feeding children, dressing them, washing dishes, laundering clothes, and so on—it is no longer shocking to see some men contributing to this work. A primary backdrop to changes in practices of fatherhood in southeastern Nigeria is the transformation of marriage described above. In modern marriages, Nigerian couples often think about limiting the number of children they have to three or four, they commonly view educating their children as their highest priority, and they frequently communicate and cooperate with regard to training children in order that they will be prepared to be successful in an increasingly urbanized and globalized social and economic environment. As the selection of a spouse has become a more individualized decision, as marriage has become more companionate and an arena of greater personal intimacy between husband and wife, and as lower levels of fertility have unfolded in consonance with greater investments in individual children (especially their education), fathers in southeastern Nigeria have become more directly involved in many aspects of parenting.

Because Ugochukwu's parenting practices struck me as indicative of a changing gendered division of labor, in the interview I asked him about how he and his wife divided domestic labor. What struck me most was how he emphasized the importance of consultation and solidarity between him and his wife regarding their children. While his wife still did most of the household labor associated with parenting, Ugochukwu—and many younger men I interviewed—went out of his way to emphasize that raising a family was a joint project in which he and his wife cooperated closely.

More pronounced than the incipient relaxing of a highly gendered domestic division of labor is the dramatic shift in the way mothers and fathers communicate to raise their children. This involves major changes in both fatherhood and motherhood, with the role of parents ascending vis-à-vis other kinship relations as the primary locus for authority and socialization. Parents were not unimportant in the past, but other kin (aunts and uncles, other wives of one's father, older siblings, and cousins, etc.) took on a more significant role in caring for, supervising, and disciplining children than is the case now. Marriage as a project of social reproduction is, of course, not new, but the way that couples view themselves—as a couple and as mothers and fathers—as the primary agents in this socialization process is something quite recent. For men, the degree of fatherly involvement is itself a change; for both men and women the focus on providing formal education and other material and symbolic resources in order to train their children to be prepared for a more modern, urban, and individualistic world involves significant shifts from the past.

In southeastern Nigeria, the notion that it is the father (but, in real-

4 Fatherhood remains a pillar of successful masculinity in Nigeria, but even as men have more intimate relationships with their children than in the past, they also need more money.

ity, the father and mother) who is solely responsible for providing for a child's education contrasts strongly with cultural norms of the past. When Victor Uchendu (1965) published his classic account of the Igbo, one of the most striking aspects of Igbo society was the degree to which entire kin groups and communities shared the responsibility for and celebrated the educational achievements of their "sons"—and in that era it was really only sons and not daughters who were educated, another feature of society that has changed dramatically. In fact, people still commonly appeal to their wider kin for help in all kinds of endeavors, including paying children's school fees. It is not unusual for a wealthier sibling, uncle, or cousin to contribute to the education of their poorer kin. But it is much less common than in the past. Today's fathers accurately perceive that, increasingly, the duties (and especially the costs) of parenting fall directly on children's actual parents.

In formal interviews and countless informal interactions, fathers I knew spoke regularly and emphatically about the priority of educating their children. Most men either suggested or explicitly stated that providing for their children's education was their greatest duty as a parent. Implicit in prioritizing education was the assumption that along with money for school fees, school uniforms, books, and so on, a father should be able to provide the basic requirements for raising a child, including food, shelter, security, and a proper social and moral foundation. Chuka, a thirty-five-year-old father of four, describing the challenges posed by the costs of formal education, expressed a sentiment I heard from many fathers: "Who else will pay my children's school fees? It is only me. As a father that is my duty." In reality, mothers and fathers in modern marriages frequently pool their resources to amass the funds necessary to pay the costs of children's schooling. But even so, it is a widely shared view that fathers ultimately bear this responsibility, and if a family can no longer afford to send a child to school, even though the mother will likely feel just as exasperated as her husband, it is the father who will be seen by kin and community as failing to provide.

The Costs and Benefits of Modern Fatherhood

Lower fertility, more nuclear family organization, neolocal residence formation associated with rural-to-urban migration, ever-more-prevalent ideals and practices associated with companionate marriage, and wider social and economic changes that have reconfigured the gendered division of labor all place fathers in a more central and more intimate parental role. For women and children, the changing ideals and practices of fatherhood have many benefits. Generally, married women I interviewed claimed to experience modern marriage as offering them more equal footing in their relationships with their husbands. The idea that men increasingly believe that part of what makes a good marriage is the quality of their personal relationship with their wives seems to provide women welcome leverage. The fact that younger married couples with smaller families and a more nuclear household organization see cooperation in the project of educating their children as one of the primary goals of their relationship, and also that many men now see their wives as key and even equal partners in this endeavor, produces and reinforces new configurations of domestic gender dynamics that most women seem to experience positively. Based on my observations, the most obvious costs to women of modern marriage are when they have a "bad" husband—one who is flagrantly unfaithful, drinks too much, or is physically abusive. The more couple-centered organization of marriage and family life makes it more difficult than in the past for a woman with a bad husband to call on kin for help, whether it is to rein in man's bad behavior or simply to seek economic assistance that her husband is failing to provide.

For children, too, modern fatherhood seems to have many benefits, but also some costs. In the many families I have come to know well over the last two decades, the degree to which children feel dependent on and more emotionally attached to their fathers seems greater among the current generation than in the past. I don't mean to suggest that children did not love or feel close to their fathers in previous generations (this would be patently untrue), but the changes in marriage, family, and fatherhood I have described in this chapter do seem to entail more communication, greater intimacy, and more direct dependence on fathers than before. As they become adults, most children who grew up in these more modern households seem to value the kind of relationship that modern fatherhood enables—though they do not necessarily spend much time consciously comparing the current situation to the past. But like for women in their positions as wives and mothers, these changing circumstances mean that children can no longer rely as much on wider kin networks for help navigating the challenges of everyday life in Nigeria. Many intertwining social changes seem to be threatening (though by no means fully undermining) the centrality of wider kinship ties for how people succeed in contemporary Nigeria. Children must rely on their fathers more than ever. The financial burden for fathers is growing even as the emotional payoffs of fatherhood also increase.

Conclusion

In courtship, marriage, and fatherhood, money looms large. The successful performance of masculinity depends on fulfilling the expected role of provider. Even—and maybe especially—in these most intimate personal relationships, having money to demonstrate manhood is absolutely essential. As I have shown in this chapter, men's most important life projects—marrying and making families—are both enabled and imperiled by the imperatives associated with money. Girlfriends, wives, and children evaluate their lovers, husbands, and fathers partly in relation to their capacity to provide money. The public performances associated with these life projects, most especially weddings, are judged based on shared standards for conspicuous redistribution.

In southeastern Nigeria, as perhaps anywhere, money alone cannot buy love and intimacy, but without it everything is more tenuous. In courtship, a man must provide for a woman's material desires as well as win her heart if he hopes to marry her. In marriage, a man with the money to provide for his family has significantly more latitude in managing his relationship with his wife. The diversity of ways in which couples navigate married life is striking, but so too is the fact that issues of money are almost always paramount. Fathers and their children commonly love each other no matter their social class, but every father and child I know in Nigeria would agree that both fatherhood and childhood would be better and easier with more money. While it is unsurprising that everyone would like more money, what is more interesting is the constant focus on *how* men spend the money they do have. In other words, even in their most intimate personal relationships, men must be seen to be spending their money in the service of sociality if they are to be seen as good lovers, husbands, and fathers. Although wealth makes it much easier for richer men to fulfill the obligations of provider love, expectations are at least partially calibrated by social class. For all men, money acts as both material and emotional currency in the performance of masculinity in their most intimate relationships.

While how men spend money on their lovers, wives, and children does not always rise to the level of conspicuous redistribution because many of these expenditures go unseen by the public, the dynamics are, nonetheless, parallel. In both public and private domains, how much money a man has matters, but even more important is the manner in which he chooses to spend it. In intimate relationships, as in more overt displays of conspicuous redistribution, such as the wedding ceremonies described in this chapter, a man is most rewarded for his money if he spends it in ways that are perceived to be in support of others. It is to men's efforts to make money and the central role that money plays in more public performances of masculinity that I turn in the next chapter.

THREE

"Money Problem": Work, Class, Consumption, and Men's Social Status

Like so many young men of his generation in southeastern Nigeria, when Chudi graduated from secondary school in 2001 he faced the daunting challenge of how to earn a living. His father was a poor farmer and had barely managed to pay his school fees, so Chudi knew there was no prospect that he could afford university. Finding a decent job in Lagos or Abuja (Nigeria's commercial and political capitals, respectively), the favored destinations of most young people, would be nearly impossible without good connections. Chudi didn't have any. But he was loath to stay at home in the village and be condemned to work as a farmer, even if it were only temporary. So he jumped at the chance when one of his mother's relatives offered to help him find work as an apprentice with a tailor in the nearby city of Aba. As I described in chapter 1, many young men unable to pursue a university education or secure a good job in an office choose to learn a trade with the hope that one day they will start their own business.

The tailor Chudi apprenticed with in Aba specialized in making men's suits (Western style). Indeed, Aba is known as the premier place to have suits sewn in Nigeria. Compared to many cases I heard about, Chudi's apprenticeship went well. After two years his master "settled" him with an amount of capital that was reasonable for Chudi to open up his own shop. The only stipulation was that he did so in Umuahia, the sleepy capital of Abia State that is about an hour from Aba and nearer to Chudi's ancestral village. His master did not want him stealing customers in Aba. Chudi obliged. By the time I met him in 2005 he had what looked like a modestly successful business that included an apprentice of his own.

Chudi became my regular tailor in Umuahia, sewing for me shirts, trousers, and the occasional suit. He was extremely friendly and always seemed happy to have me around his shop. When we went out for a beer once he admitted that he thought having a foreign customer was good for his professional reputation. We talked a lot about his life, his work, and his aspirations. His desires were quite typical of what I heard from many other young men. He hoped to marry and have children, he wanted to one day own a car, and he dreamed of being able to build a big house in his village—partly, he said, to shame those there who looked down on him and his family. Our conversations always seemed to come back to money. His words summed up what I heard from many men: "In Nigeria," he said, "money is God and money is the devil."

The necessity of money for manhood in Africa's most populous country can be narrated in idioms of triumph, aspiration, resignation, or lament. But regardless of the idiom, the need for money feels inescapable to most men. This chapter examines the multiple ways that men seek to make money, the meanings of money and work, and the ways that different livelihoods both reflect and reproduce increasingly unequal class dynamics in Nigeria. The performance of masculinity is intimately bound up with class, and especially with aspirations and anxieties about having enough money. Money is constantly a problem for men, no matter how little or how much they have, as even the wealthy bemoan the fact that "with big money comes big trouble."

To explore the importance of money in men's lives, I offer extended case studies of the livelihood strategies of the poor, the middle class, and the rich. By looking at how Nigerian men struggle to accumulate the money to pay bridewealth, settle their children's school fees, save toward building a symbolically obligatory house in their ancestral rural villages, or simply earn enough to survive another day, the inextricable links between money and masculinity are investigated and analyzed. Nigerian men regularly suggest that money is their biggest problem. A close look at their lives shows that they are so obsessed about money because their social roles as men require it, even as they are ambivalent about this central pillar of masculinity.

A Farmer

Nkem farmed all is life. He remembers accompanying his mother to the farm when he was just a small child. His father grew yams and had a large yam barn in which each year he stored his annual yield for food and for seedlings to plant during the next season. Yams were traditionally a prestige crop for men in southeastern Nigeria (Uchendu 1965; Ottenberg 2005; Korieh 2007). The more yams a man harvested the greater his perceived wealth and the more he could invest in having additional wives and children. Even today, one of the biggest traditional occasions in Igboland is the annual New Yam Festival, when the first yams of the year's harvest are cooked and eaten to celebrate the continuation of life (Coursey and Coursey 1971; Kolawole and Okorie 2008).

While Igbos still love to eat yams and men speak eloquently about the social and spiritual meaning of the New Yam Festival, the prestige of growing yams—and of farming in general—has waned over the last couple of generations. Indeed, nowadays the majority of yams consumed in southeastern Nigeria are grown in northern Nigeria, where agriculture is still a major occupation. In Nkem's village, and throughout the Southeast, almost no one in the younger generation aspires to farm for a living anymore. And while many men continue to combine farming with other economic pursuits to scratch out a livelihood, men who are farmers are generally poor. Nkem was no exception.

Nkem's father had three wives and fourteen children. With all those offspring and only a small income from farming, he could not afford to educate his children beyond primary school. Nkem stopped at Standard V one year short of completing an elementary education. He could speak a bit of English, read very simple sentences, and sign his name. But he thought of himself as uneducated—"I no sabi [understand] book" he used to tell me, when I asked him about his life and aspirations. He wanted something different for his children. He and his wife, Catherine, had six children, four girls and two boys. By the time I first got to know him in the mid-1990s, all of his children were in primary or secondary school, but Nkem and Catherine struggled to pay the fees. Eventually, over the years, all but two dropped out before finishing secondary school. The ones that finished were those Nkem described as "brilliant." Like many Igbo men I knew who had limited means, Nkem invested selectively in his children's school fees based on who seemed most likely to succeed with an education.

But this selective investment, in Nkem's mind born out of necessity, took a toll on his relationships with his wife and children. Nkem and Catherine argued when Nkem decided not to continue to support their youngest son's education. The son wasn't doing particularly well in school and was known as something of a miscreant in the community, so his father decided to stop paying his fees, instead encouraging him to think about learning a skill or a trade through an apprenticeship. The son didn't seem to mind very much dropping out of school, but his mother was furious. Despite his poor performance, the boy was her pet and Nkem told me she nagged him about it for over a year. One of his daughters was also angry when she had to drop out; unlike her younger brother, she desperately wanted to keep going. Nkem felt bad, because he knew his daughter was, as he put it, "serious" about school, but he just couldn't afford it. His real dream, though, was to send the son and daughter who had finished secondary school to university. But university fees were far beyond his means.

To give an idea of Nkem's economic wherewithal vis-à-vis the cost of a university education, each year he managed to generate the equivalent of about three thousand dollars from the surplus from his annual harvest (which included yams, cassava, and corn, as well as smaller quantities of beans, peppers, groundnuts, and various fruits from trees on his land). He also worked occasionally as a laborer helping a friend who was a carpenter. This sometimes brought in a couple of hundred dollars a month. In addition, Catherine had a small shop in the local market where she sold minor provisions like soap, biscuits, and toilet paper. At best, her shop generated a couple of hundred dollars a month. By contrast, annual tuition and fees at the state university ran close to two thousand dollars a year, and although they were farmers, Nkem and Catherine spent well more than half their annual income on food—to buy things like fish, occasional meat, palm oil, and various spices and vegetables, all of which were staples in the local diet. Further, in addition to secondary school fees, they had all kinds of other regular expenses, including occasional medical care, transportation, clothing, and house repairs. During the dry season they even had to pay for drinking water purchased from a neighbor's borehole. University tuition was simply out of the question.

Nkem and his family did not live in abject poverty as people do in some parts of Nigeria. He owned a small house built of mud bricks, but with cement floors and cement plastering on the walls. The roof was zinc pan. There were four bedrooms, each with a double bed and a foam mattress (the children slept two each in the beds). The parlor had a rickety, threadbare sofa and several plastic chairs, and also a fan and a black-and-white TV, both of which worked when the National Electric Power Authority (NEPA) brought light. Everyone in the family had several changes of clothes, including a couple outfits that could be considered "Sunday best." By 2010, Catherine and the two oldest children owned cheap cell phones (Nkem at first considered them an indulgence, but later decided that he would also acquire one). The family was never hungry, though they frequently skimped on meat and there were of course many things they would have wanted to eat that they couldn't afford.

But Nkem and his family thought of themselves as very poor. By many standards they were. But what was striking to me was the degree to which levels of expectation about what counts as adequate consumption had risen so dramatically over the past couple of decades. Nkem's children talked constantly about the value and prestige of all kinds of consumer commodities, from sneakers and blue jeans to cell phones and laptop computers. In some ways none of this should be surprising given the circulation of images, ideas, and things throughout Nigeria's globally interconnected economy. The boom in desires for consumption is fueled by the movement of people to and from Nigeria's cities, where modern lifestyles and the commodities that mark them are constantly on display. All of Nkem's children had traveled to Lagos at one time or another, and Umuahia, though sleepy by Lagos's standards, was just a twenty-minute bus ride away.

Nkem's children's growing and seemingly insatiable desires for things made him feel constantly as though he never had enough money. So did the traffic of rural-to-urban migrants back to the village. Many of these men were his peers. When they came home to the village for Christmas, or for a wedding or funeral, or simply to visit their kin, they showed off their money and their things in ways that made Nkem and many other men "stuck" in the village feel inadequate, and sometimes downright angry. Indeed, the relationship between rural men and their urban-based "brothers" was complex, contradictory, and frequently conflict-laden.

On the one hand, villages like Nkem's depended heavily on rural-to-urban migrants, not only for remittances, but also for the social, political, and economic connections that they forged across Nigeria. When Nkem and others like him sought employment or business opportunities for their maturing children, they routinely turned to their urban-based kin for help. Further, many development projects in the village, whether it was a new clinic, an addition to the secondary school, or a new section of the market, depended on the financial support of migrant kin in order to come to fruition. Men like Nkem sought good relations with their richer urban kin. Village men rewarded migrants for their wealth and spending, in some cases by supporting their bids to be conferred chieftancy titles. When successful migrant men organized lavish wedding ceremonies for their children or expensive funerals for their dead parents, villagers showed up in large numbers, heaping praise on the hosts—at least to their faces.

But on the other hand, as much as Nkem and his fellow men in the village praised—and to some extent genuinely admired—the money spent by their richer urban kin, the dynamics of money and kinship also created many discontents and some antagonism. Mostly these tensions stayed beneath the surface. Village men could not really afford to alienate their wealthier city-based brothers. But sometimes conflicts erupted. For example, I remember one annual meeting of a village development union, held near Christmas specifically so that returning migrants could attend, when a wealthy urban-based man tried to influence the location of a new clinic in a way that would clearly benefit his own family, but made little sense from a larger collective point of view. After the man insinuated that his generous support would be contingent on his favored location, one of the village-based men stood up and said, essentially, that he and others would not be "intimidated" by the man's wealth, and that they did not want his money if he only wanted to finance a private clinic for his family. A lot of shouting ensued and eventually, as was frequently the case in village disputes, tensions were smoothed over and a consensus was reached. But I know from many other conversations that strains between rural men and their urban-migrant kin were common. Almost always rural men resented it when they perceived that urban migrants tried to lord over them with their money, and urban migrants felt that their rural brothers did not respect them enough for their financial contributions to village betterment. While these tensions suggest that money can impinge on harmonious kinship ties, it is also true that in this day and age money is central to how men navigate their relationships with their relatives, good and bad.

A Vulcanizer

As mentioned already, nearly all Igbo men in today's younger generations wish to eschew farming as a livelihood and most desire to seek better lives by migrating to the city. But urban life offers no guarantee of good money or successful masculinity. I knew many men in urban

Nigeria who struggled as much as Nkem, sometimes more. Cities offered migrant men the promise of prosperity, but for most the reality was much more difficult than the dream. Even casual observation of the rhythms of everyday life in Nigeria's cities reveals the range of precarious livelihoods that migrant men rely on to survive: everything from driving motorcycle taxis (known as *okada*) in dangerous traffic, to walking around all day with a tray on one's head selling some little items that bring only tiny profits, to spending each day off-loading heavy bags of cement or rice from huge trucks parked on the outskirts of a market. The spectrum of work that involves backbreaking manual labor or tedious tasks with minimal payoff is enormous, and far more migrant men survive this way than through more lucrative pursuits. And of course many men have no jobs at all.

I learned a lot about the lives of many ordinary men in urban Nigeria, mostly in Umuahia and Owerri, places I lived in or near for many years, but also in Lagos, Kano, and Aba, other cities where I have spent significant time over the past twenty-five years. Usually I got to know these men because I needed some kind of service (a motorcycle taxi ride; a shoe repair; someone to carry a fifty-kilo bag of rice to my car from the center of the market), or because I purchased something from them (a watch battery, a kerosene lampshade, a plastic sachet of drinking water). Most of the men with whom I had these exchanges remained anonymous to me, with the completion of our transaction sending us onward never to meet again. But in many cases I became a repeat customer, and quite often I got to know individual men very well.

One place I spent a lot of time with a number of different migrant men was at the "mechanics' village" in Umuahia where I would get my car repaired. When I started dissertation fieldwork in 1995 I bought a used car, a 1983 Toyota Corolla hatchback. It was a reliable car, but given that it was twelve years old when I purchased it (and because Nigeria's bad roads knock cars around pretty thoroughly), I had to have frequent repairs. By the time the car finally died in 2004 it seemed like I was at the mechanics' village all the time. That year I bought another used car, a 1988 Nissan Bluebird. It was also pretty reliable, but again I was a regular customer in the mechanics' village before I finally replaced that vehicle in 2015.

Getting a car repaired in Nigeria is very different enterprise than what I was used to in the United States. Understanding how it works is necessary to explain why I got to know the men working in my corner of Umuahia's mechanics' village so well. The most important thing to know is that I followed the practice of many Nigerians when my car was being repaired, which was that I stayed with the car to observe the whole process from start to finish. This was preferable for several reasons. First, mechanics tended to work on whichever car they felt the most pressure to repair (and were most likely to be paid for immediately); nothing communicated urgency and readiness to pay when the job was completed better than the customer's continued presence.

Second, if the repair required a new part (or, more typically, a working used part), that part would need to be purchased in the market. Mechanics kept few, if any, parts in their ramshackle sheds. Purchasing the part necessitated cash from the customer because most mechanics wouldn't (or couldn't afford to) buy a part and be reimbursed later by the customer. Then there was the money for the mechanic to pay for a motorcycle taxi to and from the market. And for major or scarce parts, money was needed for bus fare all the way to Aba, an hour away, because the vehicle spare parts market there was vast compared to Umuahia. If my mechanic had to go to Aba for a part that meant I might spend several hours with other men at the mechanics' village before my job really even began.

The third reason to stay with the car was to assure that what the mechanic said was wrong was really the problem, and to verify that parts purported to be replaced were in fact changed. Over time, I came to trust my mechanic very much, and sometimes I even left my car with him the whole day without being there. But usually I stayed while the repairs were completed, primarily to impress upon him my urgency to get the job done. Regardless of whether I was present or not, he followed a practice that seemed to be expected in all repairs, which was that he always gave me the broken part at the end of the job to verify the work had truly been done. Over the years I have accumulated a large trove of broken vehicle parts behind the house where I park my car.

In the section of the mechanics' village where my mechanic plied his trade a number of other men provided related services. For example, one man did body work (known in Nigeria as "panel beating"). There was also a welder. He did work for both the mechanic and the panel beater, and other jobs such as constructing the metal gates that Nigerians like to have in front of their houses. Younger apprentices worked for each of these men. Another man changed oil and made wheel alignments. And there was a guy who did nothing but repair flat tires, a vocation known in Nigeria as a "vulcanizer." Also regularly present at the site was a woman who cooked food; most of the men bought their lunch from her.

I knew and liked my mechanic very well, but I got to know the vulcanizer, Nwoke, best of all. I write about him here because he represents a huge category of rural-to-urban migrants who struggled mightily to earn enough money to enable them to fulfill their most basic aspirations as men. Nwoke repaired about six to eight tires a day, though sometimes it was more or less. If the tire had an inner tube, as many Nigerian tires still do, patching one hole cost the customer the equivalent of a little more than $.50. Obviously more holes cost extra and sometimes the whole tube would have to be replaced, in which case Nwoke charged a small fee (again, only about $.50), plus a very small markup on the price he paid in the market for the new inner tube. If the punctured tire was tubeless he charged about $1.00 for each hole because the process was more cumbersome—it involved starting a fire and burning rubber. The first time I had a tubeless tire repaired I was incredulous that the method was effective, much less safe, but it seemed to work just fine. The only other source of income from Nwoke's work as a vulcanizer was when people simply wanted more air in their tires. His most expensive piece of equipment was an air pump that ran on gasoline. For a car, he charged a little less than $.50 to gauge and pump all four tires; for a motorcycle exactly half that. All in all, Nwoke was lucky to pocket more than seven or eight dollars in a day. He worked six days a week (taking Sunday off to go to church and spend time with his family), starting by 7 a.m. and closing between 5 and 6 p.m.

This was a precarious way to make a living. It was a challenge to provide for his family. Nwoke's wife, Ify, earned even less than he did as a cleaner/custodian working for a woman who ran a private primary school. Together they were lucky to bring in $300 a month. When I first met them in 1995 they had three young children, two of them in primary school and a toddler who accompanied Ify to her workplace. Most of their income was spent on the basics: food, water, clothing, kerosene (for lamps and cooking), transportation, and rent. They lived in a very modest one-bedroom apartment; Nwoke and Ify slept on a bed in the bedroom, the children on a foam mattress that they laid out each night on the floor in the parlor. Rent in urban Nigeria is typically paid in advance for a full year (sometimes two full years). Although rents are relatively modest (Nwoke and Ify paid a little more than $40 a month), the pay-in-advance method created an annual crisis. Nearly $500 in one shot was a huge burden on a $300-a-month income. Usually they had to borrow from kin or friends and then pay it back over time. Every urban-based family I knew in Nigeria dreaded the deadline for annual rent.

Even by Umuahia standards, Nwoke and Ify were poor, but with two

5 Many urban occupations, like vulcanizer, provide barely enough money to survive and leave men vulnerable to financial crises that imperil their capacity to be providers.

steady, if meager, incomes they were better off than many. But Nwoke wanted more. He wanted to be a good provider for his family. He desired to educate his children. He sought to live in a better apartment. He often talked about wishing he could afford to buy a motorcycle, as he believed that being an okada motorcycle taxi driver would be more lucrative than being a vulcanizer. But his dreams never came to fruition. I had known Nwoke for about twenty years by the time I was writing this book and he was still doing the same work. In addition to the hefty annual rent payments, three other expenses have created financial crises for Nwoke, and they are things that are experienced, at one time or another, by almost every man I know in southeastern Nigeria.

The first is school fees. As I explained in chapter 1, and again briefly in Nkem's case above, primary school in Nigeria is basically free. That's not quite true, because parents must pay for school uniforms and some minor school supplies, and schools sometimes charge small levies for various things, even though the state insists that primary education is government-provided. Secondary school is far more expensive and one of the great ironies is that the best, most selective federal schools are highly subsidized. It is the children of affluent Nigerians who are usually best prepared to do well on entrance exams (or have the political connections to be admitted even if they don't). Most Nigerians must enroll their children in state (as in state-government rather than federal-government) schools or private schools, both of which are more expensive than federal schools. By 2012, Nwoke had only been able to afford to put one of his children through secondary school. The others had to drop out. This was a source of great sadness for him. When his one son did graduate he and Ify were very proud. But they could not possibly pay for him to go on to university.

The second crisis-creating expense is health care. In theory, Nigeria has a system of basic primary health care. In practice, private providers deliver most health care, and even at government hospitals staff commonly demand advance payment before services are provided. A few years ago, one of Nwoke's children was in an accident while traveling on public transportation and she broke her leg. The injury required surgery to reset the bone. The doctors at Queen Elizabeth Hospital, the main government hospital in Umuahia, would not do the surgery until Nwoke paid a deposit equivalent to more than $200. He had to travel home to his village to borrow some money from kin and Ify got an advance from her employer to enable them to make the payment. Another time Ify's mother came to Umuahia from her village very sick and they again had to borrow money for a hospital bill. I can't possibly count how often I have observed or had people tell me about the financially ruinous costs of a health emergency.

Besides rent, school fees, and health care emergencies, the other crisis-inducing financial burden that so many men described to me was the death of their parent—or a wife's parent. In both cases a man is expected to contribute a very large amount of money to support the costs of elaborate festivities. Indeed, for many migrant men a significant measure of one's ultimate success as a migrant is the level at which one buries one's mother or father. Nwoke was no exception. I was in Nigeria when his father died a little over ten years ago and I remember the anguish he experienced trying to come up with his share of the burial expenses, not to mention the inadequacy he felt as he perceived that his kinsmen found his contribution meager. Nwoke told me something similar to what I heard from many men: "A man is not fully a man until he has buried his father." His statement signaled more than just how much money it cost, but there was no doubt that the social pressure to perform financially was one of the tests of manhood posed by a parents' death. I will return to this in much greater depth in chapter 6.

The cost of burying one's parents is but the most powerful example of the pressures on migrant men to earn and spend money in their rural communities of origin. Migrant men are expected to build a house in their natal village. They are expected to bring their families home every Christmas, and to do so in style if they can. They are expected to contribute to village development projects. But like many migrant men, Nwoke was too poor to build a house in his village. He rarely brought his family home at Christmas time. He regularly made excuses to miss meetings of his village development union to avoid the disgrace of being unable to pay his levies. His poor financial situation not only challenged his and his family's physical wellbeing, it also constantly affected his social relations and his sense of himself as a man.

A Teacher

Kelechi lived in his natal village in his father's house. As the only son, he would one day inherit the house, but for now he shared it with his aging mother and father and Adaora, his wife of ten years. Kelechi's father had recently become almost completely blind and both his parents had significant health problems. Kelechi was a teacher in his community's secondary school. Two generations ago becoming a teacher was a proud and relatively lucrative career path for a young man—something the Igbo anthropologist Victor Uchendu and others made clear in early ethnographies of the tribe (Uchendu 1965; Ottenberg 1959). Western education was highly prized among the Igbo. Becoming a teacher was also much admired because employment as a civil servant provided a secure and respectable livelihood.

By the end of the twentieth century, however, around the time I first got to know Kelechi, being a teacher had fallen in the relative hierarchy of career paths. One reason was that teachers' salaries—indeed most civil servants' salaries—had not kept pace with inflation. Another reason was that social expectations about how much money a man should earn had escalated dramatically over the past generation. While Kelechi's job enabled him to provide the basics for his family—there was never any question about whether they would eat well, have decent clothing, or be able to keep a roof over their heads, for example—nowadays, just the basics were not considered enough. Further, as female education spread and increased, and as the teaching profession became less prestigious for the reasons I have enumerated, the career became more feminized. There are still many male teachers in southeastern Nigeria, but by 2013 70 percent of secondary school teachers in Abia State (Kelechi's state) were women (National Bureau of Statistics 2014).

Despite secure employment in what was once considered a good job, Kelechi was constantly plagued by money problems. The sources of those problems were many and they illustrate well the relationship between money and the performance of competent masculinity, particularly as men try to navigate their relationships with women, family, and friends. At every turn, it seemed, Kelechi was confronted with the need for more money.

While most men I knew did not share a house with their parents—indeed, being able to establish an independent household after marriage was considered a normal and important step in achieving male adulthood—Kelechi's continuing role in assisting and helping take care of his parents was typical. Men constantly talked about the challenges of caring for their parents, and particularly the financial burdens when their parents faced a health crisis. Among his male peers any stain that living in his father's house cast on Kelechi's performance of masculine ideals seemed to be more than offset by the fact that he was obviously so committed and financially invested in addressing his parents' health problems.

I knew Kelechi from Umuahia Sports Club, where I used to play tennis many evenings and on the weekends. It seemed like almost every afternoon that Kelechi would use a break in between matches to walk out to the nearby pharmacy and pick up drugs for his father. At one point his father was hospitalized for almost two weeks in Umuahia. During that period Kelechi only came to the club occasionally and he rarely played tennis because he spent most of the time after work sitting with his father in his hospital room. As I will recount in greater detail in chapter 4, several club members discreetly lent Kelechi money during this period and club officials quietly forgave his tardy club dues. I distinctly remember the empathy other men felt about Kelechi's situation and their admiration for the sense of duty he exhibited—not to mention the willingness to incur debts—in order to take care of his ailing father.

Kelechi's financial hardships were exacerbated by another problem which no one at the club spoke of in front of him, but about which his peers sometimes spoke in his absence: Kelechi and his wife were still childless after more than a decade of marriage. When men at the club discussed Kelechi's predicament in his absence, they sometimes debated his options, and they both praised and critiqued his choices. Some suggested that Kelechi should have long ago taken another wife, one who would more likely provide him an heir. Others admired his loyalty to his wife, even as they lamented his situation. Less frequently, it was acknowledged that Kelechi himself might be the source of the couple's infertility, and the debate centered on whether his wife should have discreetly become impregnated by another man, pretending the child was Kelechi's. Here again there were arguments—and criticism and praise—on both sides. What was agreed was that everyone wished Kelechi fatherhood; the question was how best to get there.

We had known each other several years by the time Kelechi approached me and said there was something he wanted to talk about in private. I quickly obliged and we made our way to a corner of the club's lounge where no one was nearby. "My biggest problem in life," he told me, "is that I still don't have any issue ["issue" is a common Nigerian synonym for offspring]." He then went on to tell me how he and his wife had visited many doctors, traditional healers, and even recently Pentecostal preachers in search of a solution. In every case they had spent money, in some cases lots of money, but with no result. He wanted to know if there was any way I could help him and his wife obtain visas for travel to the United States, where he hoped fertility treatments would be more successful. I explained how difficult the American Embassy in Nigeria can be and also gave him a sense of how expensive such procedures could be in America—I had heard, for example, that in vitro fertilization could cost many thousands of dollars each try. I told Kelechi I'd be happy to write a letter to the US Consul on his behalf, but that there was little more that I could do. He thanked me sincerely, but didn't ever bring it up after that.

Some months later he approached me again wanting to have another private conversation. I expected it would be about the same topic. But it turned out to be something different. His wife's younger sister had just won the Diversity Visa Lottery (every year the United States awards about fifty thousand visas through a lottery system to citizens from qualifying countries). Until 2015 Nigerians were eligible and each year over a million Nigerians applied and several thousand typically won. Kelechi and Adaora were ecstatic that her younger sister, Ifeoma, had won and they hoped I would be able to advise her first how to approach the interview (winning the lottery did not guarantee the embassy would actually issue the visa), and then, if she were successful, about how to get started with life in the United States.

I was glad to help and met with Ifeoma twice before her interview. Fortunately, she was granted her visa, and—even more fortunately for me—Kelechi and Adaora had kin in Texas who agreed to host Ifeoma on her arrival in the United States. I had been afraid I would be asked to do that, something that I wasn't sure I was prepared for. Once Ifeoma settled in Texas I kept in touch with her by email and the occasional phone call. I knew she sometimes sent money home to her sister and Kelechi by Western Union. When I would travel to Nigeria each year for research, she would send me tennis gear to carry for Kelechi: sometimes a new racquet, some sneakers, or multiple tins of tennis balls. Kelechi was always most grateful to me but sometimes complained that his sister-in-law had not been able to transform their lives financially in the way he had hoped. I knew she had enrolled in nursing school—a quite common career path for Nigerian immigrants, especially women—and that it would take her some years to find her feet. I had observed many times the huge expectations that Nigerian families put on their kin who emigrate to the United States and the United Kingdom, and I knew that emigrants' lives were much harder than their Nigerian brothers and sisters at home imagined. I tried to explain the context to Kelechi and protect Ifeoma as best I could. Kelechi tried to understand, but he clearly continued to hope for more.

Eventually Ifeoma finished nursing school and she moved to California. A couple of years later she bought Kelechi and Adaora a nice used car (a Volvo) and shipped it to Nigeria. Kelechi was delighted when he learned a car was on the way and after it finally arrived he donated two crates of beer the first day he drove it to Umuahia Sports Club so his club mates could celebrate with him. Kelechi proudly drove the car for about eighteen months, until it had some major problem with the front axle. The part was not available in Umuahia or Aba, and when he asked about the price in Lagos he concluded he could not afford it. The last time I went to Nigeria, Kelechi was again using public transportation and the car remained parked in the village. Ifeoma had recently married a Nigerian man living in California and her regular remittances had mostly dried up.

Kelechi was one of many male teachers I have gotten to know over more than twenty-five years working in Nigeria. Nearly all of them lamented, at one time or another, that teaching wasn't what it used to be. The loss of prestige was palpable, but even worse was that as a teacher one simply didn't earn a salary big enough to afford the kinds of things most educated men in contemporary Nigeria aspired to have. In rural communities teachers notoriously tried to supplement their incomes by turning their students into a personal labor force, mostly by requiring them to work on their farms, ostensibly in agriculture "practicums." In urban areas most teachers moonlighted as private tutors. Arguably, this contributed to the gradual demise of the quality of public education in Nigeria—about which I heard many people complain—as teachers hoarded certain training and expertise and made them available only to those who could pay for the extra private lessons.

It was hard to begrudge Kelechi and other teachers their desire to increase their incomes. Teachers worked in a sector that exposed them to all of the most modern and global influences on desires for consumption. It was an occupation that used to be associated with being able to lift one's family, kin, and community. But in the current situation teaching's financial returns were comparatively slim, a disappointment made all the more stark because some men with considerably less education made vast fortunes and seemed to benefit greatly by flaunting their money.

A Small Business Proprietor

In southeastern Nigeria, "doing business" has long been seen as the primary alternative to doing well by getting an education and finding a job where a good education was the primary path to entry. Indeed, Igbo people are famously known throughout Nigeria for their entrepreneurial spirit, business acumen, and domination of many sectors of the market (Silverstein 1984; Meagher 2009, 2010; Peterson 2014). Further, as I explained in chapter 1, beginning around the 1990s, when employment prospects dimmed after the country's post-oil-boom economic downturn, large numbers of young men gave up the pursuit of education to seek their fortune through business. But of course business did not actually make most of the men who pursued it rich.

Linus had started in business shortly after he finished secondary school in the late 1970s, long before the current trend among younger men. His father had moved the family to Umuahia from what is now Anambra State shortly after the end of the civil war in 1970. Among the entrepreneurial Igbo, people from Anambra are especially renowned for their business orientation and within Igbo society they are often criticized for their outsized love of money—in much the same way other Nigerians pass judgment about Igbos in general. Linus's father traded in foodstuffs. He was not a wealthy man by any stretch of the imagination, but he managed to educate his three daughters through primary school and his two sons through secondary school. But when he died in 1976 Linus felt he had few options but to follow his father's footsteps and try to earn a living through trading.

At first Linus tried to make a go of his father's trade, buying and selling foodstuffs. This involved frequent trips to village markets to buy local produce in bulk, but also regular trips to Lagos, Nigeria's commercial capital in the Southwest—a journey that typically took ten to twelve hours by bus. Perhaps ironically, many foods were actually cheaper in Lagos than in local village markets in the Southeast because, with its massive population, Lagos attracted many sellers, and therefore heavy competition, from all over the country. But profits for Linus were slim and the regular travel grueling, so not long after he married in the early 1980s he made a major decision to change his line of business. He switched from foodstuffs to drinks—hard liquor, beer, and soft drinks. He invested all his savings and borrowed from some of his kin and friends to buy his initial stock. While it has not been easy, he has managed to make a living and provide for his family ever since.

When I met Linus in the mid-1990s he rented a big shop on the outside edge of Umuahia's main market. While there were many shops in Umuahia specializing in selling drinks, Linus had one of the two best locations in the market. Being on the outside rim meant not only that his shop was highly visible, but also that people could pull vehicles right in front of his place and load heavy crates and cartons for transportation without having to carry them or hire a porter. The location was also convenient for Linus. He made weekly trips to Aba and Onitsha, where soft drinks, beer, and hard liquor were sold wholesale. He too saved time and money because of his prime location, and along with the extra business, it was enough to make worthwhile the sizable rent.

Selling drinks is a reliable business because the sources of demand are multiple and steady. Igbos are famous for "offering kola" to guests (Uchendu 1964). For generations this meant that the man of the house would present actual kola nuts to male visitors in a ceremony that is still repeated in many Igbo households. But over the last few decades presenting kola has evolved to include offering a drink (while local palm wine was sometimes offered in the past, it is now routine to offer a bottled drink). Indeed, increasingly, "offering kola" does not even involve kola nuts, but just drinks and maybe some biscuits or peanuts. With drinks, as with virtually every commodity or gift in Nigeria, there is a recognized hierarchy. Malt-based drinks like Maltina and Malta are considered superior to soft drinks like Coke and Sprite. Offering a beer or stout (here too there is a known hierarchy of brands) is considered more generous than providing a malt drink. Not surprisingly, the pecking order of drinks maps neatly onto price. The whole system is complicated a bit by people's religious relationships to alcohol; some families would never offer—and some guests would never want—an alcoholic drink. Over the last decade or so fruit juices, sold in small rectangular cartons, have risen to the top status for nonalcoholic products. Linus stocked many kinds and brands. While fads and trends regarding the most prestigious drinks to offer as kola changed regularly, the need to keep drinks on hand for visitors endured and provided a main source of reliable demand for Linus's business.

The other source of demand is the central importance of drinks at major ritual occasions in southeastern Nigeria, most especially weddings and funerals. As described in detail in other chapters, men are expected to spend lavishly on their weddings and on the burial ceremonies for their parents (and for others too, but especially parents). The quality of the "entertainment" a man provides to his guests is marked above all by the food and drinks. Just like in the routine hospitality accorded to household visitors, there is a well-known hierarchy of drinks at weddings and funerals. The expectation is that drinks will be plentiful; the type of drinks they are served marks status among different guests. Most weddings and funerals in southeastern Nigeria happen on the weekends, so Linus usually sees his sales rise precipitously on

6　Small businesses are among the most common pathways by which Igbo men try to achieve their aspirations for money and a middle-class lifestyle.

Thursdays and Fridays. Sometimes customers will make specific requests in advance of an event and he will make a special trip to Aba or Onitsha to assure he stocks what is needed. In short, the central position of drinks in Nigeria's material and moral economies of conspicuous redistribution more or less guaranteed a stable demand for Linus's product.

While the drinks business resulted in a steady income and Linus has managed to provide for his family, he is by no means a rich man. Partly this is because the mark up from wholesale to retail is relatively small, but partly it is because competition is fierce. As I have already mentioned, it was characteristic of markets in Nigeria that in each line of business—whether it was foodstuffs, clothing, stationery supplies, shoes, motor vehicle parts, or drinks—many vendors sold more or less exactly the same products, typically in shops lined up one after the other. I often marveled that anyone could make a living with so many people selling the same thing in the same place. Linus complained about this too, but he managed.

The living Linus made enabled him to rent a modest two-bedroom flat in Umuahia. He was building a small bungalow in his natal village in Anambra State, adding to it little by little as he saved money. He planned to retire in the village, hoping that when he could no longer run his business he would be able live relatively cheaply there without having to pay rent. But he worried about the future. He and his wife had only one child, a daughter. Linus loved his daughter dearly and provided well for her. In 2004 she entered university and this was a major expense for Linus. Indeed, when I first knew him, Linus drove an old Peugeot 505, but by the time his daughter enrolled in university it was no longer on the road. Linus said he could not afford both university tuition and the costs of maintaining a car.

Linus anticipated his daughter's marriage with both joy and apprehension. It would be joyous to see her start her own family and he looked forward to grandchildren, especially a grandson. He and his wife had hoped for more children, including a son, but, in Linus's words, "God never agreed." He feared that when his daughter married she would turn her attention to her husband's family and that with no son there would be no one to take over his business and no one to look after him and his wife in their old age. Igbo custom asserts that it is sons who should provide for their aging parents. But in reality I observed many instances where it was in fact married daughters who did the most to provide and care for their elderly parents. I suspected Linus's daughter would do the same. In any case, Linus was a very religious man and when we talked about the long-term future he almost always said: "Somehow God will provide for us."

An NGO Entrepreneur

In many ways Obi epitomized a generation of young men who were well educated, ambitious, and possibly poised to take Nigeria in promising new directions. He was born in a village near Owerri, the capital of Imo State. When I met him in 2004 he was in his midtwenties and recently returned from completing his national youth service somewhere in northern Nigeria. Since the early 1970s Nigeria has required all university graduates to serve a year in the National Youth Service Corps (NYSC). After an initial orientation program, "corpers," as they are called in Nigeria, are typically posted to a part of the country far from their place of origin and given a small stipend for work that is like an internship. The program is designed to give young graduates job-like experience that also contributes to national development, while at the same time exposing the country's next generation of leaders to regions, ethnicities, languages, and religions different from their own. While many young people used political connections to try to assure cushy placements in Lagos or Abuja, the vast majority of corpers ended up spending a year in parts of Nigeria they had never visited and might not otherwise ever go. Although I am dubious how effective NYSC has been as national development scheme, discussions with dozens of young people who had gone through it suggested that it definitely contributed to broadening educated young people's awareness and appreciation for the diversity of their country.

Further, Obi was like a good number of recent corpers I knew in that his experience fueled a sense of idealism—if also cynicism—about issues of politics and development in Nigeria. I met him because he was working with a local NGO in Nigeria with which I had collaborated on research. Obi had been recently employed as a program officer/ field outreach coordinator on an AIDS prevention project. In practice, this meant that he did things like run training workshops for traders and businessmen and their apprentices in the Owerri main market, people who were the target of a donor-funded intervention. He handed out condoms and offered health education to commercial sex workers. He represented the organization's director at meetings with other NGOs and with officials at the Ministry of Health, with which the NGO collaborated. And he spent a good deal of time working on—

and thereby learning how to manage—the slew of documentation that even a small local NGO had to prepare to satisfy donor and government requirements. Over time, in an organization that had between five and eight full-time employees at any given moment, he became second only to the director in his skills at report and proposal writing.

Obi was a highly extraverted and jovial young man. He had strong opinions about everything and I very much enjoyed joining him for a beer after work. We talked about Nigeria and world politics and I always liked to hear his take on whatever I was working on in my own research, whether it was the "Love, Marriage, HIV" project I was conducting when I first met him or later research on the social effects of ever-more-popular Pentecostal churches. Obi's stories were colorful and he was obviously a keen observer of his own society. I always thought he might have done well had he pursued an academic career in the social sciences. But Obi's ambition was to start his own NGO.

Obi's analysis of whatever we talked about almost always suggested that people's behavior—in government, at universities, in the donor/NGO development world—was at its root much more political than these people owned up to. Further, when we discussed how people functioned in more personal arenas—in romantic relationships, marriage, or friendships, for example—he wanted to make sure I was aware of the self-serving aspects of what people did and said, even when they attempted to project something else. It was a view that I heard frequently from Nigerian interlocutors, and it typically insinuated that while such self-serving behavior might be a panhuman phenomenon, the situation was surely worse in Nigeria. Obi was not alone in this view, but he was one of its most vocal proponents.

Like most Nigerians who voiced such views, Obi usually suggested that for Nigeria to find its way out of its seemingly constant state of political and economic crisis, the basic moral orientation of people would have to change. It was therefore somewhat ironic (or maybe appropriate) that when I returned to Nigeria a couple of years later, the people he used to work with at the local NGO were saying derogatory things about his behavior and the self-serving motivations they believed were behind them. In the intervening period Obi had left the local NGO and secured a job working for the regional office of a major international NGO. He now drove a nice Toyota Camry (he had no car when I met him in 2004) and he was apparently spending a lot of time at some of the fancy nightclubs that had sprouted up to serve Owerri's growing university and young, middleclass population. His official salary working for the international NGO was undoubtedly many times higher than what he had been paid by the local NGO, but his former colleagues suggested that the main source of his vastly improved financial situation was money he siphoned off from his new position. They claimed to know of subcontracts with big budgets that had not been fully executed, workshops with phantom participants, and per diems claimed for travel that never happened—exactly the same sorts of things that Obi used to lament about the behavior of Nigerian politicians and development NGO elites.

I saw Obi during that visit to Nigeria and we agreed to arrange to meet for beer after work, as we had often done in the past. He always had a certain swagger, even when we first met. But the way he sauntered from his car to the bar this time was especially notable, as was the delight he took in ordering and paying for one more beer and an extra round of pepper soup. It was easy to see why his former colleagues found his new demeanor irritating and to understand why they trafficked in stories about the sources of his wealth. Obi himself brought up the issue of his relationship to his former colleagues and said, essentially, that they were jealous of his success. "In Nigeria," he said, "the response to others' success is to try to pull them down." Indeed, Nigerians have a phrase for this propensity, something they see as one among many national ailments. The label is "Pull Down Syndrome" (Igbinovia 2003; Shija 2016).

As an observer, it was genuinely hard for me to know how much of what his former colleagues said about Obi was true versus how much was the result of jealousies and the Pull Down Syndrome. I learned over the years they were not mutually exclusive. People could be the victims of rumors about the nefarious sources of their wealth, some of which were patently false, and at the same time there might be many stories about a man's money—how he acquired it, whether he shared it, the ways he used it to "intimidate" others—that had considerable foundation in reality. Although for most Nigerian men simply earning enough money to be a competent man is the main challenge, for anyone who has money, even quite a lot of money, navigating the interpersonal politics at the intersection of money and social relations is a never-ending challenge.

A Politician

Ogbonna's father was a senior civil servant in Nigeria's British colonial administration in the 1950s. When Nigeria gained independence in 1960 he was appointed to a top federal post. By the time the old man died, he had four wives and nearly thirty children. He was able to educate almost all of them and most of the boys went on to university and beyond. One of Ogbonna's brothers was a doctor in the United States. One was a senior civil servant in federal government, much like his father. While not all of Ogbonna's siblings had done so well, by any measure his was an elite Nigerian family.

Ogbonna himself was neither among the most nor the least successful of his father's sons. When I met him in the early 1990s, he was a lecturer at Abia State University (ABSU), a lower-tier tertiary institution in Nigeria's rapidly growing landscape of higher education. He had both bachelor's and master's degrees from the University of Lagos, one of Nigeria's premier federal universities, but he had yet to embark on his PhD—a situation common among lecturers at ABSU and similar schools. I got to know him quite well because during my dissertation fieldwork in the mid-1990s I had a Fulbright fellowship at ABSU and taught two courses there. At that time, lecturers were poorly paid and salaries were often late.

Ogbonna lived in a somewhat dilapidated house provided by the university where he and his wife and their five children shared three bedrooms, a parlor, a kitchen, and one bathroom. Water ran infrequently so they collected it in large plastic barrels each time the tap flowed. NEPA provided electricity sporadically—sometimes Ogbonna and his family would go a week at a time without light from the grid. But one of the bonuses of living in a campus house was that the university ran a generator every weeknight between 7 and 10 p.m. It was not enough to make the family's refrigerator a functional appliance, but it enabled Ogbonna to mark his students' papers, allowed his children to do their homework, and let the family watch occasional videos with their VCR and TV.

Ogbonna's car was a very old Peugeot 504 (a brand that for many years was assembled in Nigeria and up until the mid-1990s was one of the most common vehicles on the road) that one of his wealthier brothers had more or less permanently lent him. It was frequently in need of repairs and often parked for weeks at a time because Ogbonna did not have the cash to fix it. He sometimes lamented that he had it all because it proved to be such a money pit.

Ogbonna hailed from a relatively remote part of Abia State, near a place called Afikpo. As I have already noted, for most Igbos in or from southeastern Nigeria, kinship ties to one's natal community created a constant and powerful centrifugal pull. Ogbonna's village was about two hours' drive from the university on a very bad road. He went home at least half a dozen times a year to visit his aging mother. He brought his wife and kids home every Christmas, and often more frequently.

Ogbonna loved the village. But the fact that he had not yet built a house there grated on him. As a man in his forties, married with five children, with what was perceived to be a good job, and being the son of a "Big Man," it was expected that by now he should have built a house in the village—and not just some tiny little abode, but something befitting his social status (or at least the one he imagined for himself). So in recent years each trip home, despite its joys, became a reminder of his failures as well. The yet-to-be-constructed house was occasionally mentioned by his kinsmen, sometimes by his mother, and lately even by his wife and children.

Most of the money Ogbonna did earn was spent on providing for his family, and especially on school fees for his children, which were escalating as more of his kids reached secondary school. And of course there was the infernal car. It seemed to Ogbonna that at his current pace he would never be able to save enough money to build a house.

It is hard to exaggerate the social pressure in southeastern Nigeria for a man to build a house in his natal village. Traditionally, in village society sometime after marriage a man would be expected to build his own hut separate from—though nearby—his father's compound. In recent decades huts became houses (most Igbos now build houses made with cement walls and floors and metal roofs). At the same time, more and more men moved away from their villages to cities and towns for education, employment, or business opportunities. To make up for that absence, male rural-to-urban migrants face even stronger pressures than their rural kin to build houses at home in their village, and to build houses of a size and quality that reflect the social status they sought through their migration. Other than marrying and having children, for most Igbo men, there is probably no more significant marker of successful manhood than building a house at home in the village.

When I started working in Nigeria in 1989 I found it peculiar that most men aspired to build houses in their villages of origin even though they rarely lived there. Almost all the men I knew built their first (and often their only) house in their rural communities, even as they continued to rent in the city, where they actually spent more than 90 percent of their time. Eventually, I began to understand the intense cultural and symbolic importance of village houses for Igbo men. These structures were statements of continued belonging in and loyalty to their natal communities, as well as symbols of economic success. In addition, the pressure to build first and foremost in the village was accentuated by Igbos' recent history in Nigeria—specifically the civil war from 1967–70, when Igbos tried to secede from Nigeria and create the nation of Biafra.

The Igbos lost the war. A significant trauma of the defeat, in addition to more than a million lives lost, was the number of houses and businesses and the amount of property that Igbos lost in the cities around Nigeria. As I have noted, Igbos are a highly migratory, entrepreneurial tribe (Gugler 1991, 2002; Chukwuezi 2001). Before the war, Igbo men (and often their families) lived in huge numbers in cities and towns across Nigeria. When they fled back to the Southeast during the war, indigenous populations seized many of the houses Igbos had built in those places. Some buildings were destroyed and in other cases after the war Igbos could not recover their properties because of laws enacted about "abandoned property" (Tamuno 1972; Joseph 1981). Essentially, from the Igbo perspective, these regulations allowed others to steal their houses and property. Ogbonna was one of countless Igbo men who explained to me that after Biafra every Igbo man knew not to make that mistake again. One might eventually build a house in a city or in some far-flung part of Nigeria, but only after building at home, where it was safer and more secure.

But in the mid-1990s Ogbonna did not have the savings to enable him to start, much less complete, a house in his village. Indeed, like many of the lecturers I knew, he made ends meet by resorting to practices that further undermined Nigeria's already stretched and precarious system of tertiary education. For his classes, Ogbonna assigned students lengthy "handouts," which students were required to purchase directly from him. The handouts were photocopies of Ogbonna's lecture notes, as well as materials he copied from published materials (books and articles) he owned and parts of a manuscript he was working on with the intent of publishing a textbook. The library at ABSU was pitifully stocked and the campus had almost no culture of buying books (and students had little money to do so). By selling handouts lecturers provided students their primary course reading material. Because they marked up the cost dramatically and required students to purchase them in order to pass their classes, lecturers supplemented their unreliable incomes significantly in this fashion. Some faculty embarked on even more ethically egregious practices, including "monetizing" or "sexualizing" grades (as I explained in chapter 1). As I far as I knew, Ogbonna never engaged in these practices. Indeed, he openly condemned such behavior. He also lamented to me the whole business of handouts, but suggested that in the current system he could not provide for his family adequately on his salary alone.

Many university faculty members also tried to supplement their incomes through consultant work, either through the government or with donor-sponsored NGOs. Indeed, it was when I was able to hire Ogbonna as a consultant on a research project on which I collaborated with a local Nigerian NGO that our relationship was strengthened into something that long outlasted my Fulbright fellowship at ABSU. Compared to many others, Ogbonna was competent, reliable, and straight-forward. Despite selling handouts and hoping to use some of his university time to pursue consultant work, I found him refreshingly candid about his motives and admirably ambivalent about practices he engaged in because he felt he had no choice. His work on the research project was effective and I valued our growing friendship.

Toward the end of my dissertation fieldwork, the Nigerian government engaged in another round of state creation (it had done so periodically since the civil war); Abia State itself was only created in 1991, carved from Imo State. In 1996, a fifth Igbo-speaking state was created: Ebonyi State. This was in addition to Abia, Anambra, Enugu, and Imo States. Ogbonna's natal village was located in what would become Ebonyi and its creation would have dramatically positive consequences for Ogbonna's economic, political, and social standing.

The area carved off to create Ebonyi State had a reputation for being a relatively backward region in Igboland. The number of wealthy families and well-educated people was perceived to be far fewer than in the other Igbo states. Whether this was really true or not is hard for me to say, but regardless, many mutual friends and colleagues attributed Ogbonna's rather meteoric transformation to the fact that Ebonyi had relatively few men of his education and standing.

What I do know is that when Nigeria made the transition from military to civilian rule in 1999, a family friend of Ogbonna's was appointed commissioner of an important ministry in the state government. Shortly thereafter Ogbonna transferred from ABSU to the fledgling Ebonyi State University in the state capital, Abakaliki. Almost immediately his financial status changed dramatically. Two things happened. First, his friend the commissioner created a business with government money and used Ogbonna as the front man. While most of the profits went to the commissioner, he shared a significant percentage with Ogbonna for his role. Second, once Ogbonna had proven himself trustworthy, the commissioner and other state politicians awarded Ogbonna—and eventually his wife—numerous government contracts. They were not entirely bogus contracts. Usually something was actually built or supplied, or some service was rendered. But the amount of the contract typically far exceeded the cost of the job, and Ogbonna and his political patrons shared the difference.

By the time I visited him in his village in 2004 he had begun building a huge house there. When I last visited in 2012 he had completed the house in the village and had almost finished an even bigger mansion in Abakaliki. These were houses that dwarfed anything Ogbonna had even dreamed of back when he was lecturing at ABSU. The so-called "boys quarters" (which could be a guest house or servants' quarters) at the house in Abakaliki had three bedrooms—more than adequate for most families. The main house had eight bedrooms. It was opulence on a scale that Nigerian elites seemed incapable of foregoing.

By 2012, Ogbonna not only had two mansions; he also had many vehicles, a state political appointment, and a number of thriving businesses on the side. He had visited the United States twice and sent his wife on a pilgrimage to Israel. His children attended expensive schools. He often toyed with the idea of running for political office. He was now the kind of Big Man who could dole out favors and contracts rather than seek them.

I thought that with his newfound status Ogbonna might find my company passé. But for whatever reason he continued to welcome me heartily whenever I came to Nigeria. Further, he seemed to enjoy telling me about the intricacies of money and politics in this high-powered world of Nigeria's economic and political elites. As I have written about elsewhere with regard to the relationship between politics, patronage, and corruption (Smith 2007a), one of the things that struck me most about Ogbonna's story was the way in which he and men like him who use their political positions to amass wealth describe their relationships with other elite men as involving high degrees of intimacy and trust. In many ways this should not be surprising, for much of what they collude to do together is illegal. Mutual trust is at least as necessary in crime as in legitimate business partnerships. But when he described his relationships with other political elites, Ogbonna's stories evoked more than just necessary trust among criminals. Instead, these narratives evinced a profound sense of solidarity and a feeling of highly rewarding sociality. Perhaps this comradery—in most cases nearly all male—helps explain how elites justify practices that produce so much inequality and how they manage to feel good about themselves when their positions place them in such starkly disparate positions vis-à-vis ordinary people. The sense of solidarity among male elites that Ogbonna described is something that I will explore further in chapter 4.

As I alluded in to in the introduction when discussing the ambivalence around chieftancy and title taking, and as I show in many other parts of this book, the centrality of money to enable conspicuous redistribution, and the importance of provisioning and patronage for demonstrating competent masculinity in Nigeria, create circumstances where elites like Ogbonna are simultaneously admired and resented by men below them in the social hierarchy. This dynamic animates much of masculine social life in Nigeria. Ogbonna was particularly sensitive to this, having come from a prominent family, and then having struggled for many years before achieving his more recent success.

One way he coped with these conflicted feelings about the legitimacy of his wealth and status was increasingly common among elites in southeastern Nigeria: he found support in a Pentecostal church. To be fair, Ogbonna was born again before he became wealthy. But I was struck by how often he and his wife talked about and justified their new wealth and social position as the work of God, often directly tying their prosperity to their faith. I always found it a bit hard to listen to because to me it seemed hypocritical to profess faith in Jesus even as one's actions seemed so obviously to benefit one's self at the expense of others. Nevertheless, Ogbonna and his wife found common ground not only with other elites who joined Pentecostal churches, but also with many other Nigerians who genuinely believed that proper faith in God was the most important prerequisite for prosperity (Dada 2004; Ukah 2008; Marshall 2009; Umoh 2013).

But for all the respect Ogbonna gained—in his church, at home in his village, among his political peers—with his increasing wealth and success, Ogbonna's great wealth also came with suspicion, rumor, and criticism. While few people criticized Ogbonna to his face (indeed most of his old friends treated him more deferentially now), I heard many of his old colleagues at ABSU say that he had become part of the problem—a man who achieved his wealth and status through the very forms of corruption that were at the core of Nigeria's ailments. As for so many men, how Ogbonna fared socially in the face of the ambivalence about his wealth depended on how he managed his intimate relations with his kin, community, friends, and associates. It depended largely on how he spent and shared his money.

A Business Tycoon

In over twenty-five years of working in Nigeria, I've known few men as wealthy as Chima. Moreover, he was born into his wealth, so he has never known anything but privilege. He hails from the Orlu area of Imo State and I first met him at the tennis club in Owerri. He embodies a stereotype: Orlu is known as the part of Igboland that is home to businessmen who dominate Nigeria's pharmaceuticals trade. Chima's father made his fortune after Nigeria's civil war by starting a pharmaceutical company that eventually became one of the biggest producers of drugs in West Africa. Kristin Peterson (2014) has written a fascinating account of Nigeria's pharmaceutical markets and she explains how Igbos—and Orlu Igbos in particular—came to dominate the business. More broadly, one of the features of Igbo success in cornering various market sectors in Nigeria is the degree to which different regions—and what might be described as sub-ethnic groups or clans—have created virtual monopolies in various niches (Silverstein 1984; Meagher 2010).

The association of particular Igbo groups with specific businesses has been documented in scholarly accounts and is a regular feature of popular lore in Nigeria. Kate Meagher (2010) has written extensively about the shoe-manufacturing business in Aba, including the way that specific groups dominate the business and supply most of the labor. Men from the town of Nnewi in Anambra State are famous for their role in producing locally manufactured motor vehicle spare parts (Silverstein 1984). In addition to the association of certain areas or subgroups with specific commodities, in recent years I have heard many popular accounts that connect new forms of commerce to particular towns or regions. For example, many people say that Ahiazu Mbaise Local Government Area in Imo State is a hotbed for men engaged in 419 (Nigeria's notorious scams, widely associated with emails seeking advance fees in exchange for the promise of a larger payoff), and also for international trafficking in narcotics.

When I asked people what Umuahia was known for, I was intrigued to hear people say that it was increasingly associated with producing Pentecostal pastors and "new breed" churches—an allusion to the many born-again churches popping up all over the country. At first I was amused and somewhat incredulous, but when I started asking the place of origin of Pentecostal pastors in cities I visited regularly such as Owerri, Aba, Lagos, and Kano, I was amazed at what seemed to be the large number from Umuahia and its environs. Umuahia natives do not have a monopoly on starting Pentecostal churches; plenty of 419 men come from places other than Mbaise; and in businesses like motor vehicle spare parts or pharmaceuticals people outside Nnewi and Orlu are involved. But it is nonetheless true that the correlation between place/subgroup in Igboland and particular businesses is strong. Both the literature and everyday observations and discourse suggest that a big part of the reason for this subgroup dominance is the political and economic importance of personal social ties—including kinship ties. Such ties engender the trust that enables effective business relations in Nigeria's often-precarious political economy.

Chima's father groomed him to take over the company and in the process introduced him to a wide range of business contacts—in Orlu, in Nigeria, and abroad. At the tennis club he was very circumspect about his business. He spent money generously and this made him one of the club's "celebrities" (see chapter 4). But he spoke hardly at all about his work at the club. It was only when I visited him at his Owerri home, and then eventually in his village near Orlu, that he shared with me more about what it was like to run—and own—a lucrative business in Nigeria.

Chima spent a lot of time—more than he enjoyed, he said—interacting with other economic and political elites at lavish social functions. The superrich in Nigeria entertain each other often. Part of it is the opportunity to show off and enjoy their wealth, no doubt. I have always been impressed with how much Big Men in Nigeria enjoy saluting and celebrating each other's bigness. Chima could strut with the best of them. His wardrobe was phenomenal, whether it was flowing traditional dress (his preference) or tailor-made Italian suits. His many cars included both the latest Mercedes Benz and a Toyota Land Cruiser. While his house in Owerri was actually remarkably modest, he spared no expense on his mansion in the village, and I heard he had houses in Lagos and Abuja, although I never visited them.

But more interesting to me than Chima's various displays of conspicuous consumption was what he explained to me about the role that elite socializing played in his business. Attending elite social gatherings—including weddings and funerals—was absolutely necessary to cultivate and maintain business ties. So much of succeeding in Nigeria, he said, depended on maintaining these social relations. For example, he had to be on good terms with top officials in the Nigerian Customs Service to enable shipments of drugs from India and China to clear in a timely way. It was also important to have good relations with various people in the federal and state ministries of health—people who could award lucrative government contracts for the purchase of pharmaceuticals. And of course there were large numbers of wholesale and retail vendors who needed to be kept happy.

Chima acknowledged that his business sometimes required him to pay bribes to bureaucrats and political appointees in various positions of government. But paying bribes was only part of the story. He spent much more time and money, he said, on the numerous social engagements that his business ties and social position obligated him to participate in. The reality is that Nigeria's business and political elites create networks of sociality and trust, facilitated by the spending of money—based not on activities that could be labeled as overt corruption, but on social events. In many ways it seems similar to what one might associate with country clubs, golf games, debutante balls, and such things in the United States. But given Nigeria's infamous reputation for corruption, it is worth pointing out that there too a good deal of how elites reproduce their position at the top of the social and economic hierarchy is not through outright corruption, but rather through forms of sociality and cultural activities in which money is a marker of and lubricant for social connections. Even at lower levels of Nigeria's economic ladder I had long observed the way that bribes and other forms of so-called corruption typically require an underlying fabric of social relations to enable them to unfold (Smith 2001a, 2007a). One doesn't just hand over money absent the foundation—or at least the façade—of something more affective and social. For super elites like Chima, being a Big Man required a huge financial investment in sociality.

While Chima invested a lot of time and money in maintaining strong and efficacious ties to his fellow elites, like every Nigerian Big Man I knew, he also spent a lot on his relationships with a vast network of people of lower social and economic status. By now there is a huge literature in African studies about the centrality of patron-client relations in economic, political, and social life (Guyer 1995a; van de Walle 2007), including in Nigeria (Joseph 1987; Berry 1985, 1989; Clarno and Falola 1998). This literature shows the many ways that elites and ordinary people are bound by reciprocal obligations, and while these ties create important followings for Big Men that partly undergird their power, patron-clientelism can also serve to mitigate the worst consequences of inequality because elites are bound, to some degree, to help take care of their followers. I have argued elsewhere that one of the biggest gripes of ordinary people in contemporary Nigeria is that many new elites flout the traditional obligations of Big Men, spending money only on themselves, thereby making the contours of inequality sharper and the consequences less tolerable (Smith 2001c; 2007a). While I think there is considerable truth to people's sense that some Big Men aren't what they used to be, it is nonetheless the case that many elites, like Chima, still spend a lot of time and money trying to be good patrons, and therefore legitimate Big Men.

I remember one afternoon visiting Chima's house when he had invited me over for lunch. During the three hours I was there—we had our meal and watched an English Premier League soccer game on his satellite TV—no less than six different men came by to visit. Each wanted to see Chima about "something important." After observing the constant flow of visitors, when the match finished I asked him about it. He smiled and uttered a phrase I had heard many times before in Nigeria, "Dan, big money, big trouble." His visitors had included two employees at his company, two men from his kindred in his village, one man who was his "in-law" from his wife's village, and a local policeman who seemed to have no connection at all other than knowing who Chima was and where he lived. Chima explained that all of them had a financial problem of one kind or another and each was asking for money. Some asked for loans; others just wanted him to "dash" (give) them the cash. All of them presumed (or at least hoped) that because he was a rich man he could and would (or at least might) do so. I asked Chima whether he gave them what they asked for. He responded, "Even if I gave away everything I have I could not solve the problems of everyone who comes to me. But I almost always do something." Once someone secures a face-to-face meeting, he finds it hard to say no. When he does not want to deal with such requests he instructs his gateman to send people away, saying that he is out or otherwise occupied. But almost always people come back.

Despite all the time and money Chima spends cultivating social relationships of all sorts, even people who consider him a friend talk behind his back about whether his money was earned legitimately. In Chima's case the specter of counterfeit drugs hangs over his business. Some estimates suggest half of all drugs in the market are fakes. More than once I heard men at the tennis club speculate about whether Chima was so rich because his company's profits were padded by the manufacture or importation of fake drugs. Chima himself acknowledged the problem to me once, explaining that he had to be constantly vigilant about whether the drugs he imported from India and China were genuine. But he adamantly maintained that his company's drugs were real.

As with so many rumors about issues of corruption or fraud in Nigeria, I have no way of knowing whether any of those about Chima's company were true. But the larger point is that in contemporary Nigeria money is always haunted by its possible illegitimacy. While nearly every man I know in Nigeria aspired to be rich, everyone also recognized that many paths to wealth were tainted. With the continuing importance of patron-client ties and the centrality of reciprocal sociality even the most legitimate of wealth can make a rich man feel that with big money comes big trouble. The prospect that money itself is tainted only adds to the burden, both when such suspicions are warranted and when they are not. Men with money in Nigeria are constantly trying to prove that they are legitimate Big Men.

Conclusion

I began this chapter with a quotation from Chudi, my young tailor in Umuahia, who captured pithily what I frequently heard in other words from so many Nigerian men: "In Nigeria, money is God and money is the devil." Over the past couple of decades the burgeoning popularity of Pentecostal churches, particularly those espousing the "prosperity gospel," have given powerful voice to this seeming contradiction (Marshall 2009; Umoh 2013). Indeed, as I have observed Pentecostal Christianity sweep across the religious landscape in southeastern Nigeria I have been puzzled and intrigued by the way that these churches and their voluble pastors both condemn the evils associated with money and promise people that their aspirations for wealth are the will of God and can be fulfilled through born-again faith (Dada 2004; Ukah 2008).

While Pentecostal churches are reputed to be especially popular among women, in fact men—particularly young men—have also joined in droves (Meyer 2004). For many men, the messages of these churches address the central conundrums of contemporary life, not least ambivalence about money as the basis for competent masculinity. On the one hand, the primacy of money can be seen as a continuity; a modern version of the longstanding importance of providing—for one's wife and children; for kin and community; for clients if one is a patron—as the marker of successful manhood. On the other hand, the pursuit of money can appear to be a perversion of important social values, as men spend lavishly on conspicuous consumption that appears to benefit mostly only them, and as the importance of consumption as the measure of status seems to exacerbate class inequalities.

In Nigeria, great wealth, ostentatious consumption, and dramatic inequality are often suspect and frequently resented. Politicians are known to steal government money; businessmen are believed to be making or importing fake or deliberately inferior products; men whose wealth seems to appear out of nowhere are suspected of 419, drug smuggling, or witchcraft. Nearly every Big Man is the target of rumors about the origin of his money.

Yet even as nearly all wealth is suspect—and maybe especially because it is suspect—spending money to assure social and political honor and prestige is perhaps more important than ever. Men pursue chieftaincy titles even though they all know the perceived and widely disparaged problem of "naira chiefs." If they are able, they spend huge amounts of money on weddings and funerals even though everyone acknowledges its folly. Poorer men spend much more than they can afford. Rich men spend because they *can* afford it. And the very same poor men who criticize the ostentatious behavior of the rich would condemn them even more if they failed to spend in this way. Money is integral to how men perform their manhood. It enables sociality even as it threatens it.

As the cases in this chapter have demonstrated, in a world where "money makes a man," there are winners and losers. Most Nigerian men are unable to make enough money to achieve all of their masculine aspirations. The costs of marrying, paying for school fees, annual rent and health care, building a house in one's village of origin, and burying a parent—the very foundations of modern manhood in southeastern Nigeria—loom crisis-like on the horizon for poor men, and even for those who are moderately well off. The monetary costs of being a good man far exceed providing material necessities for one's family. Even for seemingly nonessential expenses, there is no chance to opt out. Money is essential not just for economic survival; it is also tied to nearly every activity and ritual through which a man's social reputation is established.

The centrality of money for performing what one might call moral sociality serves to protect elites, despite undercurrents of jealousy and resentment. Patron-client-like relations across social class assure that rich men must share some of their wealth with their kin, friends, and clients to maintain their legitimacy. This tempers class-based anger on the part of the poor against the rich. But expectations and practices of conspicuous redistribution also contribute to solidifying class inequalities. By tying moral sociality to spending money, a culture of conspicuous redistribution binds all men to a moral economy in which the wealth and behavior of elites is desired and admired, at the same time that it is also resented. As I will show in the next chapter, even in the most intimate arenas of men's lives—friendship and sexuality—the intertwining of money, sociality, and masculinity is at the core of men's aspirations and their discontents.

FOUR

"Ahhheee Club": Money, Intimacy, and Male Peer Groups

JMJ arrived at Owerri Sports Club in his new Mercedes Benz for an evening tennis game. When the men sitting in chairs arranged by the side of the court saw him enter, they chanted in unison: "JMJ, 2.6 Billion!" 2.6 Billion was JMJ's nickname at the club, a kind of late twentieth-century version of praise names that have long been a part of masculine culture in southeastern Nigeria (Ebeogu 1993; Oha 2009). Traditionally in Igbo society, men's praise names referenced attributes like skill in warfare or wrestling, excellence in farming, or some honorific associated with a man's character, such as wisdom or oratory prowess (Nwoye 2011). JMJ's praise name referred to the fact that he had a lot of money. No one knew exactly how much. But 2.6 billion was an imagined number of naira (the Nigerian currency) so large that even a very rich man would be flattered by it. JMJ's fellow club members did not, however, lavish him with so much attention simply because he had a lot of money. The praise name signaled that he was also generous in spending it.

JMJ showed off his brand new Wilson Hammer racket, then the latest model that no other club member had yet acquired. After playing a brief game of doubles, he joined the assembly of men gathered for a long evening of beer, food, and boisterous conversation that always began in earnest just after the sun set and the tennis ended.

The club's president formally initiated the evening's proceedings. He banged a large gavel that looked like it belonged in a courtroom. It was perfectly permissible to drink beer and order food from the club's kitchen before the president—or, in his absence, some other club officer—gaveled the formal beginning of the evening's fun. But once the president called the club to order, everyone was expected to join the group and participate, at least until enough alcohol pulled things again toward more informal interaction later in the evening.

A few men still talked and laughed loudly. The president reminded the group that he had the power to impose fines on members who did not respect his authority. His effort to silence the crowd—by this time probably thirty men were present—was made in a serious, severe tone. But everyone knew that any fine levied would be paid to the club. Eventually the president would order that it be converted to beer and drank by the members. So even though the gavel eventually brought order and silence, no one was overly concerned with the momentary disrespect. The men knew that, as the president himself was most fond of saying, "the club never loses." Today's infraction would contribute to the club's coffers tomorrow, and most often that just meant more beer.

Once the group came to order, the president addressed the men: "My trustee, my patrons, my vice president, my Concorde general secretary, my financial secretary, my sports secretary, the captain of tennis, my champion, all other celebrities, ladies and gentlemen." The president had looked around the assembled group to see who was present so as not to forget to acknowledge each club officeholder in attendance. The club had at least two dozen formal offices or recognized positions, and each time someone addressed the club as group it was expected that he mention each official by his title. Further, it was important to state them in their order of prestige. Because the president was speaking he did not mention himself, but normally the order would be the president, the trustee(s), the patron(s), the vice president, past presidents, and so on down the hierarchy. And every address concluded with "all other celebrities, ladies and gentlemen." The fact that every man there could be a celebrity (or at least that every man might think of himself as such) is a feature not only of the club's culture, but also of masculine social life in southeastern Nigeria more generally. Igboland is, after all, the place about which the anthropologist Richard Henderson titled his 1972 ethnography *The King in Every Man*.

Of course the fact that they had the financial wherewithal to join a club, play tennis, and spend several evenings out drinking beer with their mates meant that these particular men constituted part of the town's elite. But in reality, the men at the club varied considerably among themselves in their wealth and status, even if none was poor. Still, they often liked to point out that they were equals once inside the club premises. There was indeed some truth in this. Men of a wide range of ages and differing political and economic clout interacted with an equality that wouldn't be possible outside the club. Further, when at the club, all the men generally deferred to club officeholders, even if those relations reversed hierarchies of age, wealth, and power that prevailed outside the club. Yet, in other ways, the club not only reproduced wider social disparities, it also accentuated them. Men at Owerri Sports Club were intensely attuned to status and to the recognition that comes with it. In many respects this magnified quite common patterns in southeastern Nigeria, particularly regarding the importance of money as a marker of men's social position.

After the opening formalities the president reminded the men that the following weekend they were expected to attend the burial ceremony of the late mother of one of the club's members. Everyone was tasked with paying a burial levy that would become the club's collective contribution to the event. Members were to pay their levies to the

7   Men's tennis clubs in Nigeria are masculine spaces where money not only signals social class but also facilitates men's social relationships with their peers.

club manager (an employee, not a member) no later than the Wednesday before the burial. The president also instructed everyone that the club would leave in a convoy at 10 a.m. on Saturday morning. He encouraged members to attend in full force. He then explained that he was opening the floor for members to make additional contributions to the funeral.

Several members addressed their mates. Each speaker went through the entire list of assembled club officers and celebrities before offering a contribution over and above the set burial levy. They offered their contributions in cash or as a number of crates of beer. Everyone knew the exact price of a crate of each of the several types of beer that were available at the club. The announced contributions were followed by a collective "Ohhwaayyy!" The shout suggested mock surprise at the size and generosity of the gifts and conveyed genuine appreciation. To encourage more donations the president called for clapping in unison to thank the donors—six claps for smaller amounts, twelve claps for larger amounts. He instructed the club's social secretary to lead these collective claps, what in club parlance were known as six-gun and twelve-gun salutes. The social secretary would shout "gentlemen, twelve sharp hands, cooommmence." The manner in which he called for the claps signaled whether the final clap should be audible or silent, with violations producing more fines and more beer. Of course as the evening progressed and beer flowed, more men made mistakes.

While there was no prescribed order to offer donations, often those capable of only smaller donations would go first so as not to have to follow the richest (or most generous) men who would give the most. On this particular evening, about half a dozen men contributed before quiet descended for a bit. It was never expected that all men contribute beyond the prescribed levy, at least certainly not on every occasion. Nevertheless, over the long haul everyone observed who was generous (and who was rich) and who was not. After a period of quiet conversation JMJ stood up and asked the president for the floor.

As he stood his rotund belly protruded between his tennis shirt and shorts. Before formally addressing the club JMJ raised his hand and shouted "Ahhheee club!!" To which the assembled men chanted in unison "Club!!" He shouted again and the group responded. Then he shouted "Ahhheee tennis!!" And the men responded "Tennis!!" The "ahhheee" salutation was a dramatic mode of address. It simply meant "greetings" or "attention," but it created the expectation that the speaker had something bold or important to say. The men expected a flamboyant performance from JMJ. He began: "My president, my trustee, my patrons, my Concorde gen sec . . ." By this hour of the evening even these Igbo men, who, from my point of view, had an insatiable appetite for formal recognition, expected that conventional forms of address be cut short. JMJ obliged and followed "my Concorde gen sec" with "all protocols observed." At the beginning of the evening's festivities this would have been perceived as too curt. But later on, after several rounds of drinks, when every "celebrity" had been recognized numerous times, I was not the only one who seemed to welcome the respite from the formal protocol. So when JMJ uttered "all protocols observed," the men let out a collective "uhhhweee," signaling that they eagerly anticipated whatever he had to offer.

JMJ did not disappoint. He announced that he would contribute ten crates of beer and a whole goat to the upcoming burial ceremony. Other men had contributed between one and four crates of beer. JMJ's donation generated whoops and shouts of "2.6 Billion!!" JMJ then continued to add that all the evening's fine gestures needed to be properly "washed down." With that he ordered three crates of beer and a plate of pepper soup for everyone. At this the men whooped again. When calm was restored, the president ordered the barman and the kitchen girls to arrange the food and drinks. He then called the group to order again and instructed the social secretary to lead the men in a "twenty-one-gun salute," this number of claps reserved only for the largest and most remarkable donations. By the end of the synchronized clapping several men had lost the beat, but so much beer had flowed and was still yet to come that no one objected and the president did not impose any fines.

When the crates of beer JMJ donated were brought out for consumption, the president called on a new applicant to the club to distribute them. This man, in his midthirties, had the unenviable task of making sure the beer was distributed in order of social status. The distribution of beer (or anything shared among men) mimicked the traditional distribution of kola nuts made famous in Chinua Achebe's novels (Uchendu 1964). I had been asked to do this when I first applied to join the club, and the men took great delight in both my successes and my mistakes. The same was true for this new Nigerian comrade, though the expectations that he get it right were higher than in my case. At the club the beer had to be distributed in the same order as the formal greetings: to the president, the trustee, the patrons, and so on. Learning the hierarchy of club offices was relatively easy, but beer had to be distributed to everyone, not just club officers. Once one served the club officials the order of distribution then reverted to social status overall. In other words, one needed to know each man's perceived ranking in society. Age was a big factor, but so were money and political power. Over the years at Owerri Sports Club—and at many other clubs and venues where men share food and drink—I learned the nuances upon which masculine status is created, perceived, marked, and contested in southeastern Nigeria. As I will examine in greater detail below, monetary wealth played an ever-larger role in shaping these male peer group social rankings, but its prominence also produced conflict and discontent.

With what I have described thus far one might imagine that there were no women present that night at Owerri Sports Club, save the kitchen staff. Indeed, all the formal oratory and informal banter was among men. But, in fact, about half a dozen women were present. These were younger, single women in their twenties who were the girlfriends of some of the male club members present that evening. Nearly all the men in the club were married. But many had extramarital relationships and the club was a primary venue where these men entertained their girlfriends. Indeed, as I will also explain later, much of the motivation and many of the social rewards for having extramarital lovers came from male peer groups (Smith 2007b; Flood 2008). At the tennis club, and in many other similar masculine social spaces, married men's younger girlfriends were almost like adornments to their manhood. The women were seen and admired. Indeed, the larger group treated them cordially and often quite affectionately. But they rarely participated actively in the collective conversations.

When donated beer and food were shared, these women were offered some, but typically only after all the men were served, and only if there was enough to go around. Generally, it fell to individual men to provide for the women they brought to the club. And they did so generously, for part of the performance of masculinity associated with keeping—and showing off—an extramarital lover was demonstrating the financial wherewithal to entertain her every desire. The young women who were invited to the club enjoyed as much food and drink as they wanted (Izugbara 2004b).

The club was a particularly good place to bring one's girlfriend, not only because of the chance to show her off to one's male peers, but also because it was a relatively safe space to do so. Club members had a tacit agreement that wives were not welcome at the club, except on particularly prescribed occasions. When a man's wife did visit the club she was treated with great fanfare and respect, far exceeding anything that was done for girlfriends. This pattern of behavior reflects men's respect for marriage and for their wives, something that can appear contradictory given the prevalence of extramarital sexual relationships among these same men, a phenomenon I will explore later in this chapter.

Men's relationships with their male peers constitute a central arena for the performance and assessment of competent masculinity. Relating appropriately with other men—in school, in the workplace, at social venues and events, in the political arena, and in the myriad spaces connected with family and community—occupies more of men's efforts to be masculine than anything else. Men's concerns with what their fellow men think of them animates and explains a large array of male behavior. While men's relationships with other men are undoubtedly important in every society (Connell 1995; Bird 1996; Gutmann 1996), as noted already, in Nigeria the relatively gender-segregated character of social life means that men's relationships with each other dominate their daily lives (Cornwall 2003; Smith 2008; Chien 2015). This chapter explores the importance of men's relationships with each other, and culminates with a description and analysis of how even men's decisions, behaviors, and representations of their sexual relationships with women are deeply influenced by their relationships with other men (Smith 2007b; Flood 2008).

I use the tennis clubs in Owerri and Umuahia as central examples because they are venues I came to know so well. In particular, I focus on the connections between money and intimacy, in men's relationships with each other, but also with their girlfriends. As I have already shown in other arenas of men's lives, among male peers money—having it, sharing it, showing it off—is central to the performance of masculinity. Being able to "perform" monetarily is one of the paramount ambitions of Nigerian men and certainly having lots of money and using it in socially appropriate ways is one of the surest means to secure the admiration of other men. But as in other domains of men's lives, in male peer groups the rise of money as the most important marker of manhood comes with much ambivalence and breeds many discontents. Even as JMJ was showered with praise for his generosity, in his absence I sometimes heard his peers criticize his ostentation or speak derisively about the political corruption that enabled his great wealth. JMJ was said to be rich because of connections he had to the military government of the time, which awarded him huge (and purportedly often bogus) contracts in exchange for large kickbacks. Publicly, having lots of money appeared to bring rich men nothing but admiration; behind their backs it generated much criticism.

By about 10 p.m. the evening festivities at the club began to wind down. When JMJ departed the men stood and shouted "2.6 Billion" one last time. Eventually, only the bar man and the night watchman would remain, each of whom slept in the club hall on cardboard "mattresses." Their presence was a reminder not only that the men at the tennis club were the society's elite, but also that for most men the problems with money included simply finding enough to survive. And yet as I show throughout this book, men of all social classes aspired to be able to perform masculinity in similar ways. Money was always central to men's aspirations and ambitions. It determined their ability to fulfill expectations for intimacy and sociality with their male peers, their female sexual partners, and every other category of person in their lives.

A Gender-Segregated Social World

As should be evident by now, in many ways, everyday social life in southeastern Nigeria is highly gender segregated. While historically much of that segregation was overt—for example, in village settings men used to belong to age grades or secret societies from which women were literally forbidden (Ottenberg 1971; Oriji 1981)—in contemporary times social separation by sex is often more subtle but still powerful. I do not want to exaggerate the situation, for Igbo society was never strictly partitioned by gender, and modern life has propelled a lot of mixed interaction. For example, as I pointed out already in chapter 1, most primary schools, many secondary schools, and all universities are coeducational. In addition, the creation of a civil service associated with the nation-state and the rise of a capitalist-based labor economy have resulted in numerous occupations and workplaces where men and women work side-by-side, often doing similar jobs (Cornwall 2003; Lindsay 2003). And as I have shown in the earlier section about courtship in chapter 2, men and women interact relatively freely in Nigeria's wider social/sexual economy.

Nevertheless, in quite profound ways contemporary social life unfolds such that men and women spend much—indeed, in my experience, most—of their time interacting with people of the same sex. This is true even in contexts that on the face of it look relatively gender-integrated. For example, at Sunday church services, men and women arrive and worship together, but in practice in many (but not all) churches they sit separately on different sides of the aisle. Further, when there are church-related meetings, committees, or fundraising activities, these tend to be organized by gender. This pattern is common in many institutional settings, including in every village community that I have observed, and these arrangements extend to urban areas, where rural-to-urban migrants organize themselves into village development unions that meet frequently (typically monthly) to discuss, participate in, and contribute to the affairs of their rural places of origin (Smock 1971; Chukwuezi 2001; Gugler 1991, 2002).

Whether it is lineage meetings in village communities, migrant-led, urban-based village development unions, church groups, or even sometimes the local branches of national political parties, men and women organize themselves and meet separately. They frequently work toward common purposes, such as raising money, planning an event, or supporting a particular political candidate, but in practice men and women engage in large amounts of gender-segregated social interaction. It is noteworthy that in many cases the main male-dominated institution or organization does not carry a gendered description. The Ubakala Improvement Union is not called the Men's Ubakala Improvement Union, even though the meetings are all male, whereas the women's branch is commonly referred to as "the women's wing" or some other sex-signifying appellation. This is no doubt a consequence of—but also a means of maintaining—women's subordinate public status. The men have the main association and the women have their wing.

This relative separation of men and women in social life is evident in major rituals of the life course as well. I have already described in chapter 2 a bit about the division of labor in wedding ceremonies. This results in significant separation in terms of social interaction, with men spending their time talking to men and women conversing with women. The same is the case at burial ceremonies, as I will describe in chapter 6, and in virtually every other major social ritual or event I have observed over the years. Significantly, gender-segregated sociality operates in many informal economic and social spaces as well. Similar to the evening gatherings at Owerri Sports Club, I observed many situations where the conversational dynamic was entirely masculine even though there were plenty of women present. This was particularly pronounced at social clubs, bars, and restaurants where men would entertain their girlfriends, but it reflected wider patterns in which men created masculine spaces even when women were present. Symbolic of the social invisibility of women in male-dominated contexts is what happens during the ubiquitous practice of sharing kola nuts, which, as noted already, are offered to welcome a visitor as a sign of hospitality, but are also blessed and shared to open almost every formal social event. Women, men always emphasized, could eat kola, but they could not "see it." Formal shares were distributed only to men. It was as if they were the only full persons present. In southeastern Nigeria, men recreated these dynamics in many contexts, but especially in places and situations that they deemed to be masculine, and these were many.

It is also the case that men were peripheral in certain spheres of life dominated by women. A man might be present in gatherings of women, particularly in domestic spaces where women tended to direct activities. But it would be inaccurate, I think, to portray these as fully parallel phenomena, for men in southeastern Nigeria control many more institutions and activities than women. And men were much more likely to treat women as peripheral to important decisions or conversations than vice versa. I certainly don't want to give the impression that women in southeastern Nigeria are weak. I was often impressed by both the collective power of women and by the strength of individual women in their relationships with men. Igbo history and ethnography are rich with evidence of the agency and power of women (van Allen 1972; Amadiume 1987). But it is nonetheless fair to say that Igbo men regularly create and operate in social spaces that are male-dominated, a situation that benefits them significantly. The tennis clubs in Owerri and Umuahia illuminated many of the ways men reproduce their dominant positions in Nigerian society.

The Intoxicating World of the Men's Tennis Clubs

I discovered the masculine world of these tennis clubs not because I was looking for friends or men's company, but simply because I was in search of a good tennis game. I arrived in Nigeria to work for an American NGO in 1989 having played tennis since my childhood. Soon after I settled in I asked my Nigerian colleagues if there was somewhere I could play. The project manager, who did not play tennis, directed me to a place called Owerri Club (not the same as Owerri Sports Club). There I eventually joined in a game of doubles one evening after work. While I was delighted to play, the level of competition disappointed me. Luckily for me, one of the club members came up to me while I was having a beer at the bar after the game and told me he wanted to bring me to another place where the caliber of play was much higher. We arranged for him to pick me up the following Sunday morning. He took me across town to Owerri Sports Club.

That first Sunday morning I remember playing the current club champion, a man with the nickname "Osofia," which translates as something like "he who cuts down the bush." In Osofia's case it also alluded to the power of his tennis game. Osofia and I played just one set that noontime under a blazing hot sun. By the time the set ended in a tiebreaker most of the men at the club were watching. I had done well enough so that when we drank beers and shared food after the tennis, the president said I should fill out an application to join the club. I was happy to do so. The tennis was excellent. I observed that there were many other strong players besides Osofia. And the men all seemed welcoming and friendly. While I was eager to play there again, I had no idea that these men and those at Umuahia Sports Club in neighboring Abia State, which I would join in 1995 at the beginning of two years of anthropological fieldwork near there, would become among the most important people in my life.

I do not want to dwell on why these two clubs and the masculine culture they embodied became so important to me personally. I am much more interested, as I hope the reader will be, in why they were so significant to the Nigerian men who belonged to them. Even more pertinently, they reveal much about masculinity in Nigeria generally, particularly with regard to this book's main theme, the relationship between money and intimacy in men's lives. But I think it is necessary to explain a bit about how I came to know so much about these men and their lives. I also hope it will be instructive to explain briefly, from my perspective as a man, why this masculine world was so intoxicating. By this I refer to the appeal of this all-male comradery and solidarity, not just to the alcohol-induced intoxication that sometimes accompanied it.

After that first Sunday I made a habit of heading to the club after work as often as I could. I typically stayed for a quick beer after my tennis game and then headed home. But the men regularly invited me to stay longer, encouraging me to take part in the evening's social interaction. Eventually I began to do so. At first, the incredible formality required for addressing the club, sharing the beer, and attending to precise distinctions in status grated on me. I couldn't understand why everyone seemed to find it so pleasurable. Indeed, I never entirely overcame my discomfort with these conventions, and with men's seeming obsession with recognition. Even after twenty-five years in the clubs, I sometimes find it irritating. And it wasn't just at the clubs. I have always laughed heartily at popular Nigerian humor that parodies Nigerian men shouting in all kinds of situations: "Do you know who I am?" Igbo men recognized it as one of their own character traits, and I appreciated how readily they poked fun at themselves and their culture.

Even though I still sometimes chafe at the Igbo male preoccupation with social recognition, over time, at the club, I came to be seduced by its allure. Before my formal induction into Owerri Sports Club, when I was still an applicant, I remember the joy I felt the first time I success-fully distributed the beer according to protocol, as the men of the club openly praised my mastery of the social hierarchy. Even more mem-orable was the first time I donated several crates of beer to lubricate the evening's interaction and the president organized a "twelve-gun salute" for me. The sense of belonging it inspired was powerful.

But my full appreciation for the intoxicating feeling of belonging among these men and the psychological high that it produced only came later in the year. This happened when, to my surprise, I won the club's annual singles championship. I was one of four players who had a legitimate chance of winning. I had played the other three men many times over the preceding months. My record against Osofia, the current champion, and Emma Dike, another good player, was reason-ably even. But I almost never beat Francis, who had a crafty game full of touch and spin that gave me fits. Fortunately for me, Emma Dike beat Francis in one semifinal and I beat Osofia in the other. In the final I beat Emma Dike and won the championship without ever having to face my nemesis.

8 The author with Osofia, fifteen years after their first tennis match.

The week after my victory the club organized a big ceremony to present my trophy, which was presided over by the traditional ruler of Owerri, Eze Onu Egunwoke, who was an honorary trustee of the club. The club champion automatically becomes a "celebrity" in the club, so that every time someone addressed the club or beer was distributed I was mentioned and served because of my new status. But I found out it was much more than that. Each time I entered the club, for the entire year I was champion, every member greeted me with an enthusiastic "Up Champ!" or "My Champ!" And the ring of recognition went further. When I would run into club members around town they greeted me in the same way, with great enthusiasm. I was surprised by how good it felt and the feeling was amplified because my work colleagues and other friends in Owerri seemed so impressed that all these men in the town knew me and treated me in such a special way.

In addition to my status as club champion—which lasted only a year because in 1990 I faced Francis in the semifinals and lost—I acquired another nickname because of my tennis. As a club, we periodically played other clubs in friendly but competitive tournaments. There were four other tennis clubs to play in Owerri, but, more interestingly, we would sometimes host and often travel to clubs around Nigeria in places like Onitsha, Aba, Enugu, Nnewi, Port Harcourt, and Enugu in the Southeast, and occasionally to farther-away places like Warri, Abuja, Lagos, and Kaduna. In the first match I played for Owerri Sports Club against another team, after I made a winning backhand shot, one of my club mates shouted *"Beke wu agbara,"* which translates "the white man is a wizard." It stuck and in addition to being addressed as "Champ," when I played tennis my teammates regularly shouted it. While I received some special attention as the lone foreigner in the club, what I eventually realized was that many—in fact most—men in the club enjoyed similar recognition in one form or another. The men enthusiastically acknowledged each other at the club and around town, supporting each other's claims to social status and belonging. Every man was a celebrity his own right.

When I left Owerri in 1992 after three years working for the NGO, the club organized a big send-off party in my honor. The comradery and the special sense of belonging in this completely male-dominated social space was one of the things I missed most when I left Nigeria to go back to school in the United States for a PhD in anthropology. Indeed, when I returned to do long-term fieldwork in 1995 in the semirural community of Ubakala, one of the first things I did was find the club with the best tennis in nearby Umuahia. I joined Umuahia Sports

Club and for the past twenty years the men there have become some of my very best friends. I found the same sense of masculine solidarity and the same feeling of belonging that I missed so much when I left Owerri. And in addition to making me feel like one of the guys, all that time at Umuahia Sports Club taught me a great deal about Nigerian masculinity, and particularly about the complex and contradictory dynamics of money and intimacy in male peer groups in contemporary Nigeria. It is to that I turn now.

Money, Intimacy, and Men's Relationships with One Another

As suggested in the description above of men contributing to and attending en masse their fellow club member's mother's burial, many aspects of how men demonstrate friendship or allegiance with each other happen in very public ways. Whether one is the man who is burying a parent (or getting married, taking a chieftaincy title, launching a book, celebrating the birth of a child, or assuming a new political office) or his friend, colleague, or fellow club member trying to show support, spending money to demonstrate one's affection or loyalty to others is a key means for enacting sociality and expressing solidarity. Men's public displays of monetary backing for their peers are not only highly visible; they are also heavily scrutinized. A man's economic and political status is shaped by how much money he has. But his moral status depends, in part, on whether the amount he spends is seen as stingy or generous for his "size." In other words, while money translates into power, virtue is determined by perceptions of generosity and sincerity.

I remember once attending a book launching ceremony for man who published a history of his local community. The book was self-published and printed by a local firm. The author paid all the production costs, and neither he nor the publisher expected to make much, if any, profit from sales of the book. The man was preparing to run for public office. The book seemed to be part of a larger public-relations blitz. Not surprisingly, it portrayed the author as heir to a tradition of community leadership and presented him as the hope of this generation. A host of fellow politicians and wealthy Big Men were invited to the launching ceremony. Led by a master of ceremonies, speaker after speaker rose to express admiration for the author and donate large sums in solidarity. Many men contributed the equivalent of hundreds, even thousands, of dollars. Each donor received an ovation from the assembled guests.

When I expressed surprise at how much money men would donate at such an event, a friend with whom I attended said: "Don't mind the bastards. Most of them will never redeem their pledges." At which point it dawned on me that almost no one had paid in cash or even handed over a check. My friend added: "Even those paying huge sums by check will quickly go to their banks and cancel them. The whole thing is a charade." While I do not know how many men failed to fulfill their pledges, I heard this kind of talk frequently about various public events at which men would make monetary pledges. The sense that many Big Men made empty promises and that most of them were selfish with their vast wealth contributed to an atmosphere of suspicion about money, morality, and men's motives.

The fact that some displays of public generosity were essentially fraudulent did not mean that men could therefore shirk expectations that they demonstrate intimacy, allegiance, or solidarity with other men using money. To the contrary, if anything, most men felt intense pressure to be able to "perform" financially in their relationships with other men, just as they did with their girlfriends, wives, children, kin, and communities. Many of those performances were highly public, as men spent money on each other at major rituals of the life course, but also in smaller settings like the tennis clubs or other venues where men socialized together. Weddings, burials, and a whole range of other situations required men to spend—and share—in displays that were both conspicuous and expensive. In the face of money's association with fraud and deception, spending on sociality—performing competent masculinity for other men in the idiom of conspicuous redistribution— was all the more imperative.

But not all of the dynamics between money and intimacy in men's relationships with each other unfolded in such public ways. Indeed, one of the markers of deep friendship and intimacy between individual men manifested itself in the willingness to trust another to know about one's financial difficulties and seek help. In my many friendships at the two clubs in Owerri and Umuahia I learned about men's financial vulnerabilities and the often-quiet help they sought from each other. For example, one of the better tennis players at Umuahia Sports Club was a teacher named Kelechi, whose story I began to tell in chapter 3. On his modest teacher's salary the expenses of club membership were onerous even in the best of times. To make matters worse, at various periods during both military and civilian regimes, the Abia State government would fail to pay salaries for long stretches of time. As I recounted already, during one span of several months without pay, Kelechi's father became seriously sick and was hospitalized for several weeks. These financial shocks left Kelechi in dire straits. He eventually approached Ezeife, one of his best friends in the club, for a loan. Ezeife, in turn, approached me and a couple of other club members to contribute enough cash to see Kelechi through until the government paid salaries.

During this period many club members knew of Kelechi's situation. While people asked about his father and club members lamented and made jokes about the government's failure to pay salaries, no one ever sympathized publicly about Kelechi's financial situation, much less mentioned the fact of our loan. To do so would have been seen as unnecessarily exposing our friend's vulnerability. Until salaries were paid and Kelechi was able to right his financial situation, many people bought him beers, the president ordered the club's financial secretary to overlook his lapsed monthly dues, and no one expected him to open new tennis balls. But it was taboo to openly discuss his predicament in front of him. As ostentatious these men could be about showing off or celebrating someone's money if he had plenty, for a friend they could be equally protective when he did not.

Of course the willingness to loan Kelechi money and treat his situation discreetly was something Kelechi earned in his relationships with his friends and fellow club members. Such help and discretion could not be taken for granted. I observed other instances in which financial debts accrued in ostensibly private arrangements exploded into public disputes. When a man failed to repay a debt in the amount of time that his creditor expected, sometimes that creditor would make the dispute known to others, looking for mediation and pressure to pay the debt. I saw this many times in Ubakala, the semirural community where I lived during fieldwork, because one of the roles of the local chief, whom I knew well, was to help adjudicate and resolve such disputes. But it was rare to air such conflicts at the club because to do so was seen as shameful for both parties. When it happened a handful of times over the years, all the men lamented that money had spoiled a friendship and introduced conflict into club comradery.

In between the private arrangements in which men help their friends with money problems, tacitly agreeing to shield them from more public humiliation, and the very public displays of wealth associated with rituals like weddings and funerals, a whole middle ground of male relationships exist in which money is both a lubricant for positive sociality and a frequent cause of friction. Men at the club, for example, regularly drew on their connections with each other to seek political patronage, business opportunities, and other favors involving money.

Most of the time the common glue of club membership created good-will and these elite men further reinforced each other's relative privilege. Sometimes, of course, things went badly; for example, if a business deal went sour, if political fortunes shifted, or if individuals were perceived as just too selfish, either in their propensity to ask or in their failure to deliver. But for men at the tennis clubs, as for men throughout southeastern Nigeria, a vital part of successful manhood hinged on managing the monetary aspects of relationships with other men. As I will show below, the connections between masculinity, money, and men's relationships with their male peers also influence their relationships with women, particularly extramarital relationships.

Male Peer Groups and Men's Extramarital Sex

Alex is fifty-two years old. He owns a motor vehicle spare parts business in the town of Umuahia and is certainly one of the community's economic elite. Most evenings Alex joins several dozen other elite men at Umuahia Sports Club, where he plays tennis, drinks beer, and socializes with his peers. Alex is a married father of six. Though he hails from nearby Anambra State, Alex and his family have lived in Umuahia for almost twenty years. Many evenings, after a postgame beer, he drives off to pick up a young lady friend whom he brings back to the club for a drink and something to eat from the club's kitchen. Alex's girlfriends are typically young women, who are either attending one of several tertiary institutions in Umuahia or are employed in some kind of urban office or business. All of them are relatively "modern" girls who wear make-up, style their hair, wear fashionable clothes, and see the city as a means to a better life.

Each evening at Umuahia Sports Club it is common to see several married men meet and entertain their much younger girlfriends. In this section, I examine men's extramarital sexual behavior, untangling the complex connections between male homosociality and heterosexual infidelity (Smith 2007b; Flood 2008). I argue that men's intimacy with other men, including their desire to demonstrate their masculine prowess in both economic and sexual terms, shapes their intimate relationships with women. I am not suggesting that male peer groups provided the only motivation for men's infidelity, but it was clear that men showed off and were rewarded for their extramarital exploits when in the company of other men.

For example, at the tennis club, and in other male-dominated venues, men described to each other forms of sexual intimacy with extra-marital partners that were absent or impossible within marriage. This dynamic was fueled partly by men's contradictory perceptions and de-sires with regard to women. As I have suggested earlier, gender double standards mean that it is hard for women to be both good wives and exciting lovers, because, for many men, a wife who is an exciting lover may also be perceived as dangerously liberated, and even likely to be promiscuous. Igbo men commonly want their wives to be relatively sexually conservative in order to symbolize their faithfulness, yet they also desire forms of sexual intimacy that are perceived to be modern and exciting. At the tennis clubs men talked about these things with each other. Chinua, a forty-two-year-old merchant, described his expe-riences with sexual intimacy in extramarital relationships in contrast to his expectations for his wife.

These young girls today *na war-o* [Pidgin English, literally, "are a war," figuratively, "are incredible" or "are beyond the pale"]. I mean there are things they will do in the bed that even I, as the man, would not have thought to initiate. You would think that with these small [young] girls, you would be teaching them, but at times they are teaching you! They do things that my wife dare not. If my wife ever did some of those things, I would probably throw her out, because I would know she had become some kind of professional [a common local synonym for a prostitute].

In the full conversation, it became evident that the kinds of sexual acts Chinua was referring to included oral sex and various positions during intercourse, but also to the overt ways in which some of his young lovers directed him to satisfy their sexual desires. These were forms of intimacy that many married men found attractive, but also problematic. Indeed, men like Chinua often spoke openly of their mis-givings about and even their condemnation of the sexual morality of their young lovers. Although a strong and gender-unequal double standard is at work, most men viewed their wives as morally superior to their young girlfriends, even as these girlfriends offered forms of sexual intimacy that they boasted about with their male peers.

Young girlfriends also enabled men to further demonstrate their ca-pacity as providers. As I explained in chapter 2, for Igbo men, the ca-pacity to provide for one's family is the ultimate measure of manhood. In the precarious economic circumstances of contemporary Nigeria, even for relatively elite men, this important feature of Igbo masculinity is constantly under threat. Because providing for one's family is such a difficult task for so many men in the current economic context, men's relationships with their wives are often fraught with tensions around the family-building and household-provisioning projects. Many men experience their wives' demands and complaints as emblematic of their failures to provide as they should, and a lot of men seek extramarital lovers as a refuge from these problems. By taking care of young girlfriends, these men establish intimate relationships in which they feel rewarded for their masculine capacity to provide. Ironically, spending limited resources on an outside lover only exacerbates the economic challenges of being a good husband and a good father. Njoku, a forty-three-year-old man who owned a small shop selling office supplies, spoke of these issues.

Everything is a struggle in Nigeria. But at times my wife does not seem to understand my predicament. She will always pester me for more chop [food] money or school fees, even when the money is not there. Can I produce naira by magic? What I have, I always provide. No man wants to see his children suffer. But my wife does not always see with me. . . . [later in the interview] With Ngozi [his twenty-year-old unmarried lover of several months] I am free of those problems. She is always happy with what I provide for her. And she is sympathetic with my situation. At times, when I am having problems with my business, I will tell her things I do not tell my wife.

The intimacy between Njoku and his young lover reinforced his sense of manhood in contrast to his wife's complaints that symbolized the difficulties of achieving competent masculinity in Nigeria's struggling economy. Although my friends commonly complained among themselves about the consumptive demands and desires of their girlfriends—symbolized most recently by the growing expectations for cellular phones—it was also true that the capacity to provide these things was precisely part of what men were demonstrating to themselves and their peers in keeping expensive girlfriends.

One man's nickname provides an emblematic example of the interconnections between masculine performances of sexual prowess, socioeconomic status, and the qualities of intra-male intimacy that facilitate men's extramarital sex. A young businessman who was both one of the richest members of the tennis club and one of the most blatant philanderers earned the nickname "One Man Show." Whenever he entered the club, his mates would shout this moniker in unison with great endearment and admiration. The nickname was in recognition of the parade of beautiful women he brought to the club, but also an acknowledgement of the economic resources that are required to keep so many beautiful young girlfriends. It was obvious that One Man Show enjoyed the accolades of his male peers at least as much as the attention from his female partners.

The degree to which intra-male intimacy figures into men's extramarital sexual behavior was illustrated in a very personal way in 2004 when I accompanied my teammates from the tennis club to play a match in the city of Nnewi. In typical fashion, the host club provided us drinks and dinner after the match. Many of my teammates had brought girlfriends along for the overnight trip. These away matches were opportunities for infidelity that offered relative discretion. In addition, our hosts made sure that plenty of local young women attended the party after the match. I left the party for my hotel room around 10 p.m. because I had begun to feel feverish. By midnight, I was shivering under my covers with chills despite the hot ambient temperature. I was coming down with a case of malaria. As I huddled under my covers I heard a knock. When I opened the door a pretty young woman told me that her friend (the girlfriend of my teammate who had driven me to Nnewi) had told her I was alone and might want some company. I told her I was not feeling well and said no thank you, returning to my covers. A few minutes later came another knock. This time it was my teammate. He came to reiterate the offer of the young woman, expressing genuine concern about my lonely state. It was obvious that he had facilitated the initial visit of the young woman through his girlfriend, and it was clearly a gesture of friendship and male solidarity. I told him I thought I had malaria and couldn't manage a woman. He said that if I felt better they would all be in the disco, and he would make sure the woman stayed available for me.

My malaria helped me out of a difficult spot, as I was so feverish that I could avoid confronting the temptation posed by the pretty young woman, and save face with my teammates who would, no doubt, hear about the evening's events. Although my malaria protected me, at stake in the interaction with my teammate were both the perception of my masculinity and an aspect of intimacy in my male friendship. In addition to whatever temptation I might have felt had I not been sick, the pressure to receive the young woman would have come not only from a socially prevalent expectation regarding how to maintain a culturally acceptable masculinity, but also from my membership in an intimate male social group. While these two aspects are intertwined, I think it is important to emphasize the latter to highlight the ways in which men's intimacy with each other is part of what men are navigating in their extramarital sexual behavior.

My tennis teammates, and indeed all my friends and colleagues in Nigeria, knew that at the time I was married to a Nigerian woman. This aspect of my identity was highly celebrated. My tennis mates typically called me *ogo*, which is the Igbo word for in-law. I always felt that I was the recipient of extra affection and respect because of my in-law status. The fact that my male friends, who privileged my marriage to an Igbo woman so highly, would also go out of their way to help me have an extramarital relationship speaks volumes about the complexity of how Igbo men see infidelity in relationship to marriage and male comradery. The paramount importance of my status as "in-law" did not prevent my male peers from trying to include me in their masculine exploits on our road trip.

Although it is common to think of male infidelity as a violation of intimacy between husband and wife (indeed, many Igbo women also think of it this way), attributing men's extramarital sexual behavior simply to men's failure or incapacity to maintain intimate relationships with their wives obscures the degree to which male infidelity involves multiple and sometimes contradictory intimacies. In this section I have argued that the way men "do" intimacy in all-male peer groups contributes to producing infidelity. All of these examples demonstrate the key role played by men's relationships with each other in the motives and dynamics of male extramarital sexual behavior. Of course not all men cheat on their wives. But when men do cheat on their wives in southeastern Nigeria, it is often as much about their relationships with other men as it is about their relationships with their wives and their lovers.

Conclusion

In an interesting but mostly unknown chapter in an edited volume, John Remy (1990) argues that men's relative authority in society could be usefully understood not just as patriarchy, but also as what he called fratriarchy.[1] Whereas in patriarchy men are preoccupied with, and in part derive their power from, their status as husband, father, and provider for the family, in fratriarchy men are concerned with the self-interest, status, and reputation at stake in relations with other men. Drawing on a wider anthropological literature about men's huts, age grades, and secret societies, Remy contends: *"an extra-familial, extra-patriarchal impulse is at work in many men's associations"* (1990, 48; italics in original). It is helpful, and I think accurate, to note that when men interact together as men they often create and respond to collective interests that are not necessarily about their role and authority as fathers or husbands. Certainly at the tennis clubs in Owerri and Umuahia, and in other all-male settings I observed in Nigeria, men were performing masculinity for each other in relationships that can best be described as fraternal. Further, in these relationships men forge the economic and political ties through which power is solidified and access to social resources is enabled.

Remy suggests that patriarchy and fratriarchy result in different ethical codes, and that they sometimes conflict. While this might be true, my experience at the tennis clubs points to the ways that they are interpenetrating and mutually reinforcing. Many of the stories men told themselves at the clubs (and in other all-male settings) touted and asserted their prerogatives as patriarchs. The atmosphere in these settings was fraternal, but they also had the effect of reaffirming the legitimacy of patriarchy. Conversely, practices like men's extramarital sexual behavior, which appear obviously to be performances of masculinity that are manifestations of patriarchal privilege are, as I hope this chapter has shown, at least partly about solidifying men's social class position and their standing among their male peers—that is, about fraternity and fratriarchy. While Remy helpfully parses patriarchy and fratriarchy, it is equally instructive to put them back together and to see how each can buttress the other.

Regardless of whether men are navigating their relationships with each other or with women, their performance is judged heavily by how they spend their money. It is hard to exaggerate just how important money has become in Nigerian society, particularly for the performance of masculinity. Having and spending money are required to create and maintain just about every relationship a man has. As I have shown in this chapter, the recognition that men seek from their male peers is highly dependent on performing financially. Practices of conspicuous redistribution are partly motivated by an ethic of sharing, underpinned by a moral economy connected to kinship and patron-clientelism. As I have explained already, spending money in prosocial ways serves to legitimize wealth that can be suspect, and sharing—even in the ostentatious ways of elites in Nigeria—mitigates at least some of the discontent among men who have less. But it is also necessary to point out that practices of conspicuous redistribution establish and reinforce men's class position. In other words, these behaviors are engines and instantiations of inequality as much as or more than they are efforts to temper social disparities.

While my friends at the tennis clubs are a privileged elite, their obsession with money and their attraction to the conspicuous consumption and redistribution it enabled were widely shared across social classes. The rich embodied aspirations that most men in southeastern Nigeria shared. Poorer men envied elites' cars, leisure activities, and pretty girlfriends. And although not all men of lesser means wished to belong to social clubs or keep girlfriends, hardly anyone I knew, no matter how poor, did not aspire to be able to pay for lavish weddings for their children or extravagant burial ceremonies for their parents. A big part of the explanation for these seemingly ubiquitous aspirations is that Nigerian men's desire for money is not only, or even mainly, about individual greed. Instead, it is deeply tied to sociality and to the yearning for and rewards of social recognition.

Yet even as one must acknowledge the social work that money does for men, it cannot be denied that Nigerians also perceive money as a fundamental threat to morality and sociality. It both symbolizes and facilitates forms of behavior that violate values about sharing and reciprocity that gird even relatively unequal social relations in southeastern Nigeria. People recognize that immense wealth in the country is the result of a political economy marked by corruption and deceit. Those who have lots of money, like JMJ, face the constant challenge of trying to legitimize it. As noted, conspicuous redistribution eases not only the discontents engendered by inequality, it also mitigates some of the concerns about how money is made. But the specter of money's immoral aspects always looms, even in seemingly successful performances of masculinity.

In Nigeria's gender-segregated social world, male peer groups are major arenas in which men spend their time and money and seek social recognition and rewards. Despite its dark side, spending money animates and lubricates many important social networks to which men belong. The sense of belonging—which, for me, became so palpable in the tennis clubs—often triumphs over the discontents that money can bring. Despite the challenges posed by money, most of what I have described so far in this book are instances in which the intersection between masculinity, money, and intimacy could be described as primarily prosocial. But of course some men and some performances of masculinity are seen in Nigeria as antisocial, immoral, and even criminal. It is to these more troublesome examples of how men navigate money and intimacy that I turn next. But even these more problematic cases are better understood when analyzed as a product of the same cultural circumstances and social aspirations that characterize men and masculinity in Nigeria more generally.

FIVE

Masculinity Gone Awry: Intimate Partner Violence, Crime, and Insecurity

Brutus introduced himself to me near the beginning of my dissertation fieldwork in the mid-1990s as I was walking back to my house following an afternoon interview with one of Ubakala's elders. He seemed nice enough. He asked where I came from, what I was doing in Nigeria, and where I stayed—very similar to what many Nigerians asked in our first interactions. Further, he identified himself as the son of an elderly woman I had met on several occasions. I thought it might be interesting to talk to him again. But when I got home and said I had just met a man named Brutus everyone in the house shrieked and warned me to avoid him at all costs.

Brutus, it turned out, had a reputation for being the worst criminal that the village had ever produced. Many people thought his family should not allow him to live in the community. But his mother always let him come home. Despite all Brutus's escapades and regular warnings from her other children, she still had a soft spot for her baby boy. At the time, Brutus was in his early thirties. He had a wife and two children who lived in the family compound with his mother, along with one of his older brothers and his family.

I was told that Brutus was an armed robber, and that he and his gang were notorious for violent home invasions.[2] He was caught once, but he was never convicted—rumor had it that his relatively affluent and well-connected family had paid off the police to have him released. Fortunately, people also said that Brutus's gang operated outside Ubakala. But many people suspected that he only stayed out of sight during crimes committed there because he could be easily identified. Some believed his group was behind a string of robberies that had occurred in the community over the past year.

Brutus's life of crime seemed improbable given his family background. One of his senior brothers was a successful businessman in Port Harcourt. Another was working in the United Kingdom. One of his sisters was a doctor in California. With some assistance from his siblings, Brutus had himself migrated to Libya in his twenties. He stayed there for a couple of years but came home without much to show for it. Shortly thereafter his mother begged his brothers to set him up in some sort of business. Reluctantly, they bought him a small bus with the idea that he would use it to earn income by driving a local route. He crashed the bus beyond repair within four months of its purchase, apparently while drunk. Among Brutus's bad habits was that he was a notorious alcoholic. He also supposedly smoked marijuana and used other narcotics.

In addition to helping him try to start a business and getting him out of trouble with the police, Brutus's siblings also assisted him to get married. They paid for most of the bridewealth and for his wedding ceremony. In the years since Brutus married Chigo she had complained to her brothers (and his) many times about Brutus's behavior. Not only did he drink and use drugs, he frequently failed to provide any material support for her and their children. Further, he sometimes physically abused Chigo, something she protested about many times to her in-laws. I saw the outcome once myself when Chigo came by our house with obvious bruises from a beating he'd apparently given her a few days before.

In the years after my dissertation research, when I would come back to the community almost annually, sometimes Brutus would be there, sometimes he would not. I talked to him on many occasions, but only casually and about trivial things. I never invited him to my house or told him any details about my movements—advice I heeded from his own relatives. During one visit in the early 2000s, when I hadn't seen him for a couple of years, I learned Brutus was around. I was shocked to hear that he'd converted to Pentecostal Christianity and started his own small church. He spent much of his time recruiting new members to his tiny little flock. Given that I found many new-breed Pentecostal preachers to be veritable charlatans, I found it humorous and fitting that the most notorious criminal in the village was now trying to become a Pentecostal pastor.

But in truth Brutus was far worse than any pastor I could think of, and what I heard about him that trip confirmed it. People in the community discovered that he had been having sex with some of the young women whom he recruited into his fledgling church and in at least two cases he allegedly raped them. From what I heard, these were teenage girls, and one was supposedly only fifteen years old. The girls and their families did not press charges. As is the case in many settings, in Nigeria rape often goes unreported because systematic gender inequality and stigma for the victim make the social costs of doing so too high. But the community was outraged and there seemed to be a consensus that something had to be done.

With the rise of vigilante justice and extrajudicial killings in Nigeria during this particular period of time, I wondered whether people in the community might arrange for the Bakassi Boys, a notorious local vigilante group, to "deal with" Brutus (Baker 2002; Harnischfeger 2003; Smith 2004c; Meagher 2007). Nothing happened during the remaining weeks I was in Nigeria that summer, but when I returned the next year I learned that Brutus was in prison. It was not for rape, however, but for robbery. I was told that Brutus's family had arranged to have him imprisoned. They apparently paid the very people they used to bribe to keep Brutus free—the police and the judicial authorities—to make sure he was locked up without a chance of getting out. People said the family had negotiated Brutus's life in exchange for removing him permanently from the village. Everyone seemed happy that he was gone, and his kin retained their position as a respected family—though Brutus's mother was apparently heartbroken. I did not see her for some years after this; she was said to be living with her son in Port Harcourt.

The vast majority of men I have gotten to know in Nigeria over twenty-five years try to achieve their masculine aspirations through socially acceptable means. As I have shown in previous chapters, the paramount importance of money for being a successful man in modern Nigeria puts all men in potentially awkward positions vis-à-vis collective morality. Few, if any, successful men escape suspicions about their motives and their actions, including where their money comes from and what they do with it. But most men are genuinely trying to be good men.

As in any society, however, Nigeria has men who act well beyond the boundaries of acceptable behavior—men like Brutus who rob, rape, and even kill. The tendency is to see such men as far outside the norm, and of course in some ways they are. But in this chapter I argue that men who are deviant—even men who are criminals, rapists, and killers—can also be usefully understood through the same interpretive lens I have applied to men generally. Further, I will suggest that in many ways these men are not as different from ordinary men—from "good" men—as they might appear. Looking at the lives and behaviors of "bad" men can illuminate masculine projects more generally.

I think it is probably true that in every society bad men—examples of what one might call masculinity gone awry or gone too far—are more similar to other men than is typically acknowledged. But it is perhaps especially important to show this in Nigeria, and in Africa as a whole, because there seems to be a tendency (in its most simplistic guises completely misguided) to blame many of Africa's problems— wars, crime, corruption, etc.—on bad men and a crisis of masculinity (Ekpenyong 1989; Lambo 2005; Uchendu 2007; Ukeje 2013). As with many stereotypes, there is an element of truth in seeing Nigeria's struggles as connected to problems with men. Men's behavior contributes to reproducing the challenging social conditions that they and others face. But whether men are good or bad, the social contexts that shape the performance of masculinity, its meanings, and its consequences look remarkably similar.

Below I examine a range of problematic performances of masculinity—problematic not just from my perspective, but also from the point of view of many Nigerians. First, I look at the private realm of intimate partner violence and marital rape, showing how such behavior is enabled and in many ways justified by sexual and gender norms in Nigeria, even as attitudes are shifting gradually in the direction of collective opposition to such behavior (Pierotti 2013). New and contradictory attitudes about intimate partner violence and rape illustrate not only a changing landscape of gender norms, but also the ways that particular shared ideas about masculine privilege produce bad behaviors by men. Rather than simply branding individual men or particular behaviors as criminal or immoral, however, I try to explain the social context and masculine projects that produce them. I follow this section with case studies of four men whose public behavior can be described as illegal or violent (or both). But in each instance I also show how their stories further illuminate the complex geometry of money and intimacy in the performance of masculinity in Nigeria.

Intimate Partner Violence and Marital Rape

Adaku's husband, Ifeanyi, was a notorious drunk. When he drank he sometimes beat her, especially when she complained about his philandering and his frequent failure to provide money for food and for the children's school fees. Despite the beatings, Adaku did not relent in her criticism. On the contrary, she frequently carried her complaints to her family and to Ifeanyi's kin. She made no pretense of "loving" her husband. She simply wanted him to meet his obligations to provide for her and their children. In her mind, the chief obstacles to his doing so were his drinking and his infidelity. On one occasion she said to me, "What sort of useless man spends all of his money on beer and girlfriends? I will not allow him to forget that he has a wife and children." Ifeanyi's primary objection to his wife's conduct was that she had no appreciation for his efforts to provide for his family nor sympathy for how difficult that is in Nigeria. In his words, "My wife disrespects me seriously. She demands money when I have none, shames me in front of my people, and never offers the support that a man should have from his wife."

Their respective kin had made many interventions to try to make peace between them. During these mediations Ifeanyi would promise to curtail his drinking and better support his family and Adaku would vow to try not to provoke her husband's temper. But the cycle of violence and reconciliation continued for many years. Sometimes, Adaku would move out of her husband's house to stay with her natal kin for weeks, and even months, at a time. But, eventually, she always went back. While separations are common, divorce is rare and stigmatized in southeastern Nigeria. In addition, Igbos are mostly patrilineal and children formally belong to a man and his lineage. A woman who divorces her husband will likely lose custody of her offspring. Even in her awful circumstances Adaku saw the permanent dissolution of her marital union as untenable.

My impression is that most men in southeastern Nigeria do not beat their wives. Indeed, excessive violence by men against women or children is culturally unacceptable. But the idea that a man has the authority to slap his wife or children if they defy him is widely accepted, or at least tolerated, as long as he does not do so too frequently and he does not cause undue injury. In this context, instances of intimate partner violence within marriage often go unreported. Further, even if friends, neighbors, or kin are aware of violence, it can stay at the level of the unremarkable so long as the effects are not too brutal.

Over many years of research, I have had the opportunity to witness the aftermath of several instances of intimate partner violence. These were all cases of men who beat their wives. I observed the ensuing interventions (and frequently the lack thereof) and resultant conversations among kin and community members. It is notable that I never heard a wife complain specifically of rape or sexual violence on the part of her husband, nor did I hear others in the community talk about their concerns regarding domestic violence in these terms. It is indeed unclear to me how frequent marital rape really was. This is partly because many people in southeastern Nigeria—especially men, but also women—do not recognize the category of marital rape. While the problem of rape in general is deeply shrouded in Nigerian society, marital rape in particular is commonly considered an oxymoron. Men, by and large, reject the very concept of marital rape. They see women's sexual consent in marriage as taken for granted. Many women either share the cultural logic that marital rape is a contradiction in terms or they recognize that given prevailing social norms, such a complaint would be unrecognized, and even counterproductive.

Men who beat—and perhaps even rape—their wives must be seen in the larger context of the challenges to Nigerian masculinity. I don't mean to excuse or justify men's ill treatment of women. I only argue that like other examples of men behaving badly, intimate partner violence can be better understood if it is seen in relation to larger projects of masculinity, albeit manifest in ways that most readers—but also many Nigerians—would condemn. As with other men I will describe and analyze in this chapter who engage in theft, perpetrate fraud, or traffic in drugs, men who beat their wives are less different from their better-behaved peers than one might imagine. They are caught up in the challenges to manhood created by the importance of money and its relationship to forms of sociality and intimacy integral to the performance of modern masculinity, particularly as husbands and fathers.

In the last decade or so, the topics of domestic violence and marital rape have begun to be addressed by both scholars and advocates in Nigeria (Fawole et al. 2005; Oyediran and Isiugo-Abanihe 2005). As feminist discourses have circulated globally in the same era that gender relations themselves are changing due to increasing levels of education, growing urbanization, rising female participation in the formal labor force, and a range of other interconnected factors, it is now common to find local civil society groups such as NGOs advocating for greater awareness of intimate partner violence and more measures to protect women (Onyejekwe 2008). NGOs promoting women's rights tend to be based in the national capital, Abuja, and the country's commercial capital, Lagos, and sometimes in state capitals. Many run projects and do advocacy work in smaller cities and rural areas, but rights-based language regarding domestic violence and rape has not yet reached places like Ubakala with significant effect.

Further, all efforts to specifically outlaw marital rape through federal legislation or statutes have failed. In fact, the Nigerian Criminal Code expressly legalizes marital rape by exempting any sexual relations between a husband and his wife from the category of rape. Section 6 of the code clarifies the definition of rape as follows: "unlawful carnal knowledge means carnal connection which takes place otherwise than between husband and wife" (Chika 2011, 42). While it is surely not the case that a law against marital rape would by itself be sufficient to address the problem of marital rape in Nigeria, law—as Sally Engle Merry (2006) has shown—can be a significant force in social and cultural change. But as Saida Hodzic (2009) has observed in Ghana, getting national legislatures dominated by men to pass laws against marital rape can be highly politicized and difficult. The four rationales opposing marital rape laws identified by Kwaku Ansa-Ansare (2003) in Ghana are common in Nigeria as well: (1) such ideas are foreign-imposed; (2) such laws would threaten African family and culture; (3) domestic violence is best adjudicated privately, within families and communities rather than by the federal government; and (4) traditional authorities should mediate such disputes. As Hodzic notes for Ghana, in Nigeria it tends to be men who hold and promote these views, and who dominate the corridors of legal power, though I sometimes heard women voice these ideas too.

Data on marital rape in Nigeria is scant, in no small part because of the difficulty of measuring a phenomenon widely believed to be a conceptual paradox. But one study conducted in two communities, one rural and one urban, in the same general region in southeastern Nigeria as Ubakala suggests that domestic violence is common and the incidence of rape in general is high (Okemgbo, Omideyi, and Odimegwu 2002). This study found that nearly 80 percent of women had been battered by their male partners (with battery defined as anything from a single slap to more violent beating). Most people in Ubakala would not consider a slap to be battery; the local norm that men should not be excessively violent with their wives that I mentioned earlier does not apply to all forms of physical abuse. While I find it hard to believe that 80 percent of men in Nigeria have ever slapped their wives, much less beaten them, the study does suggest a contradiction between scholarly and local definitions of what counts as violence.

The same paper further documents that approximately 21 percent of women reported having ever been forced to have sexual intercourse against their will. However, imprecision in the way the data was collected (or reported) make it difficult to parse violence and rape that occurred before marriage versus within marriage, or whether women's understandings regarding what qualifies as rape were different inside and outside marriage. Indeed, one might imagine that because of the cultural belief that women must be sexually available to their husbands, they might frequently have sex with their husbands when they don't want to, but without any explicit issue of consent. It seems evident from this study and others in Nigeria that marital rape is difficult for Nigerian women to prevent or report, and perhaps also even to identify (Onyejekwe 2008; Aihie 2009; Esere et al. 2009).

A report by a women's advocacy group headed by a Nigerian law professor enumerates not only why the Nigerian government has failed to criminalize marital rape, but also why it remains so difficult to address more generally:

First of all, the fact that marital rape is not known to be a serious social offence, because although such cases exist, most of them go unreported. Second, women that live with their husbands feel that reporting marital rape would have a negative impact on the marriage, family reputation and children. Third, the fact that it is extremely difficult to establish any case of rape in Nigeria and this means that marital rape, which occurs behind closed doors, is even more difficult to establish. Fourth, the culture dictates a situation in which married women are controlled in all respects by their husbands including in their sexual reproductive lives, therefore the idea of forced sex does not exist because the wife is expected to always submit to the husband's demands in all instances regardless of her own feelings. (Okonkwo 2003, 18)

While I would contest the idea that men's control of women is understood by ordinary Nigerians to be so complete (my observations of exertions of female agency in southeastern Nigeria suggest something different), I would nonetheless be hard pressed to offer a better summary of the situation. My goal in the remainder of this section is try to explain why this situation persists, and in particular to connect it to the performance of masculinity in contemporary Nigeria.

It is common in southeastern Nigerian discourse for masculine authority in the domestic sphere to be justified on the grounds of a model of marital relations symbolized by men's payment of bridewealth. As described in chapter 2, when a couple marries, it is almost universally expected that the husband and his family will provide agreed-upon

gifts in cash and in kind to the wife's family in exchange for their consent and participation in the socially shared project of a marriage. This
occurs regardless of whether the union is deemed a love marriage or
one that is explicitly arranged by the couple's families. Anthropologists have been insistent for decades that bridewealth payments are not
tantamount to purchasing a wife (Comaroff 1980; Bledsoe and Pison
1994). Bridewealth systems are complex social arrangements in which
extended families and communities create social ties rather than simply transferring a women's reproductive capacity from her natal family
to her husband and his family (Ogbu 1978; Tambiah 1989). Bridewealth
payments mark the beginning of relations rather than the conclusion
of a single transaction. Most Nigerians I know can comfortably and
fluently explain the socially embedded character of bridewealth and
marriage in their society.

But it is nevertheless common to hear people explain and justify
masculine authority and a man's privileged sexual access to his wife in
terms of a simplified notion that bridewealth (and therefore marriage)
entitles a man to certain rights over his wife. Indeed, on the occasions
when I asked men about the possibility of marital rape in their society,
I was commonly told that there could be no such thing because a man
was entitled to sexual access to his wife whenever he wanted or needed
it. While most men agreed that a man should not have sex with his
wife in a given moment if she did not consent, this was usually overrid-
den by the belief that a woman should always consent. When consent
is presumed, rape is difficult to conceptualize, much less prevent. With
regard to the invocation of bridewealth as the justification for men's
sexual access to their wives, I think it is best understood as symbolic
in people's minds of a larger set of norms and practices rather than the
actual reason for them.

The fact that the preponderance of intimate partner violence—in
marriage and otherwise—is perpetrated by men against women suggests that such violence is an overt manifestation and enforcement of
patriarchy. But in southeastern Nigeria, as in many settings around
the world, a combination of complex social changes such as political-
economic and demographic transformations, and also the rise of femi-
nism and the circulation of rights-based discourses, have made the
maintenance of male privilege and power through violence increasingly untenable (Pierotti 2013). Even as many Nigerian men justify intimate partner violence and deny the very possibility of marital rape
based on ideas about masculine authority, the spread of formal educa-

tion and the inclusion of women in a capitalist labor market intersect with more intimate transformations in gender dynamics, such as the rise of love as a relationship ideal for marriage described in chapter 2, to challenge hegemonic masculinities. Despite these ongoing changes, however, it is clear that in southeastern Nigeria gender inequality remains strong, domestic violence is still a serious issue, and marital rape continues to be a mostly unacknowledged problem.

Two aspects of masculinity in southeastern Nigeria are relevant to explain these circumstances: (1) nonviolent performances of masculinity undergird widely shared ideas of manhood that allow intimate partner violence and marital rape to remain acceptable, if increasingly contested, behaviors, and (2) perceived threats to masculinity that men experience in Nigeria—many of them tied to anxieties about money— create insecurities that contribute to male violence. Although my evidence and argument focus on masculinity in southeastern Nigeria, it should be obvious that domestic violence and marital rape are not unique to this region, country, or continent. While the universality of the problem should perhaps be unnecessary to note, delving into the social conditions and cultural context that situate masculinity and enable intimate violence can sometimes be misread as blaming culture— something unfortunately all too common in accounts of African social problems. It is important to distinguish between putting a problem in its context and simplistically blaming victims (and perpetrators).

In southeastern Nigeria, men are in positions of dominance over women not primarily because of violence or the threat of violence; instead, male violence against women is tolerated (though, of course, also contested) because masculine power achieves its relative hegemony through other means—political, economic, social, and symbolic—that do not require overt violence. An extensive system of patriarchy and a widely shared social construction of masculinity create the circumstances in which men's perpetration of domestic violence and marital rape is possible and, at least to some extent, culturally protected. That being said, actual incidents of domestic violence and marital rape seemed to be tied, and sometimes triggered, in nuanced ways to men's perceptions that masculinity is threatened, not just by the women against whom violence is perpetrated, but also by larger forces that appear out of men's control. Many of these same threats also undergird male violence in more public arenas, and men's criminality more generally. It is to these more public arenas of male criminality and violence that I turn now.

A Drug Smuggler

Anyanwu approached me several months into my dissertation field-work, saying he had a family problem he wanted to discuss with me. The tone of his request was similar to what I experienced when people came to me asking for a loan or some kind of favor. But I knew Anyanwu to be a relatively prosperous businessman. As the first son of a wealthy chief who had owned many properties in the city of Aba, Anyanwu appeared to be doing quite well with his various businesses. He didn't need money. In fact, his problem was much more intriguing. His brother, Ikechukwu, was in prison in the United States on some kind of drug charge, and Anyanwu was hoping I might be able to offer advice about an appeal, or at least more information about how long Ikechukwu might remain incarcerated.

Anyanwu didn't explain much that day—or ever—about exactly why Ikechukwu was in prison. He was at best ambiguous about whether he thought his brother was guilty or not. He didn't assert his innocence, but he also said certain things that suggested he thought his brother might have been wrongly convicted. What I did learn was that Ikechukwu had an American wife and two half-American children. Anyanwu insinuated that it was perhaps the wife's influence and social networks that got his brother in trouble. While I didn't glean much more from Anyanwu, or from anyone in Ikechukwu's family about his case, over time I heard many things from others in the community. Local perspectives varied and they revealed much about the complex construction of competent masculinity in southeastern Nigeria, particularly with regard to the relationship between criminality and morality as they are inflected by the interplay of money and sociality.

Most people in the community believed that Ikechukwu had been trafficking in cocaine, organizing smugglers, or mules—people who carried drugs between Nigeria and the United States. By the 1990s, Nigeria had a global reputation as a transit point in the international illicit drug trade (Bayart, Ellis, and Hibou 1999; Ellis 2009, 2016). Nigerian organized crime networks, many allegedly masterminded by Igbo men, were said to play a large role in these operations (Ellis 2009; Meagher 2014). According to scholars and law enforcement authorities, a combination of the much-renowned Igbo entrepreneurialism and the relatively decentralized, acephalous structure of the syndicates (mirroring traditional Igbo political organization, about which much anthropology has been written [Ottenberg 1971; Njaka 1974]) made these networks particularly hard to catch and crush.

About five years after Anyanwu approached me about Ikechukwu's case, I met a Nigerian resident of the United States who was the brother of a friend of mine. The man, Obioma, was home in Nigeria for summer holidays to visit his family. When I inquired what Obioma did in the United States he said he worked for the government. When I followed up to ask what exactly he did, at first he demurred. But after his brother (my friend) assured him that I was trustworthy, Obioma explained that he worked as a translator for the FBI, part of some sort of task force assigned to combat Nigerian criminal networks. He didn't explain very much, except to say that he often helped authorities translate communications in Igbo recorded on wiretaps. It was dangerous work, he said, because the Nigerians who run these lucrative criminal networks would have no hesitation to kill him for what he was doing. He also insinuated that these criminal networks were linked to and protected by powerful people in the Nigerian government. He offered no proof of that, but it was a rumor I had heard many times from others.

Given his line of work, I told him about Ikechukwu's case and asked if he knew anything about it. To my surprise, he said he knew all about it. Obioma explained that Ikechukwu was fairly high up in a Nigerian drug smuggling syndicate. According to Obioma, the authorities had arrested one of the mules Ikechukwu had recruited to carry drugs. In a deal with US authorities, the person agreed to act as an FBI informant. Ikechukwu was then caught up in some kind of sting in which he and others were recorded organizing illegal drug importation. Eventually, Ikechukwu was arrested in possession of a large amount of cocaine. I asked how long he would be in prison and what would happen on his release. Obioma didn't know how long remained on Ikechukwu's sentence, but he said that he would probably be released in a few more years and then most likely deported to Nigeria. What would happen when he returned to Nigeria, I asked? Obioma smiled and said that would depend on "the Nigerian factor" (an allusion to the importance of connections, corruption, and money in how the state functions in Nigeria). In theory, Nigeria could also pursue some sort of prosecution, but in practice, he said, it almost never happened.

Sure enough, just a couple of years after I met Obioma, when I returned to Nigeria for a brief visit I heard that Ikechukwu had been released and was back in the country. I was very curious about the reception he received, both from his family and in the community more generally. I was also interested in what Ikechukwu's post-incarceration life would be like in terms of his work and his personal relationships.

Ikechukwu was not in Ubakala during my visit that year, so I did not meet him. But I talked with lots of people about his return. Pretty much everyone knew that he had been in prison in the United States and that it had something to do with drugs. But opinions differed about how to interpret his incarceration and his return to Nigeria. Some people rejoiced that he was home. Most of those repeated, more or less, the family mantra that Americans, perhaps especially his wife, had duped him. Notably, neither she nor his two half-American children accompanied him back to Nigeria. I was told that he and his wife had split up while he was in prison.

Others were agnostic about whether Ikechukwu was guilty of the crime, but it didn't seem to affect their view of his return. He was a son of the community, they said, and would always be welcome. Some holding this view also added that if he sold drugs in the United States, it was the American appetite for such things that was the source of the problem, not a Nigerian's willingness to sell it to them. Over the years I'd sometimes heard people voice similar sentiments about Nigeria's global reputation for 419 scams: that it was foreigners' greed that made the whole enterprise possible, and hadn't white people exploited Africa for centuries, after all? Turnabout was fair play.

But a significant fraction of people I spoke with lamented Ikechukwu's behavior and his return to Nigeria. "Such men are the reason Nigeria has the bad reputation it does. The government should not have allowed him back in the country, or when they did they should have locked him up on arrival," one elder told me, expressing a sentiment I heard from quite a few people. Some also extended their criticism to Ikechukwu's family, and especially Anyanwu, who, as the eldest son of their late father, was the head of the extended family. Anyanwu knew what his brother was doing in the United States, they said, and he happily accepted Ikechukwu's large remittances with which he bought cars, invested in his own business, and built an addition to the house he inherited from his father. Anyanwu's position as a Big Man in the community was criticized as based on his brother's illegitimate drug trafficking profits. Indeed, more than a few people compared Anyanwu negatively to his father, who had been a respected chief in the community.

I heard one rumor that Anyanwu and Ikechukwu were not on good terms because Anyanwu had spent much of Ikechukwu's money that he was meant to hold for him while he was in prison. That was the reason, I was told, that Ikechukwu decided to reside in Lagos on his return, rather than come home to the family compound in the Southeast. It was impossible for me to sort out how much of what people said was true versus what was gossip fueled by various rivalries and jealousies in the community. But questions about whether a man's money was legitimate or tainted were characteristic of wider patterns that I have already documented and analyzed in earlier chapters, even in cases where the menace of overt crime, embodied in Ikechukwu's case by conviction and imprisonment, was less glaring. Also emblematic of much wider dynamics were the tensions and conflicts that emerge between kin over money. On the one hand, people relied on ties of kinship to create and sustain the trust necessary for certain kinds of financial relationships. On the other hand, the temptations of money often led to strains and fissures among family. In southeastern Nigeria, men constantly face the dual and competing realities that close ties are the most important ones for making and securing money, while at the same time money puts those very relationships at risk.

The rumors and diverging views about Ikechukwu and Anyanwu also highlight the way that wealth and money both create solidarity and foment conflict in Nigerian communities more generally. Big Men like Anyanwu recruit and support allies by sharing their money in patron-client relationships. But those patron-client relationships are always fraught. Some men feel excluded; others grumble that the ways they are benefitting are insufficient. And sometimes even some of a Big Man's closest allies will feel and express discontents behind his back. Ikechukwu's imprisonment for drug trafficking and his eventual return to Nigeria stirred this combustible mix in powerful ways, by highlighting the specter of illicit wealth and by raising again questions about exactly how much money Anyanwu had, as well as about how he used it.

But as I have indicated, just as money can be the source of discord between men, among families, and within communities, it can also be the most effective lubricant for maintaining effective sociality, healing strained intimacies, and enabling a man to perform masculinity in ways that reap social rewards. In the years after Ikechukwu returned to Nigeria he seemed to be able to do just that. A couple of years after his initial return from the United States, I learned that he was about to marry a Nigerian wife. Though I did not attend the wedding, I heard that it was lavish affair. I was also told that Ikechukwu had established a successful (and purportedly legal) business in Lagos. When I finally met him in the village during the Christmas holidays, he was extremely friendly. He said he had heard all about me from his kin and friends in the community. He wanted to talk about the upcoming NFL playoffs. I did not ask about his experience in prison or about drug trafficking and, not surprisingly, he did volunteer anything. He did not seem like a man troubled by his past. From all I could tell he'd done everything he needed to in order to ensure that his money was still good in Nigeria.

A 419er

Nwakere was rich. Not only was he rich, he delighted in showing it off. His house in Owerri was enormous, including what looked like a small tower at the front gate where an armed security man served as his watchman. He owned many cars and usually traveled in a small convoy. For a couple of years in the early 1990s one of the vehicles even had a siren, so when he moved around town it was similar to how the state's governor traveled. After riots in Owerri in 1996 in which numerous alleged 419 men had their properties ransacked and burned by an angry mob (Smith 2001c), he stopped using the siren and minimized travel by convoy. The Owerri rioters had not burned Nwakere's house, though one of the hotels they torched was allegedly his property.

As I have explained and illustrated amply throughout this book, many men face suspicions about the source of their money, especially if their wealth is considerable and their occupation or business less than transparent. For rich men who have come into big money seemingly overnight, the common rumor is that they are 419ers, men who make fabulous profits by duping people (mostly foreigners) in elaborate scams. I have written extensively elsewhere about 419 (Smith 2007a) and do not intend to repeat what I have already said. Here my aim is to use Nwakere's example to focus directly on the relationship between 419 and masculinity, and specifically on 419ers as emblematic of wider dynamics regarding the relationship in men's lives between money and social intimacy that is elemental in Nigerian politics.

Nwakere was an occasional visitor to Owerri Sports Club. His calls at the club were memorable because of his flamboyant behavior. Not only did he buy copious amounts of beer and meat for everyone present, he also spoke extremely loudly (even by Igbo men's voluble standards), usually about himself. I didn't like him, not only because of his arrogant and ostentatious style, but also because even after being introduced to me many times by name he always addressed me as *onyeocha* (Igbo for white man). The tennis club was the one place in Owerri where everyone knew my name, so Nwakere's insistence on never learning it irked me.

I never actually got to know Nwakere very well. He never invited me to his house. I never visited his office. In fact, I only saw him a very few times outside the club, at an occasional wedding or a funeral. I do not actually know how he managed many of his most intimate relationships—with his wife, his children, his kin, his community of origin, and his friends outside the club. I don't think many, if any, of the guys at the club thought of him as a friend, but that might be my own dislike coloring how I observed others' interactions. But despite not knowing Nwakere very well personally, I heard a lot about his failed bid to morph himself from a rich man into a powerful politician.

When Nigeria was undergoing a transition from military to civilian rule in the late 1990s, Nwakere ran for governor of Imo State. He was one of about half a dozen candidates that people speculated had a chance—in Nwakere's case because he was believed to have so much money. The process for becoming a governor (or president or almost any elected official) in democratic Nigeria involves first getting the nomination of one of the contesting parties and then winning the popular vote in the election. Nigerians commonly believe—accurately, I think—that money is a prerequisite for political success in Nigeria. But as Nwakere's case illustrates, it is not just having enough money (there are many fabulously rich men in Nigeria), it is also how you use that money in political relationships. In Nigerian elections the main parties' nominating process determines who will even have a chance to succeed, and it is in this phase that money and politics intersect most centrally. When Nigerians lamented in the first decade after the restoration of democracy in 1999 that their political process involved "selections not elections," this was literally true of the nomination procedures.

The process of creating a handful of viable national political parties (just two or three) had already taken place by the time Nwakere and others officially declared their intentions to run for office. The task for him and his rivals was to secure one of the coveted party nominations. Nwakere attempted to secure the nomination of one of the main parties. Ultimately he received very few votes from the delegates at the state party convention that selected their party's nominee. I did not observe any of this firsthand, but men at the club told me that Nwakere had botched his chances by thinking that he could simply buy support. All of the men seeking the nomination had money and spent lavishly on their political peers. But apparently it was how he spent his money—arrogantly, presumptuously, and carelessly—that alienated the party's kingmakers.

One story I heard symbolized Nwakere's arrogance. My tennis club members relayed it as an example of why he failed in his bid for the governorship. Apparently at one of the meetings of the party's elites, Nwakere insulted an elderly politician who no longer had much money or real power, but who had established a reputation as a fierce advocate for the people after the Biafran civil war. Allegedly, Nwakere said something along the lines of: "Why should we listen to an old man with no more money and no more potency [said in Igbo in a way that could mean political power or sexual potency]?" Most of my friends said Nwakere never had a chance anyway; he had the money but he lacked the political skills and social connections to make it. The remark to the respected elder only epitomized why he failed.

None of this negates the incredible importance of money in politics in Nigeria. But it illustrates that many of the dynamics at play in more everyday performances of masculinity are also integral to the connections between money and success in political relationships. As in virtually every arena of men's lives, money's value (and its stigma) is closely tied to the social work that it does (or fails to do) in human relationships. 419 men are suspected of accruing their wealth through endeavors that are themselves threatening to appropriate sociality. But ill-gotten money can be somewhat cleansed in the way that it is spent. Nwakere seemed to fail on both fronts. The source of his wealth was suspicious; the way he spent it was seen as selfish and antisocial.

419 men have become iconic figures in Nigerian popular political discourse because they symbolize collective anxiety about the state of affairs in the country. If one peruses the titles and contents of the thousands of videos produced by Nigeria's popular Nollywood film industry, literally hundreds of films each year have the intersection of 419, politics, and intimacy as central plot lines. These themes appear in much Nigerian fiction as well. For example, I recently read an entertaining novel about 419 called I Do Not Come to You by Chance (Nwaubani 2009). One of the main characters in the novel is a super-wealthy fraudster, nicknamed Cash Daddy, who succeeds in becoming a governor. He is presented as an even more distasteful character than Nwakere. But while in fiction such a man might use his illicit wealth to buy political office, in actual fact men in Nigeria who seek political power must use their money carefully to build the necessary social and political ties. I am not suggesting that money cannot buy power in Nigeria. In many ways it certainly does. But the masculine life proj-

ects of seemingly criminal politicians, whether they are 419ers or other political elites, entail similar dynamics between money and intimate sociality that I have described for Nigerian men more generally. Money is ultimately valuable for what it does socially; if he is seen as too selfish and arrogant, even a very rich man will struggle to turn wealth into power.

A Bakassi Boy

By the time I had worked in Nigeria for a decade, I had seen a lot of disturbing things: dead bodies on the side of the road in Lagos, left alone as many thousands of people passed by in cars and buses during the morning commute; toddlers with kwashiorkor showing up at clinics in communities that, at least on the surface, looked too prosperous to have such an awful affliction; beggars who were the victims of polio navigating heavy city traffic using flip-flops on their hands to push skateboard-like contraptions, hoping that better-off Nigerians might roll down their windows and offer alms. But the day in Umuahia that I came upon the Bakassi Boys carrying out a vigilante operation—what Nigerians called "jungle justice"—I saw the beginning of something that I could never forget. It made me feel sick to my stomach. The vigilantes had apparently caught a thief in the market. A huge crowd gathered as they doused him with gasoline, put an old tire around his neck, and prepared to burn him alive. I knew they would do it. The Bakassi Boys were by then infamous for their extrajudicial killings, which included not only "necklacing," but also chopping off heads and other body parts. As grisly as the impending execution appeared, at least as disturbing was the mood of the crowd. People watched almost as if it were entertainment. Of course, I could not know the actual thoughts of those present. But I did know that for several years the Bakassi Boys were very popular in southeastern Nigeria, including in the Abia State capital of Umuahia, near where I was doing research at the time. I think it was revulsion at my own temptation to watch that ultimately made me turn away and leave before the vigilantes set the young man alight. Watching, I thought, would somehow make me complicit.

Although I didn't watch, I had become fascinated with the Bakassi Boys. Why were they so popular? What did their popularity reveal about Nigerian understandings of crime and justice? How were they entangled with politics and the state (because I learned they most definitely were)? How can one explain their rather quick demise, and the fact that about three years after they first rose to almost super-hero status in southeastern Nigeria, they were eventually branded as criminals—disbanded, arrested, and some of them killed? The same public and the very authorities that had actively supported them applauded their downfall. I have written previously about the Bakassi Boys (Smith 2004c, 2007a). In those publications I tried to answer the above questions. But I never got to know any vigilantes personally. I could not ask anyone what it was like to be a Bakassi Boy.

Then, in 2010, I met a man whom I was told had been one of the Bakassi Boys in Aba. When the Nigerian government sent the mobile police to break up the vigilante group in 2002, he had been shot and arrested. He was imprisoned for a couple of years and then released without ever being charged. He moved back to Aba, near the Local Government Area of Isiala Ngwa from which he hailed. His name was Chidubem. A friend whose business took him regularly to Aba introduced us. My friend knew that I had been interested in the Bakassi Boys and had written about them. One day, out of the blue, he asked me if I wanted to meet a former vigilante. I joined him on his next trip to Aba.

Perhaps fittingly, Chidubem was working in the shoe section of the main market area in Aba, the place where the Bakassi Boys first started (Baker 2002; Harnischfeger 2003; Meagher 2007). I expected to meet a large, muscled, confident—even aggressive—man. The fearsome image of the Bakassi Boys definitely left its imprint on me. Instead, Chidubem struck me as rather slight, unimposing, and even shy. He was almost thirty-six years old when we met, which meant that he was in his midtwenties when he was part of the Bakassi Boys. My friend had told him that I was interested in interviewing him about his time with the group and he agreed. We started our conversation at a small canteen where we had lunch and continued it over several weeks in other meetings we arranged in Aba.

Chidubem moved to Aba when he was seventeen, having dropped out of secondary school less than halfway through. His father was a farmer in the village and had died when Chidubem was about fifteen. His mother didn't have the money to continue to pay his school fees and none of his uncles would help, he said. In Aba, he tried various ways to make a living. For a while he sold eggs from a small stall owned by a man with a bigger business. The man provided him a room to sleep in and a meager and unpredictable wage. Chidubem said he sometimes slept hungry. Then he managed to get an apprenticeship with a welder in Aba's vast mechanics' village, but an eye injury while welding left him unable to work for some weeks. During his absence his master replaced him with someone else. He hadn't learned enough yet—much less accumulated the capital—to be able to start out on his own.

When Orji Uzo Kalu was elected Abia State governor in the transition to civilian rule in 1999, he promised he would provide thousands of motorcycles to young men in Aba on a no-interest "hire-for-purchase" (lease-to-own) basis so they could become *okada* (motorcycle taxi) drivers. Kalu was wildly popular among Aba youths and swept to victory. But Chidubem did not get a motorcycle. He said it was the Nigerian factor—that is, he did not know the right people. By late 1999, he was working as a tout in a local lorry park. Lorry park touts are young men who are paid commissions to recruit passengers onto buses and load cargo in Nigeria's hectic, competitive, and furiously busy system of public transportation ("public" being something of a misnomer because nearly all the buses and lorries are privately owned).

Not long before this time the Bakassi Boys formed in response to crime and insecurity in Aba's markets. Less than a year after they first emerged in Aba they began spreading their "services" to other cities in the Southeast, especially Umuahia and Onitsha, the teeming market city along the Niger River in Anambra State. Chidubem had a friend who lived near him in Aba who was one of the original Bakassi Boys when they emerged in Aba's shoe market. As the group began to expand, they needed more members and Chidubem's friend asked him if he was interested in joining. When his friend told him how much money he made every week, he could not resist the offer. Chidubem had never been a criminal, he said, and he had never before fired a gun, but through his work as a motor park tout he was accustomed to the rough-and-tumble ways of Aba's underbelly.

At first, he said, they patrolled various areas of the market, especially at night, to scare off thieves. The criminals they caught were mostly as the result of tips from informants. The police, Chidubem reminded me, were often in collusion with criminals—or so at least many Nigerians believed (Alemika 1988; Hills 2008). The Bakassi Boys were needed, he said, to catch criminals and punish them publicly in order to deter crime. Over time, the vigilante group cultivated a reputation for being able to judge an alleged criminal's guilt or innocence through magical means. Being able to judge guilt and justify their violent punishments was necessary to legitimate their work because they rarely caught criminals red-handed, instead relying, as noted, on information passed to them.

As the vigilantes gained popularity, local politicians, especially the governors of Abia and Anambra States, coopted them for their own purposes. Further, the Bakassi Boys evolved into something of a mafia, collecting money from local traders for their security services through levies that were enforced, many local traders told me in Umuahia, with implied threats. In some cases, people allegedly hired the vigilantes to intimidate rivals in disputes. All of this led to a reversal in public support and widespread relief when they were disbanded in 2002. As crime and insecurity have continued to plague southeastern Nigeria since then, there have been various attempts to bring back the group, but nothing has materialized into anything like what prevailed in those first years.

I was interested in particular in how Chidubem conceived of his involvement in a group that was once celebrated and ultimately condemned for its violence. He said that when he first joined the Bakassi Boys he felt like he was doing something valuable with his life. In theory, the identity of members was supposed to be secret, but of course many people knew who was involved. Chidubem recalled being treated with respect, almost reverence, in Aba when the vigilantes were at their pinnacle of popularity. People were afraid of him, he said, but many people also thanked him for the work the Bakassi Boys were doing. Word even spread of his role to his natal community in Isiala Ngwa. When he went to his village to visit his mother, boys and young men came to his house to see him as if he were some kind of celebrity.

He also had more money than he had ever dreamed possible. As a motor park tout he barely scraped together enough cash to feed himself. As a Bakassi Boy he could afford to buy nice clothes, spend money on women, and give his mother big envelopes of naira each time he saw her. But the culture of the group was not focused on the usual goals of social reproduction. Only a handful of the older leaders were married and had children. Most of the members were young and single. Further, the group's norms emphasized immediate enjoyment. Buoyed by mutually reinforcing male peer pressure, they spent most of their money quickly—on alcohol and drugs, on women, on fashionable clothes, on videos and CDs, and so on. So when the government eventually broke up the Bakassi Boys, even those who escaped and avoided prison began their post-vigilante life with almost nothing. Popular rumors suggested that many former Bakassi Boys became full-fledged criminals— schooled, as they were, in making money by using violence.

I was curious especially about Chidubem's experiences with violence. In our next-to-last meeting I asked whether he ever took part in one of the extrajudicial executions. He said he had, but he emphasized that in all the cases he took part in, the people who were killed were definitely guilty—implying that the Bakassi Boys, as alleged, sometimes killed people who were innocent, or at least whose guilt was unproven. He didn't seem to want to talk more about violence or killing, except to tell me that the problem with the Bakassi Boys in the end was that they spawned imitators, groups of vigilantes who called themselves by the famous name, but who were not "real." Chidubem suggested that his group was the real one and that the violence they'd perpetrated had been for the noble purpose of combatting crime. Some acts of violence were more justifiable than others, he suggested. But he didn't say more and I did not push him.

Chidubem explained that two years in prison gave him a lot of time to think about his life. While he was locked up his mother died and he missed her funeral. When he got out he vowed that he would move as far away from crime as he could—from prison, from doing anything illegal himself, and also from any role in vigilantism. After his release in 2004 he got married and he had two children. But he is poor. He is worried that he cannot give his children a better life. While he says would not return to the Bakassi Boys, it is clear that it fulfilled a desire for respect, and a wish to somehow make a mark on the world. He did not seem haunted by what he did as a vigilante; rather, he seemed regretful that the moment passed without anything changing in the end—for him and for so many other men struggling to survive in Nigeria.

An Area Boy

Lagos is notorious for massive traffic jams, what Nigerians euphemistically call "go slows." While bad roads, reckless driving, and a huge volume of vehicles account for much of the congestion, people also commonly blame the city's infamous "area boys," who supposedly create obstacles to slow or stop traffic to collect informal (and illegal) tolls, to extort drivers, or simply to increase the level of mayhem, thereby creating an environment conducive to a range of nefarious activities. The term "area boys" is an appellation applied to a wide swath of young, unemployed men in Nigeria's megacity (Omitoogun 1994; Momoh 2000, 2003). In its most specific application it refers to bands of youths who are at least somewhat organized, and who control various aspects of the urban landscape in many communities and neighborhoods across the city. Most residents think of them as a nuisance, as when they slow traffic. Sometimes they are perceived as a menace, as when they extort money from local residents or shop owners, ostensibly in exchange for keeping peace—though most people assume that the peace they are buying is from harassment by the area boys themselves. Seemingly paradoxically, area boys are at once most feared and most appreciated in relation to crime. This is because they are known to be, at different times, both criminals and vigilantes (not so different, in that way, from the Bakassi Boys). For everyone, though, including area boys themselves, they are symbols of the struggles of young men to survive, much less thrive, in the country's commercial capital.

Most times on my arrivals and departures from Nigeria over the past twenty years, I have stayed with a family in a part of Lagos known as Oshodi. It is near the airport. It is also notorious for maddening traffic jams and renowned for the dense sea of humanity that pulsates in its main outdoor market along the railroad track and Agege Motor Road. The widely circulating photos of impossibly dense populations of people in Lagos are usually shots of Oshodi market, taken from the traffic-choked highway bridge that passes over it. Oshodi is also one of many neighborhoods in Lagos infamous for area boys.

I first saw Nduka by the large, iron gate that was closed each night around 11 p.m., blocking vehicle entry and exit on the street where I stayed in Oshodi. Such gates are now common all across Lagos and in many cities around Nigeria. They are meant to deter crime by making it impossible, or at least difficult, for criminals to use motor vehicles to carry out their activities. But of course legitimate residents sometimes needed to drive in or out after the gate was locked so someone had to be able to open and close it after hours. Some communities hired watchmen. In this neighborhood the task was taken up by a group of area boys who collected a small fee from anyone who needed the gate opened after hours. The area boys knew everyone in the neighborhood. Residents in the neighborhood thought that it was better to give these idle youths something constructive to do that would also earn them a little money, lest they become the thieves everyone feared. But of course people still worried—and rumors circulated—that this is exactly what sometimes happened.

After seeing Nduka a couple of times late at night, one morning I saw him filling a bucket of water from a borehole tap in the neighborhood. He greeted me and introduced himself. He was an Igbo from the Southeast and he was surprised, as many Igbos are, that I could comfortably exchange pleasantries in his native language. When he laughed and asked how I could speak Igbo, I responded that I could also speak Nigerian Pidgin English, the lingua franca in linguistically mixed places like Lagos. After some brief banter and much laughter on his part, he called to some of his mates who were playing cards on a bench down the street, saying in Pidgin: "make una come see dis oyingbo where de knock Pidgin like say na Lagos dem born am" (you need to come observe this white man who speaks Pidgin as if he were born in Lagos). Such comments often served to break the ice with people whom I might not otherwise have had a chance to talk to.

Nduka's mates beckoned me over to where they were sitting. They proceeded to interview me. (In anthropology we don't examine nearly enough how important all the ways people interview us are for our research—not only to build rapport, but also as the source of important insights.) Nduka accompanied me to the bench, delaying the bucket bath he seemed to be preparing. The group of young men proceeded to ask me a barrage of questions: where I was from, what I was doing in Oshodi, wasn't I afraid, how had I managed to master Pidgin and learn so much Igbo? Why was it so difficult to get a visa to America? Was it true that everyone there carried a gun? Each answer led to another question.

After almost an hour, they seemed satisfied that they had penetrated some of my strangeness. So, after a pause, I asked whether it would be okay to ask them some questions. They said yes. Given how little time I spent in Lagos relative to the Southeast, I figured this was my best chance to learn something about the everyday life of Lagos area boys. So I launched right in. I'd heard a lot about area boys in Lagos, I explained. "Are you guys area boys?" I asked. They laughed uproariously.

They seemed incredulous that I knew what an area boy was. But I think their fascination with my awareness regarding seemingly local knowledge, combined with their assumption that I really didn't know all that much about the true realities underlying my apparent familiarity, created an atmosphere where they felt compelled to tell me more. Their reaction was something along the lines of: "You may think you know what's going on in Nigeria, but wait until you hear the real story." It was a dynamic I encountered often and it helped me immensely in my research.

They said they didn't like the area-boys moniker. They were not boys, after all; they were men. Indeed, each of them was between the ages of twenty-five and thirty. Nduka's story was similar to the rest of them. The life he described since he migrated to Lagos after dropping out of secondary school was one of frustrated aspirations—a series of roadblocks getting in the way of his ambitions for employment, income, and a level of consumption that would enable him to fulfill his ideals of masculinity. As insulting as they found the label "boys," it captured the extent to which their livelihood strategies and lifestyles were evidence of an unfinished trajectory to full manhood.

When Nduka moved to Lagos he first lived with a maternal uncle who worked at the wharf in Apapa. But he failed to find steady work and after about six months his uncle asked him to move out. I asked whether he thought about going back to his village at that point and he said, "There is nothing for me there—no jobs, no money, no future." So he moved into a room in Oshodi that he shared with one of his Lagos friends. The room was in a "boys' quarters" (a small back house behind a larger residence, named for the fact that such structures used to serve as accommodation for servants, but now are typically rented out to people like Nduka who can't afford anything better). The term "boys" in both "area boys" and "boys' quarters" is not a coincidence. It both cases it signals inferior status to "men"—it is men who have the money to live in the big house, marry, and have children. Like so many young men in sub-Saharan Africa frustrated by obstacles to education, employment, and a decent income, Nduka's transition to full manhood was stalled (Sommers 2012; Honwana 2012, 2013).

9 Most "area boys" desire legitimate work, but informal employment options like cart pushing offer little money and scant hope of allowing them to fulfill their aspirations to manhood.

Nduka and his mates described daily life as a hustle. Besides the turns they took as unofficial watchmen at the community gate, they each constantly sought employment. While they dreamed of permanent positions with regular incomes, in practice they skipped from one temporary job to another: off-loading trucks, working as day laborers on construction projects, selling various items to passengers in vehicles stuck in traffic. It was clear they all worked—or tried to work—as often as they could. But the area boy hustle also included less savory activities. For example, in election season they sometimes worked for local politicians running for office. They would be paid token amounts just to show up at rallies and even more if they broke up events and chased away supporters of rival candidates. Occasionally, local government officials would hire them to create roadblocks where the officials could check for tax receipts, customs clearances, and various other forms of bureaucratic documentation required for transportation, commerce, and other activities of everyday life in Lagos. They said that sometimes they were hired by landlords to intimidate tenants whose rent was long overdue or who ignored eviction notices. In other cases they threatened debtors on behalf of creditors. Sometimes they "worked" as vigilantes on behalf of the neighborhood to find and punish a troubling criminal.

Of course looming in the background of our conversation was whether they themselves engaged in crimes such as robbery. Nduka and his friends asserted that they were loyal to their neighbors, suggesting that they would never commit crimes in their own community. They were less transparent about their activities elsewhere. While I cannot say exactly what, if anything, these area boys did beyond what they told me, it was clear that they would have rather had good jobs, steady incomes, and secure futures than survive through hustling. Nduka's words captured the sentiments of his peers: "I want a good job. I don't want to be poor. I want lots of money. I want a woman to marry me because she respects who I am. I want to go home to my village at Christmas and have people admire my car and the huge house I am building in my father's compound. Anyone would rather be a Big Man than an area boy. I don't live like this by choice."

Conclusion

People in Nigeria—men and women—commonly perceive everyday life to be perilously insecure. Mostly this is a perception related to difficult livelihoods and frustrated economic aspirations: money problems. But it is often crystallized and voiced in terms of fears about an escalation of fraud, corruption, and crime, especially violent crime—almost all of which are perpetrated by men. In many ways, men whose behavior signifies the worst of the country's problems are simply more extreme versions of all men; it is not just men who commit crimes or perpetrate violence who are suspected of greed, selfishness, and socially problematic motives and actions. The fact that the performance of masculinity requires money and the reality that money is always potentially tainted, even as it is also socially worshipped, mean that men's social relationships are constantly colored by the possibility that things are not exactly what they seem.

This chapter has examined the lives of men whose behavior fuels the popular perception that Nigeria is increasingly violent, criminal, and insecure. Using examples of a wife beater, a drug smuggler, a 419 man, a Bakassi Boy, and an area boy, I have shown how these "bad" men and their behaviors exemplify the challenges of masculinity in contemporary Nigeria, particularly as these men navigate the intersection of money and intimacy. Their cases also suggest that it is possible to move beyond the misunderstandings produced when Nigeria's social problems are explained by blaming a presumed crisis of masculinity. Attributing the country's pathologies to a problem with masculinity is the gendered version of blaming Nigerian "culture" for corruption, inequality, or any other social or political problem. The question is not whether masculinity has something to do with crime and insecurity, or whether culture has something to do with corruption and inequality. Without a doubt they do. The issue is what sort of explanations these are.

Even as this book challenges many of the assumptions associated with the assertion that there is a crisis of masculinity in Nigeria, or Africa, and rejects the idea that Nigeria's social problems reflect some fundamental problem with men, it is necessary to acknowledge, examine, and understand the various ways in which problematic masculine behavior both results from and in some ways contributes to many of Nigeria's most difficult social problems. While virtually all men face challenges and experience ambivalence with regard to the expectations associated with modern Nigerian manhood, only some men resort to crime or violence. And while manhood alone does not explain these behaviors, such conduct is nevertheless just as gendered as the more prosocial aspects of masculine behavior.

Most men in Nigeria are not like Ifeanyi; they are not drunks who routinely beat their wives. And yet the relative social tolerance for intimate partner violence, not to mention the fact that marital rape is a kind of cultural oxymoron, cannot be explained without placing it in the context of a larger system of patriarchy and men's anxieties about social changes that are challenging that system. Most men I know in Nigeria reject the idea that a man should beat his wife or force sexual intercourse without her consent. Yet many—I think most—of these same men have spoken and behaved in ways that uphold the patriarchal ideas that preserve the gender inequalities that protect intimate partner violence from more overt challenges. Similarly, most men who condemn drug smuggling and 419 have nonetheless happily attended lavish weddings, funerals, and chieftaincy ceremonies paid for by men widely known to have made their money this way. In a sense, they reward and perpetuate such behavior.

Men in general, one might say, have an interest in preserving patriarchy. Perhaps. But it is not as easy to assert that all men have an interest in perpetuating systematic class inequality in Nigeria. Nonetheless, many men who are clearly not benefiting from the current situation behave in ways that seem to protect the status quo. Poorer men who reward—or at least tolerate—elites' practices of conspicuous redistribution seem to be acting as much against their own interests as in them. The fact that men without much money both depend on wealthier, more powerful men and in some ways envy and admire them makes it difficult to pursue alternatives.

Further, the rise of money as the medium through which the masculine performance of sociality and intimacy is evaluated has put all men in a difficult position, albeit with much harsher consequences for the poor. Money as a measure of manhood inevitably threatens the perceived sincerity of every relationship it enables, whether one is poor or not. But as the case of Ikechukwu (the drug smuggler) illustrates, for the rich, ill-gotten wealth can be cleansed, at least somewhat, with the right kind of spending. Dirty money is less dirty when it is used for seemingly prosocial purposes. Conspicuous redistribution is available to men with money, not only to entrench their elite status, but also to turn bad money into good money. But for men without money— men like Chidubem (the former Bakassi Boy) and Nduka (the Lagos area boy)—it is difficult to construct a socially acceptable manhood. While men with money are almost always suspected of something bad, because money is the currency of intimate social relations, even a man whose money may be tainted is better off than a man with none. Indeed, the awareness of this reality is arguably what pushes some men to become "bad" men in the first place.

SIX

Becoming an Elder, Burying One's Father

De Chiemeka sat on his verandah in an easy chair that one of his grandchildren moved there every morning from its overnight spot indoors in the parlor. As he took his seat each morning, De Chi, as he was known in the village, inspected not only how well the verandah was swept, but also whether the entire front of his compound appeared immaculate. If there was sand on the steps or a weed sprouting somewhere in the hard red dirt that constituted the front yard, he would yell for one of his grandchildren, and, if they had gone to school, for his daughter-in-law, or even his equally elderly wife.

At some point in the morning he would be served his breakfast on a small table placed in front of his easy chair. If any crumbs or kernels from his meal spilled on the ground while he ate, someone would be called to sweep again. De Chi maintained this perch throughout the day, a position that enabled him to overlook a main thoroughfare in the village, including many of his neighbors' houses. Usually late in the morning he would get up and walk with his cane as far as the Anglican church, about a third of a kilometer from his compound. It was a difficult walk because De Chi suffered a stroke when he was in his early seventies that rendered the left side of his body partially paralyzed. After his walk he would sometimes retreat to his bedroom for a brief nap, but otherwise he was reliably stationed in his chair on the verandah from shortly after sunrise until just before sunset. His location meant that De Chi interacted with many people in the village through-out the day, as Igbo culture dictates that one greets and briefly chats, even in passing, all the more so if one encounters a respected elder. The result was that De Chi stayed up to date on community events, troubles, and gossip.

De Chi was born in one of the eleven villages of Ubakala and mar-ried a woman from a neighboring community. He lived in his village all his life, with the exception of about half a dozen years in the 1960s, when he worked as a laborer for a company operating in northern Ni-geria. Among his four living children, one of his two sons resided in Lagos. That son was married and had four children of his own. Both daughters were married and lived away from the village with their husbands and children, one in Port Harcourt and the other in Abuja. He was fond of his first daughter's husband but thought his younger daughter's spouse was something of a scoundrel. Only his youngest son remained in the village. He lived in De Chi's compound along with his own wife and three children. This son was a "contractor," a com-mon descriptor for a man whose livelihood revolves around trying to reap some benefit from a friend, kinsman, or acquaintance who might steer some government money his way—to build something, supply something, or provide some sort of service. De Chi lamented that his son struggled financially, but he liked having some family at home, especially the grandchildren. He had many age mates who lived in empty compounds, all of the children and grandchildren having mi-grated away.

My conversations with De Chi spanned the full gamut of themes that animate everyday life in southeastern Nigeria, but I was particu-larly interested in his understandings of the experience of becoming old and what that meant as an Igbo man. Predictably, he thought that many of the behaviors of young people undermined important tradi-tional values and customs. It must be some sort of cross-cultural uni-versal that a significant fraction of the elderly see the youth as leading society toward hell in a hand basket. Some of De Chi's complaints could be chalked up to his place in the developmental cycle—more indicative of his stage in the life course than of anything about actual histori-cal changes. But I found, nonetheless, that the substance of De Chi's discontents—and those of other elders—was a revealing window onto the nature of social change. Even if De Chi's grievances about the young were partly the inevitable grumbling of the aged, the content of those criticisms nevertheless reflected a good deal about the times.

Not surprisingly, I was especially intrigued by the ways that money and intimacy figured into De Chi's commentary about contemporary Nigeria, and particularly about what that was like for an old man. He didn't talk much about intimacy explicitly, perhaps itself a reflection of his generation's approach to the issue. But I knew—from a couple of times that he'd called me into his bedroom when I stopped by to greet him and he wasn't on the verandah—that he and his wife kept separate bedrooms. His son confirmed that they always had. This was common in De Chi's generation and even for some in his son's age group, though most young married couples now share one bed and one bedroom, even in a village community like Ubakala. I never felt it was appropriate to ask De Chi about his sleeping arrangements with his wife, but I was able to ask about his marriage. Theirs was an arranged marriage, he said, but he was quite happy when his parents proposed his wife as his future bride. He thought she was beautiful and she had a reputation as a hardworking girl. He believed she would make a fine wife. In more than fifty years of marriage nothing had changed his mind.

At one point, when I was working on the aforementioned "Love, Marriage, HIV" project, I tried to explain to De Chi what I was researching. He was probably in his early eighties at the time, though he did not know his birthdate. After explaining the project as best I could, I asked him whether he loved his wife. He laughed heartily and then answered: "Of course I love her. She is a good wife and a good mother." I then followed up to ask whether he thought the now-common practice of young people choosing their spouses based on being "in love" was a good idea. He scoffed and said: "A person's character is only revealed over time. The young are not good at seeing the signs, which is why it is important to have the elders involved. But now young people do as they please. We can only investigate [alluding to the common Igbo practice of looking into the family background of the person one's child wants to marry] and hope the match is a good one."

While I had to prompt De Chi to talk about love and marriage, it took no prodding to get him to speak about his children and whether they lived up to his expectations of filial piety. It was a topic about which he opined easily and frequently. The things he said were in some ways contradictory. Part of what accounts for the contradictions is the complex intertwining of money and intimacy. Specifically, an elderly father and grandfather like De Chi wants his children to remain close to him, but a big variable in determining whether they can do so in ways that please him is whether they have enough money. De Chi frequently lamented how rarely his Lagos-based son came home to the village, a grievance highlighted especially when a year earlier he did not come home for the Christmas holidays, as is the Igbo custom. And yet he also regularly praised the same son for his contributions to the family. In recent years the son had, for example, built an addition to the house and bought all new furniture for the parlor. When De Chi spoke of these things he inevitably noted with pride that his older son was "doing well."

In contrast, the younger son who lived with him in Ubakala took care of many of the day-to-day needs of De Chi and his wife. For example, this son arranged for and accompanied De Chi on his visits to a doctor in Umuahia; he—and, of course, his wife and children—took care of almost all the daily tasks of maintaining the household (farming, shopping, cooking, fetching water, sweeping, and so on) and he represented his father and family in village affairs. But despite all of this intimate caring, the Ubakala-based son's lack of steady employment or business success created constant money problems that De Chi lamented. When De Chi talked about his second son, he often described him as "having nothing doing"—a common Nigerian shorthand for having no means to make money. In an ideal world, De Chi would have liked to have both his sons (and their families) at home and making good money, but of course in contemporary Nigeria it is almost impossible for young men to make enough money to meet their or their fathers' expectations by staying in the village.

De Chi also offered more general opinions about the situation in contemporary Nigeria. For all that he wished for his sons' success, and for all that he enjoyed it when they were able to enhance his wellbeing with their money, he nonetheless shared with many older men a sense that Nigeria's youth were so enamored with money that they had led the country into a moral morass. Corruption and crime were the two problems De Chi (like many other Nigerians) dwelled on regularly. For example, once during my fieldwork a prominent man who had a lot of money came home to the village for an early retirement and his townsmen asked him to manage the funds for a community development project. Allegedly, the man siphoned off some of the money for his own personal use. While the community celebrated his financial success outside the village even though many knew, or at least suspected, that his wealth was the result of corrupt contracts he managed for cronies in the government, stealing from his kinsmen was an abomination. De Chi talked about the case regularly when it was going on. "The young men of today," he said, "are blinded by money. Our forefathers would have dealt seriously with such behavior." De Chi was aghast that the offending man simply lost his position in the development union, but there appeared to be no other consequences. While De Chi did not say so, it appeared to me that the man's real offense was stealing too close to home; stealing from the government brought rewards at home rather than opprobrium. But that was part of De Chi's point: when the obsession with money is so all-consuming that you steal from your own people, then "Nigeria is in trouble"—as I commonly heard men say.

De Chi's laments about corruption were matched perhaps only by his dismay about crime, particularly crime in the community. When Brutus (with whom I opened chapter 5) and his criminal gang were operating, De Chi more than once told me that in his youth the community would have organized itself and had Brutus killed. He lambasted the ineffectiveness of the police, he decried the failure of leadership in the community, and he said many times that had Brutus's father been alive (he died almost two decades ago and he was renowned as a strong chief; De Chi clearly respected him greatly) he would have put a stop to it himself. While De Chi saw criminals like Brutus as embodying a socio-pathology in which monetary greed leads to egregious violations of socially acceptable practice—all the more so when perpetrated against one's own kin and community—more interesting was his harsh criticism of Brutus's brothers. "They are too busy chasing money outside [meaning outside the village] to notice the evil in their own compound," he scowled.

Sometimes, when De Chi would become most vexed about the problems in the community and in contemporary Nigeria more generally, he would note, almost with relief, that his days were numbered. "Soon," he said, "I will be in God's hands." On one occasion, a couple of days after I had seen him at the funeral of one of his peers—a lavish affair because one of the man's sons was a well-to-do lawyer in Abuja—I asked De Chi about his opinion regarding the seemingly ever-escalating costs of burials in southeastern Nigeria. As with so many other topics regarding the current state of affairs, he expressed concern that the obsession with money had undermined socially and morally appropriate motivations and practices. "God forbid my sons put me in the mortuary for six months while they find the money to bury me well," he said, referring to the common practice of postponing funerals in order to raise the funds to perform a "befitting" burial. But for all his unease about the way that showing off money has come to dominate men's aspirations and behaviors, I couldn't help note that De Chi's observation was about not being left in the mortuary; he still wanted to be buried well.

This chapter is about the experience and performance of masculinity among the elderly. As life expectancy has increased and fertility rates have gradually fallen, the age structure of Nigeria's population has shifted such that a growing proportion of people are old. Demographic transformations have been accompanied by other social changes—not least high levels of rural-to-urban migration—that have created new challenges for old people and for their children who feel obligated to help take care of them (Adamchak 1989; Darkwa and Mazibuko 2002; Makoni 2008; Nabalamba and Chikoko 2011). These changes have affected how elderly men and women experience their senior status and how they relate to younger generations (Udvardy and Cattell 1992; Baiyewu et al. 1996; Oppong 2006; Adeboye 2007; Whyte, Alber, and Van der Geest 2008). For elderly men, recent social and demographic transformations intervene at the time of life when they expected to enjoy the full benefits of their lifelong performance of masculinity.

For earlier generations of men in southeastern Nigeria, reaching the status of an elder marked the culmination of successful manhood (Meek 1950; Green 1964; Shelton 1972). Increasingly, however, older men find that the respect accorded to seniority is undermined by ongoing social changes, perhaps especially the youthful obsession with and glorification of money. And yet in many ways older men also measure their children's performance of filial piety by their capacity to provide for them financially. Even as the status of senior men is diminished by the all-consuming importance of money, older men's experience and assessment of the quality of their relations with their children is mediated by the central role of money in the provision of care.

For many men, the experience of being an elder involves migration, whether it is returning home to one's rural place of origin to retire or facing the reality that most (and in many cases all) of one's children have moved away from the village. Below I present three cases illustrating how elderly men experience the intertwining of money, intimacy, and migration. The first case is a man who lived all his life in the village only to find that his children had moved away at the time he felt he needed them most. The second is a man who had a successful and lucrative career outside Ubakala and decided to try to take a position of political leadership in the community when he returned home to retire. In the process, obstacles and resentments he could not easily navigate continually frustrated him. The third case describes a poor migrant man who worked until the end, dying before a hoped-for return home.

After examining the dynamics of money, intimacy, and migration in the lives these elderly men, I close by showing how Igbo burials— the last ritual in a man's life course—embody many of the tensions and contradictions between money and intimacy that characterize the entire trajectory of manhood in contemporary Nigeria. Arranging a befitting burial for one's parents remains one of the most important obligations that any man experiences in his life. Indeed, as noted already, many Nigerian men will say that one is not fully a man until one has buried one's father—not simply because it marks one's transformation to being an elder, but because of the social pressures, financial burdens, and the personal and emotional work involved. These end-of-life rituals now include expectations for expensive and lavish ceremonies involving extreme amounts of conspicuous consumption and redistribution that often strain families and kin-groups, creating both financial hardship and social disharmony. The escalating expectations around burials exemplify the challenges of social changes in Nigeria for men, as the twin aspirations of performing the duties of kinship and exhibiting success in the arenas of wealth, consumption, and social class make men deeply anxious and ambivalent about behaviors they nonetheless feel utterly incapable of avoiding.

An Empty Compound

De Okeke was seventy-eight years old when we met. He was proud that he knew his birthdate. He said that white missionaries had told his parents that it was important to know the date, so they kept the certificate they were given and passed it on to De Okeke when he grew up. He stored it in a plastic bag in a small metal box he kept under his bed, along with all the other official documents he had accumulated over his lifetime and deemed important. September 26, 1926.

Among the other papers he still had was his Standard VI leaving certificate, evidence that he had completed primary school. That was as far as he went with his education, but even so, he pointed out, it was better than most boys in his day. When we started talking about his life, it was clear that he was proudest of the fact that his own children—all six of them—had completed secondary school. Indeed, two of his sons and one of his daughters had gone even higher. The sons attended what were known then in Nigeria as "polytechnics": two-year programs geared toward more professional training as opposed to the broad curricula of four-year universities. One son read civil engineering, the other read accounting. One of his daughters went to a teacher's college and is now a secondary school teacher.

De Okeke was proud not only that all of his children were educated, but also that *he* had educated them. Until he stopped working just a few years earlier because of a bad back, De Okeke was a mason. This meant that he constructed foundations, walls, and floors for houses and other buildings, almost all of which are now built in southeastern Nigeria with cement. In his most prosperous years—he was never rich, but had a solid, steady income—De Okeke ran a side business molding the cement blocks used in local construction. His wife, Da Ezinne ("Da" being the female equivalent of the honorific "De" for senior men), kept a small shop in the local market selling various foodstuffs. And of course they farmed De Okeke's family land.

De Okeke never lived anywhere besides Ubakala. Local construction kept him busy most of the year. His own house was a modest three-bedroom cement bungalow that he built adjacent to his father's compound. It looked slightly better maintained than most village houses, but by and large it was similar to others owned by men who had respectable livelihoods—his house was that of a man who was not rich, but also certainly not poor.

Now that he was retired—"retired but not tired," he used to say, emulating something I heard from many retired men in southeastern Nigeria—De Okeke spent a bit more time visiting his farm plots; he attended community social occasions and meetings more frequently than he had time for when he was working; and he sat regularly under the shade of a big tree not far from the market with a number of other older men playing (or watching others play) draughts (the British name for checkers) for hours at a time. As they watched and played, the men talked about politics, about the latest community gossip, and about their families. Most of the men's children were living outside Ubakala, having migrated in search of education or employment, or relocated at marriage (in Igboland, a woman traditionally moves to her husband's community, or follows him if he is a migrant).

In De Okeke's case, all six of his children had migrated away to various cities and towns across Nigeria. Only he and his wife and two of his grandchildren (sent home by one of his daughters to help them out while they also attended primary school in the village) lived in De Okeke's compound. Even as De Okeke was notably proud of his children's education, his biggest lament was that none of them was around now.

He sometimes complained that the two grandchildren living with him were too small to help with heavy work. They were perfectly capable of sweeping the compound, fetching water, running errands to the local market, or delivering a message to someone elsewhere in Ubakala. These things they did on a daily basis. But he grumbled that they were too little to do serious farm work or help with house repairs. At least as problematic as the diminished labor power was that none of his sons was home to represent the family at important occasions, meetings, or disputes. De Okeke still attended most of these events, but he worried what would happen if he became too ill or too frail, not to mention when he died.

Like for so many elderly couples whose grown children had migrated away from the village, foster children—sometimes, but not always, grandchildren—provided not only youthful labor, but also regular company and living symbols of the continued commitment and investment of their absent children (Isiugo-Abanihe 1985). Even though he was sometimes quite stern with his charges, it was obvious that he loved them. When they weren't being disciplined for their own good—at least as he saw it—he was often quite affectionate with them. As in so many cultures, Igbo grandparents seemed free to spoil their grandchildren in ways parents were not (Duru 1983; Alber 2004; Whyte, Alber, and Geissler 2004; Ngwudike and Otieno 2012).

Like De Chi with whom I began the chapter, De Okeke took great satisfaction in the fact that his children had done well enough to be able to find livelihoods outside the village, and yet he simultaneously wished they—or at least some of them—lived at home. But the reality is that in many rural households only the least successful children end up living in the village with their parents. At least all of De Okeke's children "had something doing," he would sometimes console himself. His children went to great lengths to make sure their relative success in the world made its way home to their father and mother. All of his offspring provided remittances. In Ubakala, as in much of Nigeria and Africa, it is still the case that children are expected to take care of their parents in old age (King 2008; Agulanna 2011). De Okeke's sons and daughters sent home regular envelopes of cash, carried by kin and neighbors returning to Ubakala. They brought money, clothing, food, and medicine on their own visits. While I heard many older men (and women) complain about neglectful adult children, De Okeke and Da Ezinne seemed fortunate to have especially dutiful offspring. Nevertheless, two problems that De Okeke faced during the first year I got to know him encapsulated in his mind the challenges of having no children "at home." In one instance, Da Ezinne became very ill and was hospitalized in Umuahia. In the other, the son of one of his late friends began planting crops on a plot of land De Okeke claimed was his own.

One afternoon when De Okeke returned home after a few hours with the men playing draughts near the market, hoping that Da Ezinne would have his lunch prepared, he found her lying on her bed listless and weak. She said she felt dizzy and that if she tried to get up she became faint. He worried but hoped it would pass once the cool of the evening arrived. It was the hot season and the sun could make even a healthy young person feel weak. But by nightfall Ezinne appeared to be worse, to the point where she wasn't communicating clearly. De Okeke walked across the village to the house of one of his kinsman who had a car and explained the situation. The man came with two of his teenage sons and they helped Da Ezinne into the car and took her to the community's health center near the market. The nurse on duty (there is no doctor posted at the health center) took Da Ezinne's blood pressure and discovered it was extremely high. She also noticed that her feet were swollen. She recommended that they take Da Ezinne to Queen Elizabeth Hospital in Umuahia. De Okeke pleaded with his neighbor, who agreed to transport them.

At the hospital the admitting staff noted Da Ezinne's very high blood pressure. They explained that no doctor was immediately available, but suggested that she be admitted and observed until a doctor could examine her. The staff said that a deposit would be required before she could be admitted. As I explained in chapter 3, deposits are commonly requested before admission to hospitals in southeastern Nigeria, even at government hospitals. De Okeke had hardly any money in his pocket, but since it was night and it was obvious that no banks were open, he and his neighbor prevailed on a nurse to admit Da Ezinne with the promise that they would pay the next day. De Okeke slept—or tried to sleep—in a chair next to his wife's bed.

In the morning a doctor examined Da Ezinne and said he was ordering some blood tests. When the doctor left, one of the staff informed De Okeke that the deposit would have to be paid before the lab work could be completed. De Okeke took public transportation back to Ubakala where he had left his cell phone, a present he recently received from one of his sons.

At that time De Okeke was barely conversant with using his phone. Cell phone service had only recently become available in Ubakala. His children typically called him and he answered, but he never initiated calls himself. Further, charging the phone was a chore since electricity was sporadic in the village. He usually took it along to play draughts and asked one of the shopkeepers with a generator to recharge it for him. Fortunately, on the morning after Da Ezinne was admitted to the hospital his phone was charged and one of his grandchildren assisted him to dial his eldest son. In a scenario typical of how migrant children mobilize assistance for their parents in their absence, the son called one of his friends (in fact, also a distant relative) who lived in the village but who worked in Umuahia to ask if he could bring the necessary cash to the hospital to be refunded later. The friend obliged and by midmorning the deposit had been paid.

Two days later, another son, who was able to arrange to miss work more easily than his older brother, came home and spent several days in Ubakala and at the hospital with his mother. After Da Ezinne was released the son had to leave to go back to work, but his visit was followed by one from his sister, who stayed nearly a week to look after her mother, cook, and help with other household chores. Da Ezinne had been prescribed medication for high blood pressure and apparently the doctor said something about diabetes, though it was unclear to me from my subsequent conversation with De Okeke whether she had diabetes or was at risk.

For nearly two weeks a flurry of visitors and phone calls enlivened the Okeke compound. De Okeke and Da Ezinne's children had mobilized quickly and effectively to manage their mother's care. De Okeke didn't spend any money himself. The children took care of everything. To me it looked like a remarkable example of filial piety—of Igbo kinship mobilized effectively even as families are separated by migration. I was impressed not only with the way De Okeke's children responded, but also by the agility of these informal networks to arrange transportation, the transfer of money, and the provision of care. The cell phone revolution made it easier, no doubt. But I had seen many examples in my first fifteen years working in Nigeria, before there were cell phones. Migration stretches and strains Igbo kinship networks, but it does not break them (Chukwuezi 2001; Van Den Bersselaar 2005; Smith 2011).

But De Okeke experienced Da Ezinne's health emergency as an example of the vulnerability he faced in his old age because none of his children lived "at home"—by this he meant in or very near Ubakala, not literally in the family compound. He was certainly grateful that his children were so quick to assist, but he worried that as he and his wife grew even older and potentially more infirm, the children's absence would become more problematic. He seemed concerned about both the concrete problems that might arise—with health clearly at the top of the list—and the fact that it was awkward to have to rely on others besides one's children, even if it were only until the children could get home. "A man shouldn't have to cry for help from his neighbors when he has a family of his own," he said.

The vulnerability of being an old man, even in one's ancestral community, where one has many kin and lifelong neighbors, was further driven home by a land dispute that erupted between De Okeke and the son of a recently deceased man who had been one of De Okeke's close friends. One day, De Okeke explained to me, he went to visit one of his farm plots and discovered that someone had encroached on his land. The intruder had made mounds for cassava that reached almost ten feet into his property, spanning the length of a plot that was almost sixty feet. De Okeke was shocked and befuddled. He couldn't imagine who would do such a thing, especially given that the adjacent land belonged to the family of one of his best friends, who had died only about a year before.

The next day he walked to the house of his late friend so that he could tell the son who lived there that they had an intruder. He was glad his friend's son lived in the village, he said, for it would be useful to have a younger man present when they caught and confronted the guilty party. De Okeke said he experienced one of the greatest shocks of his life when his friend's son informed him that it was he who had made the mounds and that he was simply reclaiming land his father had lent De Okeke many years ago. He left his friend's compound dumbfounded but determined to fight.

Soon after, De Okeke went to the village headman and then to the eze (the overall chief of all the villages in Ubakala) with the case. There were several meetings with chiefs and other elders to try to resolve the dispute. At these meetings De Okeke was always present and in a couple of instances one of his sons was home and joined him. Both sides had people who testified on their behalf. In the end the village chiefs said there was insufficient evidence to rule on the case, but since De Okeke's friend's son had already planted on the plot, for this year he should be allowed to grow and harvest those crops. De Okeke was infuriated, as were his sons. On the advice of the eze, they filed a case with the local magistrate court in Umuahia. That was in 2005. Each year since, the case has come up for hearing once or twice annually, and each time one of De Okeke's sons comes home to represent the family at the court—or if he cannot make it asks his attorney to request a continuance. A decade later the case is still in court and no one farms that little strip of land. Both parties have probably spent more on attorney and court fees than it would have cost to buy a similar plot.

De Okeke is now too infirm to pursue the case. But his son has taken it up eagerly, mostly out of a sense of righteousness, but also in solidarity with his father. When the case started, and in many conversations since, De Okeke told me that he was sure that his late friend's son was

10 For many elderly men in southeastern Nigeria, the quality of their relationships with their urban-migrant children is central to the experience of getting old.

deliberately exploiting the fact that all of his own sons lived outside the village. "He would never have tried it if my sons all lived at home," he told me. Perhaps this was true, but the fact that his sons were educated and relatively successful meant that they had the wherewithal to see the case through the judicial system. And in this instance the disputed piece of land became symbolic for De Okeke's sons of their continued sense of belonging in their place of origin and their loyalty to their father.

Most elderly men in southeastern Nigeria experienced and assessed the quality of their senior years based, in part, on the relationships they had with their offspring. In comparison to some other old men I knew, De Okeke had remarkably loyal and helpful children. Typically, men had some children they could count on and others they could not. Some men felt like their children had failed them almost entirely.

Their children's migration away from the village meant that older men in rural areas often felt that their empty compounds left them vulnerable to acute crises like a medical problem or more chronic ones like a land dispute. Of course many old men were themselves migrants. But among aging men who once lived in cities, old age frequently plays out in rural communities, as most men return to their communities of origin to retire and live out the last years of their lives. It is to an elderly man who was a migrant himself that I turn in the next case.

Retiring in the Village

De Ufomba returned to Ubakala when he retired from his job with a bank in Lagos. By all appearances he had lived something like an Igbo man's ideal life. His parents had educated him well. He started in an entry-level job at a bank when he was in his twenties, rising to an executive position by the time he was in his forties. He survived in a sector that has been periodically plagued by crises, scandals, defaults and closures, and regular government reorganization, all of which had cost many men their jobs. By the time he retired in 2004, De Ufomba had finished educating his three children, his only daughter was married, he had buried both his parents in grand style, and he had long since built a befitting village house where he planned to retire.

In the years he worked for the bank—mostly in Lagos, but also stints in Warri, Port Harcourt, and Ilorin—he had been a regular visitor to Ubakala to see his parents, to monitor the construction of his house, to participate in the annual Christmas festivities, and to attend as many of the weddings and funerals of kin and community members as he possibly could. In addition, he had been a faithful member of the Ubakala Improvement Union (UIU) in each place he lived. UIU was the community association through which migrants contributed to and participated in development-related activities and projects at home. Nearly every Igbo community has one and there are branches in any place with a significant number of migrants, not only in cities and towns across Nigeria, but also in the United States and the United Kingdom. In Lagos, De Ufomba held various executive positions in UIU's biggest branch for several years.

I met De Ufomba on several occasions before he retired, in Lagos and when he visited Ubakala. Well before he actually moved back to his village, he told me about his plans to retire there. It was the same thing I heard from almost every aging Igbo male migrant I met anywhere, whether in Lagos, Abuja or Kano, or in the United States. For men of the generation that grew old during the twenty-five years I have worked in southeastern Nigeria, migration was almost universally seen as a means to an end—or rather to various interconnected ends. As I have already shown many times over, men migrated in search of education and employment, to be able to earn enough money to marry and educate their children, and to be able to build a house in their place of origin. For nearly every Igbo migrant man I've ever met, successful manhood involved a continuous circulation to their place of origin, with the imagined end goal of retiring comfortably at home, and ultimately dying and being buried there.

As the lives of the men I have already described in other chapters attest, migration is by no means a guarantee of success, either in place of destination or at home. But nearly every man's assessment of his own life's successes and failures is measured, in large part, by how he perceives his standing in his village of origin. This is true even among men who spend remarkably little time there. Among men who are first-generation migrants, few things loom larger in their masculine projects than their status at home.

The shared ideal is that all the toil and suffering of working, raising a family, and saving to build a house at home, even as one lives modestly in a city, will pay off in a comfortable and dignified retirement at home. Of course not all men are able to make that dream real. Indeed, when I was carrying out a research project in 2001–2 studying Igbo migrants from Ubakala in Kano, the largest city in northern Nigeria, an Ubakala man died there. The local branch of UIU had a special fund that all the members contributed to that would pay for the transportation home of any member who died in Kano, so that he could be buried appropriately in the village. The man who died wasn't able to retire at home, but at least he was buried there. During my second summer of fieldwork for the project, another migrant died. This man was one of the very few Ubakala migrants in Kano who did not belong to UIU. He was buried somewhere in Kano. His fellow migrants viewed this as sacrilegious and a big tragedy. For them it epitomized why belonging to UIU and staying connected to "home people" was so important.

In contrast to the unfortunate migrants who died in Kano, De Ufomba seemed to be on an ideal trajectory and poised to live out the typical Igbo man's dreams for his latter years. But it didn't work out exactly that way. The move home from Lagos was smooth. He had spent several years preparing his village home to become his permanent residence, including elevating the wall around his compound to increase his sense of security, digging a borehole so that his household would have its own water supply, and installing a large electricity generator that was much more powerful than the small one he used during his trips home in the past. In addition, his social reintegration into the community was eased by the fact that he had been a regular visitor home all his adult life. Those visits and his devoted membership and relative generosity to the Ubakala Improvement Union meant that his kin, neighbors, and fellow community members saw him as a loyal "son of the soil," as Igbos commonly put it. It was only when De Ufomba turned his attention to local politics that his experience as a return migrant took a turn toward the more unpleasant.

In Nigeria, there are three officially recognized tiers of the state: federal, state, and local. But at the local level there is actually a fourth tier, below the Local Government Areas (of which there are 775 in Nigeria). The fourth tier is made up of what are known as Local Autonomous Communities (LACs), which typically have a single traditional ruler who occupies a customary position that is also recognized and supported by the state. In contemporary Igboland that person is usually known as an eze, which is often translated as "king"—though there is a proud tradition in much of the Southeast saying that the Igbo have no kings (Onwumechili 2000; Harneit-Sievers 2006). The emergence of ezes and other forms of chiefship goes back to colonialism and the imposition of indirect rule by the British, when the colonial authorities confronted the Igbos' largely acephalous, republican political system. Essentially, the literature suggests, the British invented chiefs and imposed them on the Igbos (Afigbo 1972; Harneit-Sievers 1998).

It is a rich and complex history, but fast-forward to the early twenty-first century and Igbo communities like Ubakala had become the stage for tremendous competition over these invented positions as traditional rulers. At the new millennium, Ubakala was a single local autonomous community (LAC) made up of eleven villages. The villages were divided between two equally large wards. Shortly after the return to civilian rule in 1999, a new eze had been appointed after some years of a vacant stool. Each ward had lobbied for its favored candidate and in the ward that did not have its candidate selected there was much discontent. After contesting the outcome (and failing to have the decision changed), the villages in the losing ward adopted a new strategy, which was to petition to become an independent LAC. The state government eventually granted this petition and the second ward crowned its own eze. This led several of Ubakala's eleven villages in both wards to decide to petition to become LACs themselves, each with their own eze. All this unfolded not long after De Ufomba returned home to retire.

When the possibility emerged that his village might become an LAC with its own eze, De Ufomba decided to vie for the position. The competition to become the village eze brought De Ufomba into conflict with many in his community, as the contest came down to a choice between him and another senior man who had lived more or less his whole life in the village. De Ufomba tried to persuade people that with his experience in the bank, his years of living outside the community, and all his work with the UIU over the years, he would bring a forward-thinking, development-oriented leadership to the village in its new status as an LAC. His opponent emphasized his local roots, his deep knowledge of the community and its problems, and his known trustworthiness.

I heard from people in the village that De Ufomba belittled his opponent's lack of education and his relatively modest means. Apparently, De Ufomba spent handsomely on food and drink at various meetings he hosted for people as he lobbied for their support. It was even rumored that he promised influential men and women money and positions on his council in exchange for their support (ezes typically appoint a council of advisors who are officially unpaid, but who garner prestige and a small share of revenue from various local fees, levies, fines, etc.). I have no idea if this was true, but it played into the narrative that his opponent wanted to construct, which was that De Ufomba was a relative outsider trying to buy his way to power in the village.

Ultimately, the community decided to put forward De Ufomba's opponent as their preferred candidate, though the process of becoming an LAC became stalled and the contest became moot in terms of producing an actual eze. But for De Ufomba it was a bitter experience. He saw himself as a devoted native of the community and interpreted his compatriots' choice of someone he viewed as obviously less qualified as a slap in the face. To him, it was a sign of the worrisome backwardness of his "home people." For me, it symbolized a more common challenge that migrant men face as they navigate their intimate relationships with kin and neighbors in their communities of origin: namely, how migrant men handle money in their relationships with home people is a central factor in how they are perceived and received. And these men—including older men like De Ufomba moving home to the village to retire—face an almost impossible set of contradictory expectations.

The challenges can be summarized as follows: (1) migrate and make no money and one is more or less a failure; (2) migrate and make money, but don't share it widely enough through appropriate contributions to kin, clients, and community projects and one's riches might torpedo one's social standing at home rather than help it; and (3) spend money too ostentatiously, or in ways that appear too overtly self-serving, and even seeming generosity can leave one criticized. The third risk was the one to which De Ufomba fell prey. His failed venture into community governance reflects the difficult balance that must be struck in pursuing conspicuous redistribution as a political strategy to navigate the complex geometry of money and intimacy, and inequality and sociality more generally.

But even if De Ufomba had not pursued the chief's stool, many of these same dynamics would have surely characterized his relationship with his community and kin. How much money did he have? How much was he sharing? Was it enough? No matter how much it was, what were his motivations for sharing and spending? These are questions faced by all migrant men that become everyday challenges when they return home to retire.

Working until the End

The three men whose lives I have discussed so far—De Chi, De Okeke, and De Ufomba—all experienced a period in old age that could be conceptualized as retirement. As a migrant returning home to the village, De Ufomba explicitly planned for and imagined what he was doing in those terms. For De Chi and De Okeke, who lived their whole lives, more or less, in Ubakala, the notion of retirement was less salient. But they too recognized that their latter years involved a diminution of work and, in the context of southeastern Nigeria, an increasing reliance on their children for financial support. It is worth noting that even for many men who were rural-to-urban migrants, support from their children was crucial in their old age. De Ufomba was relatively exceptional in the wealth he accumulated in his lifetime. I knew plenty of older men of lesser means who retired (or simply couldn't work anymore) without much of a nest egg at all. For example, men who had been civil servants all their lives were, in theory, entitled to a gratuity from the government (a kind of onetime severance package) and a monthly pension. But it often took years of visits to the pension office (and some said it required bribes) before one received the gratuity. Further, pension payments were relatively meager and often disbursed sporadically, running months (or longer) behind schedule.

Many older men never retired at all. In Ubakala—and in villages across southeastern Nigeria—lots of elderly men farmed until sickness or death made such labor impossible. For the poorest among those men such farm work was a necessity, while others continued to farm partly to supplement their livelihoods and partly because they couldn't imagine their lives without it. As I have noted already, nearly every Igbo migrant man I have ever known, regardless of social class, aspired to retire in his ancestral village. But in cities and towns many older men, mostly the poor, also worked until the very end, dying before they could retire and move back to their communities of origin.

De Joseph was one of the gatemen at Umuahia Sports Club. When he started the job he looked to be in his late sixties. His work involved opening and closing a heavy iron gate when club members entered or exited the premises in their vehicles. This task required some vigilance because the club was located directly across from Umuahia's main market, and shoppers with vehicles were always trying to find somewhere to park in the area's impossibly choked environment. Joseph was somewhat deaf, so club members blew their horns long and loud to get his attention over the din of the traffic. Joseph's job also included sweeping leaves off the tennis courts each morning, weeding the grounds, and running various errands for members.

Every day he wore the same green uniform. He seemed to prefer bare feet to the flip-flops that he only occasionally donned. Joseph always seemed to be at the club. At first I wondered whether he ever went home—until I discovered where he slept. Every night he laid out a small foam mattress in the main club hall.

Joseph's salary was staggeringly small, only about $30 a month. I'm sure he made more from the small tips club members gave him when he ran errands, and from the times he let vehicles park in the club's lot for a fee (something he could get away with in the morning because almost no members came to play tennis or drink beer then). But even including all this, Joseph was a very poor man.

Being poor comes with lots of indignities in southeastern Nigeria. Wealthy men command poorer men in ways that appear highly patronizing from my perspective. And poor men's responses often seem remarkably obsequious—though countless times over the years I heard men who were servants or laborers or service providers of various sorts grumble about the arrogance of the rich. Sometimes a poor man would resist, and I occasionally heard heated arguments that erupted, essentially, when a poorer man demanded greater respect from a richer man. But the reality is that richer men *are* more powerful and poor men mostly perform their inferior positions faithfully. Joseph addressed the club members as "sir" or "*oga*," or "*nna*," all terms of respect. The latter term, nna, is perhaps the most interesting here. In Igbo it means father. I often heard Joseph address club members this way, even men who were obviously younger than he was. Indeed, it was something I observed much more widely in Nigeria: terms of seniority used to acknowledge class and power differences rather than age. Wealth and power increasingly trumped age as the measure of social prestige, but never entirely. Club members frequently addressed Joseph as just "Joseph," but also as "De Joseph." The fact that they didn't always use "De," as they should have by custom, illustrates the triumph of class over age. But that they used it at all suggests seniority still counts for something, even in the context of dramatic class inequality. Indeed, as often as club members gave Joseph orders, it always struck me that the tone was more moderate than with younger employees, like the men who ran the bar.

Joseph had worked at the club about six or seven years when one day I came for an evening tennis game and learned that he had died the night before. The club president announced a collection to contribute to Joseph's burial. Over the next few days, members donated a substantial sum that was handed over to Joseph's family. He was buried a little over a week after his death. Given how burials in southeastern Nigeria have become performances of class and exercises in creating, reinforcing, and showing off social and cultural capital, it should not be surprising that, in general, the poorer one is the faster one is buried. Ordinary folk do not have the money to arrange the lavish funerals requiring long preparations.

About a week after Joseph's burial one of his daughters came to tell club members a formal "thank you" on behalf of the family. To my surprise, I recognized her. She was the same young woman who had long sold *moi moi* (a snack made from cow peas) and other food to club members as they drank beer. She was probably about twenty-five years old and was as tall and slender and Joseph was short and stocky. The only resemblance that I could see was that each had a jet-black complexion. After she thanked the club and took her leave, the president told us that she had requested that she still be allowed to sell snacks

11 While most urban-migrant Igbo men aspire to retire in their villages of origin, many poor men, like De Joseph, the watchman at the tennis club, are unable to achieve that goal.

now that her father had passed. I was happy to learn the president had said yes. Apparently Joseph left behind a wife and four daughters, only one of whom had so far married.

Death and Burial: The Final Measure of Manhood

Even for a poor man like Joseph, a remarkable rallying of resources occurred at death in order to provide a befitting burial. While many Nigerian men (and women) complained about the arms-race-like escalation of costs associated with burials, few dared flout social expectations when it came time to bury their own kin, particularly if the person had lived a long life. Elderly Igbo men hoped that their children would bury them well. Middle-aged men realized that burying their parents would be a major milestone in their own achievement of manhood. The complex dynamics between money and social relations are on full display in Igbo burials, with all the associated aspirations and expectations and jealousies and resentments infusing each moment of preparation and performance. As in so many endeavors in which men must spend money to solidify sociality and intimacy, burials are rituals in which the blurry boundaries between conspicuous consumption (which can be seen as selfish and aggrandizing) and conspicuous redistribution (which is imperative if one is to be seen as a good man) are continuously navigated and evaluated.

Over twenty-five years of working in Nigeria, I have attended more than two dozen burials, including at least ten in which the deceased was a senior man. In several cases, I followed events from the first word of death through to the completion of burial ceremonies. In this section I examine the main features of Igbo burials as they relate to masculinity, for both the older men who have died and, especially, for their sons who must bury them. Following the main theme of this book, I focus particularly on explaining how, in each step of the burial process, the tensions between money and sociality are manifest. At the core of these tensions, and the ambivalence generated in Igbo burials, is a fundamental contradiction in the social structure of Igbo society, wherein kinship, friendship, and other social ties are marked by inequalities that trouble trust and intimacy (Geschiere 2013). These inequalities are highlighted and exacerbated in rural-urban relations and of course they are manifest in differences in wealth and symbolized above all by money. Burials crystalize paradoxes I have discussed throughout this book: men are both rewarded and resented for success, encouraged to show off their wealth and jealously begrudged for their achievements, and expected to pursue ambitions beyond the village but also frequently suspected of betraying their loyalties to "home." Burials as rituals reflect these social structural contradictions, sometimes helping to resolve them but also serving to highlight and intensify them.

Burial Preparations

In Ubakala, where more than half of the burials I have attended occurred, news of death travels quickly. After the death of a senior man, the immediate family begins mobilizing resources for the funeral and related events. A key element in understanding the social pressures around burials is realizing that the expectation for grand festivities surpasses what is prescribed by local custom. Each village, indeed, in many cases, each lineage has clear rules for the amount of money and the specific gifts and commodities that particular individuals and associations are customarily required to contribute to a burial. While these contributions can be substantial and can create their own burden, particularly for poorer people, when Igbos lament that the costs of burials have gone out of control, they are referring mainly to expectations that go beyond local customary obligations.

Briefly, some of the common features of contemporary Igbo burials that are *not* required by traditional customs but that have, nonetheless, taken on the aura of obligation include: (1) printing posters and banners to announce the death and burial arrangements, and, if the family is wealthy enough, taking out newspaper, radio, and TV advertisements for the same purpose (Lawuyi 1991; Ogbuagu 1989; Omoruyi 1988); (2) arranging a convoy of vehicles to accompany the body home from the mortuary on the day preceding the burial (including an ambulance that serves as a hearse to carry the coffin and corpse) and, often, hiring buses to carry mourners; (3) hiring a generator to produce electricity for the night vigil, the burial, and the ensuing celebrations; (4) renting chairs and tarpaulin tents to accommodate guests and protect them from the rain or the sun; (5) contracting a photographer and video cameraman to record the entire performance; (6) arranging dancers, singers, and musicians (often both traditional performers and a modern electric band) to entertain guests; (7) sewing expensive (often silk) clothes for the corpse and preparing an ornate platform for the body to be viewed; (8) sewing new, fashionable, matching clothes for the immediate family to wear for the burial; and (9) procuring an expensive coffin and preparing an elaborate gravesite, often with a headstone, in the family compound. In addition, the amount of food cooked and the soft drinks, beer, and wine procured to entertain guests almost always exceed what is required by local custom.

Very few families have savings great enough to finance what is necessary for a burial. In the mobilizing of resources, the unequal dimensions of kin and community relationships are accentuated, and the importance of rural-urban relations for the accomplishment of a successful funeral is clearly manifest. Every Igbo burial I have witnessed involved both rural residents and returning urban (and, frequently, international) migrants. The relationships between rural and urban kin in burial preparations illustrate the conflicts and interdependencies that characterize these ties. For example, when Pa Chima died at the age of eighty, his sons were relatively poor and living in the village while one of his daughters was married to a wealthy Igbo businessman in Lagos. To give their father a befitting burial, Pa Chima's sons both needed and expected that their sister and brother-in-law would make a very large contribution to the costs. Yet at the event the sons resented the self-aggrandizing way in which, in their view, their brother-in-law made it widely known that he had "underwritten" the burial of their father. In a discussion with some of his kin and neighbors, Chima's eldest son, a fifty-one-year-old father of five asked, rhetorically, about his brother-in-law: "Does he think we could not bury our father without him? Because he has money and lives in Lagos, does he think he can intimidate us? Are we not the ones who gave him a wife?" Chima's son's expression of resentment relied on an idiom of affinal reciprocity to criticize his brother-in-law. But as a later conversation with the brother-in-law demonstrated, the tensions that emerge in kin-based patron-client relationships run in both directions. The brother-in-law said about his contributions to the burial: "I paid for 90 percent of the expenses but my in-laws barely acknowledged my contribution. They wanted to bury their father in a big way, but did not want to admit that they could not have done it without my assistance. Sometimes pride is foolish." Tensions around money and the associated inequalities in kinship and affinal ties are not uniquely rural-urban, but patterns of rural-to-urban migration and levels of inequality associated with it are central to the unfolding dynamics of kin-based clientelism in places like Ubakala.

All the while that people are mobilizing family resources, soliciting gifts and loans, and pledging or selling land to raise the money for the burial, the body of the deceased is kept in a mortuary in town. Typically, bodies stay in the mortuary for at least two weeks while the family and the community prepare for the burial, but often the stays are much longer.[3] Many circumstances can delay a burial. Most commonly, it may be necessary to wait for family members who reside in faraway cities like Lagos or Kano, or, even more significantly, overseas, to arrange to come home. The reasons it is important for relatives in the city and overseas to return home for a burial are manifold. In addition to emotional ties, chief among the pragmatic social explanations are the prestige that their presence provides for the dead man and his family and the resources they are expected to contribute. Successful migration of a son or daughter to a big city—and, even more, to Europe or the United States—is considered among the greatest achievements of a man, something that will yield benefits to the whole lineage (Chukwuezi 2001; Uchendu 1965). Igbos returning home from far away for a burial are at once proud showpieces for the family and the objects of tremendous pressure to provide material assistance.

The dynamics of the relationship between urban patrons and rural clients that play out in Igbo burials reflect the ways in which money and inequality are intertwined with a morality of reciprocal obligation that characterizes kinship relations. Families who must bury their dead rely on wealthy relations and other patrons to fulfill social expectations to perform grand burials. For patrons, burials are ideal-typical cases of the manner in which prestige is generated through an obligatory sharing of one's wealth with one's clients. For the wealthy urbanites, burial ceremonies are opportunities to assure continued identity with place of origin, solidify political bases, display their achievements, and bask in the recognition of being successful (cf. Geschiere and Gugler 1998; Lentz 1994). For the poor, especially in the village communities of the deceased, burial ceremonies are chances to enjoy a moment of conspicuous redistribution of resources. Inherent in the dynamics of the whole enterprise is a great ambivalence, as burials exemplify and lay bare the intertwining of inequality and interdependence that characterizes clientelistic kinship in communities, especially as they extend across rural-urban boundaries.

The Journey Home

The strength of the obligation that relatives of the deceased come home to bury their dead is exceeded only by the power of the expectation that the dead should be buried at home. For Igbo men who die away from their place of origin, the journey home involves the literal transportation of the corpse back to the village. The institutional mechanisms in place to facilitate this journey attest the centrality of "home" and "home people" for Igbo migrants (Chukwuezi 2001; Gugler 1991). As I have noted already, in all the major cities across Nigeria that constitute common destinations for Igbo migration, migrants have organized local branches of hometown associations (Chukwuezi 2001; Smock 1971; Wolpe 1974; cf. Trager 2001 for Yoruba-speaking Nigerians). Among the most practical and symbolically significant functions of these associations is to assist in the transport home of migrants who die "abroad." These associations levy themselves and contribute significantly to the transportation costs and, to a lesser degree, the burial costs of their deceased members. Even Igbo migrants overseas maintain such associations and members frequently contribute to the costs of transporting dead bodies back to Nigeria.[4]

For men who die in the village, and for deceased migrants once their bodies arrive home, the journey home is symbolic and begins with the transport of the corpse from the mortuary in town to the family compound in the village. The symbolic journey home is itself an important performance. Outside the mortuary a large convoy of cars and vans assembles, led by an ambulance hired as a hearse to carry the coffin.[5] Included in the convoy are relatives, townspeople, friends, and associates of the deceased from all arenas of his life, as well as people connected to other members of the family.

It is important to recognize that the social ties being displayed, strengthened, and reaffirmed are as much those of the family, especially the sons of the deceased, as of the deceased himself. Indeed, many of the most extravagant Igbo burials are performed by wealthy men for their deceased fathers (and mothers). For urban Igbo men, the burial of a parent is an opportunity to exhibit to "home people" the strength of one's ties in the city and to display to one's urban peer groups the level of one's status in the village. For the men whose status is at stake, the bigger the convoy from the mortuary, the greater the prestige conferred upon the family.

Along the journey home the procession may stop at several significant places in the deceased's life to allow the people of that place or organization to pay their respects, as well as to recognize that group. A burial program might literally read "the body will lie in state at . . ." giving the time and place. The actual duration of the stop may be as little as ten or fifteen minutes. A body may "lie in state" at a place of work, a business, a town home, one's maternal village, and, possibly, at the locations of any associations or social clubs significant in the person's life. At the tennis club in Umuahia, when a prominent member died we were instructed to await the body at the club dressed in full tennis attire on the day of his journey home. When the procession arrived some members put on a symbolic two-minute tennis exhibition. Within twenty minutes the procession moved on to the next destination. The more places a body stops to "lie in state," the more prestigious the burial.

Of course, the majority of men are buried without so much fanfare but almost all aspire to it. Most families spend well beyond their means to put on a good show. Ultimately, these conspicuous displays are about demonstrating, and, indeed, solidifying and assuring, the continuation the family's important ties to a range of social networks. The displays of wealth and the efforts to demonstrate up-to-date fashions that characterize Igbo burials are meant to testify to the achievements of a man and his family in the world—achievements that are seen as arising from, above all, relationships with other important people, especially people with connections to navigate the opportunity structures of contemporary Nigeria.

In large measure, burials demonstrate to the world a family's intention to maintain its status. The specific arrangements at the night vigil that precedes the burial, and at the burial itself, make it even clearer that burials are tremendously significant symbolic moments for recognizing and celebrating the importance of "having people," and for renewing those ties as one individual departs the world of the living. Indeed, Igbos have many proverbs that emphasize the importance of "having people," including *"onye were madu were ike"* and *"onye were madu were aku,"* which, respectively, translate as "somebody who has people has power" and "somebody who has people has wealth." The irony in contemporary Nigeria is that as people aspire to greater wealth and success, they increasingly resent the very individuals who symbolize their aspirations and on whose patronage they depend to uphold the appearance of success.

The Night Vigil

In pre-Christian times, Igbos buried their dead immediately—within a day or two of death (Ottenberg 1968). Then, usually a year or more later, the family performed a "second burial," during which obligations to lineages, age grades, title societies, secret societies, and other community associations were concluded, and important sacrifices and rituals to appease ancestors and gods were fulfilled. Traditional practices had a built-in period during which the family could prepare for and muster resources to discharge community and religious obligations. It was the advent of Christianity that compressed the period within which burial obligations must be completed; Christian churches preached against the second burial as idolatrous. As Igboland has become almost universally Christian, nearly every community has adopted the single ceremony model, dropping most, but not all, of the rituals oriented to ancestors and the deities of traditional religion, but retaining most, if not all, of the obligations to lineage, community, and association. With rising expectations for burials coinciding with the pressure to fulfill all burial obligations in one performance, people have felt compelled to delay burials to mobilize the necessary resources.

Somewhat ironically, given the historical role of Christianity vis-à-vis Igbo burials, many churches now sanction members who do not bury their dead within two weeks. By refusing to grant Christian burial rites if ceremonies take place more than two weeks after the death of the deceased, churches hope to help rein in the costs and extravagance of burials. Perhaps not surprisingly, some families now resort to keeping a death a secret from their church for as long as possible to avoid the start of the two-week clock, announcing a relative's death only when within two weeks of being ready for the burial. Of course such "secrets" are often public knowledge, creating some awkward situations.

In contemporary Igboland, most funerals of senior men are preceded by a night vigil, and like the other phases of the burial process, there are many degrees of pageantry, depending on the wealth and stature of the deceased and his family. The night vigil begins after dark but does not really get going until around 10–11 p.m. People from all the groups and associations to which the deceased belonged, and from the groups and associations of his immediate relatives, assemble at the family compound to stay up throughout the night, praying, singing, drinking, dancing, eating, and socializing. It is impossible to overemphasize the degree to which invitations to and attendance at burial ceremonies— including night vigils—are important symbols of connectedness. People endure what often appear to be extreme inconvenience and even significant risk in order to put in an appearance at a night vigil. For example, people generally see driving between cities and villages in the middle of the night in Nigeria as highly dangerous because of fears of armed robbers; yet such risks are routinely undertaken to fulfill obligations to attend night vigils.

The accoutrements of the night vigil are similar to those of the burial itself (tents, an electric generator, performers, etc.). Indeed, most of them are retained throughout the burial ceremonies. At some point in the night, it is expected that all of the guests will be provided food and drink. Similar to what I described for weddings, there is tremendous variation in the quantity and quality of food and drink. But it is universally expected that something will be served. At a minimum, everyone will be served at least a beer or a soft drink and a plate of yam pepper soup. But often the "entertainment"—when Igbos speak of entertainment at any public function they mean, above all, the food and drink—is much more sumptuous and elaborate. The major costs come by including more protein—beef, goat, fish, or chicken—with whatever staple is served. The more meat people are served, the more they will praise and admire the hosts. As I have discussed earlier, drinks are similarly ranked and distributed in ways that mark the recipients'—and the hosts'—perceived status.[6]

More than likely, wine and brandy will be displayed conspicuously on the "high table" for all to see, but only shared with a select few. The high table is a feature of nearly all Igbo public ceremonies and occasions. At the high table the most important guests are honored with special recognition, special service, and more expensive entertainment. They are fed superior food and given a wider choice and larger amounts of drink. Feathers are often ruffled over who is and is not selected to be at the high table, as omissions grate on the strong Igbo pride about recognition and appropriate sharing. Selectivity and consequent resentment with regard to distribution is not restricted to the high table. Among other guests definite distinctions are made, with more prestigious individuals and groups getting better treatment. Generally, special attention is paid to those coming from farther away—for example, the urban work colleagues of a deceased civil servant (or of his son) will be given better seats than, and superior entertainment to, local villagers. At one level, the Igbo notion of hospitality makes this exceptional service provided to outsiders acceptable to locals. But I often heard local people grumble that they were shortchanged because the hosts pandered to status.

The Funeral Ceremony

Funeral services usually commence around 11 a.m. the morning following the night vigil. Burials typically take place on a Saturday morning, as this maximizes attendance, especially by city dwellers who must travel to the village for the ceremonies.[7] Most families contract the printing of a burial program that includes the schedule of burial events from the journey home through the night vigil and the burial itself (Omoruyi 1988). Usually included in the program, in addition to a schedule of events, is a reproduction of a photograph of the deceased and a brief biography. Any living spouse and all direct descendants of the deceased are listed, and if any descendants have prestigious jobs or titles, or are resident overseas, this is almost always indicated. The programs are usually printed completely in English, though some families include Igbo versions of hymns or prayers. Often, in typical village settings, many older people are illiterate and cannot actually read the programs, yet everyone wants one and complaints are heard if the programs are not enough to go around. The programs—like the posters, banners, and media announcements described above—are markers of material wealth and cultural capital, but they are also commodities that must be shared.

The Christian part of the ceremonies is performed at the local church of the deceased or is officiated by a pastor in the family compound. Once the Christian service is completed, the body is taken back to the family compound for interment, or simply moved within the compound if the service was done there. Before the interment, one or two people are asked to give orations. The orations usually take the form of a stylized biography of the deceased, in which only his positive accomplishments are acknowledged. The content of the orations illustrates again the great value of "having people" in Igbo society, and the importance of a man fulfilling his obligations of kin-based patron-clientelism. Orations enumerate all of the organizations and associations to which the deceased belonged or contributed. The magnanimity of the deceased is also highlighted, particularly his assistance to relatives and contributions to the village community.[8] For those men who were migrants, the extent to which the migrant used his urban connections to help "home people" is emphasized. Achievements lauded include paying school fees for junior siblings or the children of siblings in the village, finding relatives employment in the city, and using urban connections to bring development projects to the rural community. In other words, the deceased is represented as a good patron—a man practiced in the art of conspicuous redistribution who used his money appropriately in relations with kin and community.[9]

After the orations, the coffin is moved to the place of interment, which has been dug in advance. Almost all Igbos bury their dead within the family compound. Occasionally, the moment of interment can be particularly tense because unresolved conflicts in or between various groups to which the deceased belonged can explode into a contest over ownership of the corpse. I have witnessed several burials delayed for periods of between a few minutes and many hours because of conflicts between competing factions. De Sylvester's burial was delayed because his urban church's members claimed Sylvester had renounced his membership in the local men's secret society when he became "born again." Church members and Sylvester's urban-based "born-again" daughter did not want the secret society members to perform the rituals they usually undertake at the interment of their members. Rural-urban conflict was pronounced.

Igbo people work hard to make burials into events that symbolize the strength of social connections. But the underlying tensions in social relations are frequently exposed in funeral ceremonies. Family quarrels and resentments, land conflicts, anticipated inheritance disputes, and problematic relations between rural and urban kin are among many strains that sometimes explode around a man's burial. Inequality and the perceived failure to fulfill the obligations of reciprocal kinship ties and patron-clientelism are commonly at the heart of these resentments.

Entertainment and Status Recognition

Immediately after the interment, announcements are made over a public address system regarding where various groups and associations should proceed for their entertainment. Numerous tents are labeled with signs bearing the names of, for example, church groups, in-laws, the maternal lineage, a workplace, an old boys association, or a social club. In addition, extended family members and neighbors usually agree to make their homes available to entertain certain groups of guests. A definite hierarchy characterizes where guests are asked to go, with houses being more prestigious than tents, and some houses being more prestigious than others. At the various venues of entertainment the guests wait to be served with food and drink, with differences in the quality of food and drink indicative of the perceived status of the guests.

In some respects the entertainment phase of the burial is most illuminating, because many of the essential and often conflict-laden dynamics between money and sociality that energize Igbo social life come to the surface. It is during the entertainment phase that the various factions, groups, organizations, and associations are most readily identifiable and segregated, and where individual rank and status are most openly flaunted, celebrated, and resented. People are instructed where to go to get their food and drink and everyone knows which venues have the best food, and which people are being shown the greatest respect. To some extent, Igbos would not have it any other way. Were one to suggest that a local farmer holding no chieftaincy title should be seated in the same place and served with the same food as a state government official visiting from city, most Igbos would find it preposterous. But while a poor farmer might not necessarily be rankled over the urban-based official's extravagant entertainment, he will pay close attention to the meat on his peer's plate, the brand of beer others are served, and who is offered a chair. Perhaps not surprisingly, the visiting urban elites often become more upset over perceived slights than poor villagers because the higher one's status the more that appears to be at stake in assessments of appropriate recognition.

Once, at the burial of a friend's father, members of my tennis club were so insulted by their treatment they nearly left in annoyance. They felt they had not been offered adequate seating and were not provided with enough food and drink. These men seemed genuinely outraged that they were not entertained properly. After one member found our host and informed him of the neglect, our host (the son of the deceased and fellow tennis club member) went himself to the kitchen to assure that more food was dished for his tennis mates, but for this too he was criticized. What, after all, was a Big Man such as himself doing in the kitchen with women dishing food? This was interpreted as another sign of poor arrangements. The entertainment phase of a burial seems inevitably to produce tensions over whether people are being accorded appropriate recognition and given their fair share. Big Men are never treated big enough, and given that nearly everyone perceives himself as a Big Man in some sense, the ubiquity of dissatisfaction is striking.

Even when the entertainment is so grand that everyone can eat and drink to his fill, the hosts might be accused of flaunting their wealth or using their urban connections to "intimidate" village kin. But for all the complaints about recognition and sharing, and all the resentments rooted in perceptions of inequality, most burials succeed in some fundamental sense. To fail completely is unthinkable, which is why people suffer such incredible pains to perform them. They have no choice. Not to comply with expectations would be tantamount to saying: "We do not need our people." Neither rural Igbos nor their urban brethren would dare say it, because it is simply not true.

Much as the burial of one's father is a defining life event for an Igbo man, and much as the successful completion of this rite of passage is in many ways a kind of final marker of full manhood, the completion of a burial is not necessarily liberating. There are debts to be repaid and land pledges to redeem. Adult male children of the deceased may face all kinds of antagonisms and disputes that were postponed while the parent was still alive. In addition, many disputes erupt over inheritance, especially if a late father was polygynous. Death can crystallize long-simmering fissures in the fold. Further, relatives resident in the village often use the death of an old man as an opportunity to grab his land, especially if the sons are based in the city and do not visit family farmland on a regular basis. Many disputes between village residents and their migrant relatives emerge after the death of an elder. So while the burial of one's father is a great accomplishment for any man, it is also the beginning of another phase of life problems, problems tied—as so many challenges of masculinity are—to the intersection of money and social relations.

Conclusion

Funerals offer a particularly revealing window onto the complex and sometimes contradictory processes whereby Igbo men—and surely many other Nigerians—negotiate kinship, community, and patron-clientelism across rural and urban settings in an era of economic inequality. Burials are opportunities for men to display their money in the most universally expected—but also often the most flamboyantly executed—examples of conspicuous redistribution. These ritual performances are moments for people to build, solidify, and show off social and cultural capital, including connections to migrant kin and other patrons and clients in the world beyond their communities of origin. The paradox that all Igbo men must confront in burying their fathers is that their home communities demand of them displays of wealth that are often simultaneously resented. In mobilizing and showing off the support they have from migrant kin, or the support they provide as migrant kin, men must navigate—and they sometimes ignite—the underlying tensions produced when kinship relations are also patron-client relations (i.e., unequal and mediated, in large measure, by material wealth).

At the heart of these tensions is the fraught dynamic between money and morally acceptable sociality. As at every other stage in his social life, at a man's burial his sons (and to a lesser extent his daughters) experience an inevitable conflict between "performing" financially and behaving appropriately among one's kin and community. Almost without fail, burials augment and exacerbate the everyday debates and social strains regarding whether money is being spent in socially productive or socially destructive ways. Spend too little on one's father's funeral and one risks being seen as a failure. But the flip side is being accused of excessive ostentation, what I often heard Nigerians describe as intimidation. Conspicuous redistribution is the strategy men adopt to navigate this fine line: money needs to be seen as shared and as contributing to kin and community. Conspicuous consumption for its own sake, conversely, is often perceived as self-aggrandizing and socially damaging. As should be evident by now, the boundary between them is blurry. And it is worth emphasizing again that even as conspicuous redistribution offers the rich an opportunity to spend their money in prosocial ways, and even as poorer men frequently envy and emulate as best they can many of the masculine behaviors associated with wealth, practices of conspicuous redistribution clearly serve elite men's interests more than ordinary men's interests, be they young or old.

As the cases in this chapter attest, elderly Igbo men in contemporary Nigeria are highly attuned to the complex geometry of money, intimacy, and sociality more generally. In today's world, these forces play out most starkly in relation to migration in men's lives—whether it is their own mobility or their children's. For senior men who are or were migrants, intimate social relations in old age are affected deeply by how much money they have and how they use that money, particularly when they decide to retire in their communities of origin, which is the ideal for almost every Igbo man. For men who never moved, their children's migration is crucial to understanding how money and intimacy intersect in their later lives. As in their youth and in midlife, for older men, the experience and performance of masculinity hinges significantly on money and its pivotal role in sociality. Even in death men cannot escape it.

Conclusion

My intention in this book has been to describe and explain manhood in contemporary southeastern Nigeria. I have examined the main phases and spheres of men's lives through case studies that support my contention that the relationship between money and intimacy—and money and sociality more generally—is the central dynamic in Nigerians' performance of masculinity. Further, I have shown how this dynamic and its manifestations in men's behavior offer a revealing window onto economic, political, and social life.

In the conclusion, I draw together the pieces. First, I look again at what performing masculinity means in practice, particularly as it plays out in the complex intertwining of money and sociality. Then, I offer some thoughts to refine the concept of conspicuous redistribution, which I introduced at the beginning and which has provided useful analytical leverage throughout. Next, I briefly revisit the contributions of the individual chapters to the overall argument, with an eye to tying the geometry of money and intimacy not only to masculinity, but also to the nature and consequences of relevant social changes in Nigeria. Finally, I end by considering the misconceptions created when Nigeria's—and Africa's—difficulties are reduced to a "crisis of masculinity." Such a perspective misdiagnoses the problem, eliding the deeply social motivations for men's behavior and the fact that almost all men want to be good men.

Performing a Befitting Manhood

The notion that masculinities—and, for that matter, all identities—are performative is firmly established in the social sciences (Goffman 1959; Connell 1995; Gutmann 1997). In many cultural contexts, the reality that identities are enacted is submerged in order to mask their performative character (it is as if to acknowledge performance somehow undermines authenticity). In contrast, one of the most interesting—and, frankly, entertaining—aspects of masculinity in southeastern Nigeria is the strikingly overt manner in which men perform their manhood. Anyone who has spent significant time there cannot help but have noticed men's exaggerated behaviors, whether it is the magnificent strut of a man dressed in his most flamboyantly flowing and colorful traditional dress, the boisterous tones in which men argue, their ostentatious displays of wealth, or the vociferous assertions of the right to recognition and respect (I would be rich if I had a dollar for every time I heard an Igbo man shout "Do you know who I am?"). Men in southeastern Nigeria perform their masculinity exuberantly, especially, of course, if they have the money to back it up. And while I have presented considerable evidence to show the challenges and ambivalence that Nigerian men face and feel about contemporary expectations for manhood, I hope it has not been lost on readers the degree to which so many of these same men understand and embrace the performative dimensions of being a man.

As I noted in the introduction and illustrated in the ethnographic chapters, Nigerians themselves commonly employ the verb "perform" when assessing an array of behaviors associated with masculinity. The uses of the word support my argument that money is central to how men fulfill social expectations and obligations. When Nigerians say a man has "performed," it can refer to the monetary performance of sociality across a huge spectrum of domains, from sexual and romantic relationships with women to the ties of patronage and political cronyism that animate politics, even at the highest levels of the Nigerian polity. It is no coincidence, I suggest, that when a young woman assesses the quality of her relationship with an older married male lover, for example, she speaks explicitly about whether he has "performed," thereby using the same term by which clients assess their patrons or citizens evaluate whether a president or a governor is doing a good job. Across this wide range of masculine endeavors, whether a man uses his money morally—to further intimacy, sociality, or the collective good as opposed to enriching and benefitting only himself—stands as the single most important criterion to determine how well he has "performed."

If the competent performance of masculinity in Nigeria entailed nothing more than spending money on others in the pursuit of the collective good, however, understanding why men behave as they do would be more straightforward than it actually is. But in reality, men spend money on intimacy, sociality, and politics not simply to be seen as generous, but also to reproduce both patriarchy and patron-clientelism. A successful man—patriarch or patron—must spend a certain amount on his own aggrandizement in order to show that he has the wherewithal to perform as a man should, whether it is as a sugar daddy, a husband, and a father, or as a political patron or a politician. Further, in both gender and politics, even Nigerians who are not Big Men are invested in the system that produces them. I do not mean to suggest that Nigerian women like patriarchy or generally benefit from it, or that ordinary Nigerian men enjoy patron-clientelism and think it is best for them. This situation is more complicated. But I do think that the reproduction of expectations about masculinity in Nigeria cannot be fully explained without seeing how women and ordinary men are at least partially invested in a system that valorizes a performance of masculinity that does not ultimately benefit them.

Another common Nigerian English word helps elucidate these seemingly paradoxical dynamics. Nigerians are obsessed with whether a whole range of social—and in so many instances masculine—performances are undertaken in a "befitting" way. Like the verb "perform," the meanings and uses of the adjective "befitting" provide a telling perspective on Nigerian social life. The entire panoply of significant social ceremonies in southeastern Nigeria is judged by whether such events are performed in a befitting manner. Although an array of factors play into whether a wedding, a funeral, a title-taking ceremony, or some other celebration is deemed befitting, including the way that that hosts or sponsors handle social relationships with guests, kin, and community, always central to the assessment is money. How much has been spent? Was it generous and lavish enough to befit the status of the sponsors? As I have shown, in many circumstances it is the social standing of a particular man that is most obviously on stage in these ceremonial performances.

Judgments about whether a man has performed befittingly extend well beyond significant public rituals and ceremonies, though I hope I have demonstrated that manhood is especially at stake in these performances. A man is also judged with regard to whether he builds a befitting house in his community of origin, provides a befitting education for his children, drives a befitting car, has a befitting cell phone, or provides his wife a befitting wardrobe (to name just a few examples). Of course social class calibrates expectations about what is befitting. Everyone realizes that not all men can afford a smart phone, a car, or a big house in the village. But the connection between successful masculinity and social class is precisely one of the most significant features of modern masculinity in Nigeria, creating aspirations that nearly all men share, but also considerable discontent because only very few men can achieve the status and accrue all the benefits of being a Big Man. The close and troubled relationship between money and intimacy, and money and sociality more generally, is at the core of this complex constellation of aspirations, expectations, ambivalence, and dissatisfaction.

Conspicuous Redistribution

For men who have money in Nigeria, their exuberant performances of masculinity are nothing if not conspicuous. Wealth in contemporary Nigeria is displayed ostentatiously. Men with lots of money build houses too big for even the largest family, drive (or rather are driven in) the most expensive SUVs, and throw lavish parties. Among the very richest class having a personal jet has become a status symbol in a country where literally millions of people still live in abject poverty. Many Nigerian elites—mostly and especially men—engage in a level of conspicuous consumption that could be described as grotesque. It is no wonder that the popular media, Nollywood films, and, most significantly, huge swaths of the ordinary Nigerian public regularly produce a condemnatory discourse about the behavior of elites, most typically in complaints about corruption (Smith 2007a; Obadare 2016; Pierce 2016).

But more surprising, more interesting, and more salient for explaining the production and reproduction of inequality in Nigeria—and, for my purposes here, the central role that the performance of masculinity plays in these processes—is the degree to which ordinary Nigerians reward men for these behaviors, even as they simultaneously condemn them. To accurately describe and analyze these circumstances, I find the term "conspicuous redistribution," introduced at the beginning of the book and illustrated throughout, to be conceptually productive. By distinguishing between conspicuous consumption and conspicuous redistribution, one is better placed to notice and understand the social work expected and achieved through the spending of money, even in situations where the lavishness and obvious inequalities displayed can appear outlandish and offensive.

Conspicuous redistribution in southeastern Nigeria (and I suspect in many other settings) involves a complicated intertwining of seemingly contradictory dynamics. Clearly, when a man spends money on a wedding, a burial, a title-taking ceremony, or any other event where large numbers of people are invited, part of what he is doing is converting wealth into prestige. The expenditures of wealth associated with social ceremonies not only convert money into prestige, they also transform monetary wealth into wealth in people. As a long lineage of scholarship about Africa has made clear, social prestige and political power have historically been—and are still—heavily dependent on having wealth in people (Nyerges 1992; Guyer 1995a; Smith 2004a). Part of what men are doing in performing the festivities I have described is showing off, and also cementing, their webs of social and political connection. The people who attend these ceremonies constitute a man's wealth in people, whether they are his superiors, his equals, or his clients (as d'Azevedo [1962] noted long ago, in Africa everyone is patron to a lesser person and a client to a more powerful person).

The phenomenon of wealth in people is closely tied to the structural and interpersonal dynamics of patron-clientelism. Steven Pierce's (2016) recent book about the history of corruption in Nigeria offers evidence of the importance of conspicuous redistribution for patronage politics in much of Nigeria's history, albeit without using the term. Pierce examines what he calls "moral economies of corruption" (see also Olivier de Sardan 1999). The nature of Nigeria's moral economy of corruption—and of politics and power more generally—is such that the conduct of Big Men is judged socially based largely on how well such men's behavior is perceived to use their power and (especially) their money for productive social and political purposes, rather than for purely selfish aggrandizement. The multiple opportunities for men to engage in conspicuous redistribution are key moments in such a moral economy. To be an effective patron and Big Man, building and solidifying wealth in people (and thereby prestige and political power), a man must strike the right balance between spending ostentatiously and yet doing it in a way that isn't perceived as intimidating or oppressing the very clients (and fellow elites) he is trying to impress.

In the context of contemporary Nigeria, where wealth is often suspected of being of dubious origin, the process of converting monetary wealth into prestige (and wealth in people) is typically only partially successful. It is important to emphasize that practices of conspicuous redistribution primarily benefit elites. Such performances attempt to make more socially acceptable massive disparities, while in fact they promote and perpetuate inequality. But the critical discourses that circulate behind the scenes at the weddings, funerals, and chieftancy installation ceremonies sponsored by Big Men, which I have amply illustrated in the preceding chapters, attest to the extent to which ordinary Nigerians are not fooled. And yet nonelites not only continue to participate in these spectacles of conspicuous redistribution, they also expect them—even demand them. There are several reasons for this, which, when properly analyzed, elucidate the concept of conspicuous redistribution and show why I think it is a useful idea for explaining these social dynamics, particularly as they manifest themselves in the performance of masculinity.

Perhaps even more striking than the lengths to which rich Nigerian men will go to show off their wealth to perform befitting weddings and funerals is the extent to which less wealthy men do the same, often accruing huge debts in the process. As Nigerians themselves often articulated to me, the expenditures necessary to meet social expectations regarding weddings and funerals feel like an arms race in which all see that the costs are unsustainable and yet no one is willing to unilaterally disarm. The result is that everyone participates in processes that they simultaneously lament. But why this is the case is less clear. I think that it has to do with how expectations for conspicuous redistribution are embedded not only in the moral economy of patron-clientelism (and corruption), but also in relations of kinship and the implicit expectations of generalized reciprocity that undergird them.

When a typical Nigerian man decides what he will spend on (or borrow for) his wedding, or to bury of his father, for example, he is thinking implicitly about all the weddings and burials he has attended, and about what others have done. My observations and discussions about these matters with men in southeastern Nigeria suggest that underlying such calculations is not simply a desire "keep up with the Joneses," but also a fundamental sense of reciprocal obligation. As Lévi-Strauss (1969) argued long ago, and others have elaborated more recently (Bearman 1997), kinship as a stable social and moral system is buttressed by expectations and practices of generalized reciprocity. A man spending to host and entertain his community does not know when the next wedding or funeral will occur, but he expects that it will happen, and that his peers will perform similarly. He certainly knows that others have done so before him. The expectations of generalized reciprocity associated with kinship ties (and also, it must be said, with patron-clientelism—because, of course, kinship and patron-clientelism overlap tremendously in places like southeastern Nigeria) help explain the powerful feeling of obligation men experience in relation to performances of conspicuous redistribution. They are not simply showing off—though they certainly are doing that. They are fulfilling a deep sense of duty.

While much of what I have explained so far about conspicuous redistribution has emphasized the political, social, and moral foundations of these seemingly outlandish (and for poorer men unaffordable) displays of monetary wealth, I would be remiss if I did not also include in my explanation a mention of the desires and pleasures Nigerians share when it comes to the "conspicuous" part of conspicuous redistribution. Much as a man runs the risk of behind-the-scenes criticism if his performances of conspicuous redistribution seem mismatched to his actual behavior as a kinsman, a patron, or a politician (in other words, one cannot overcome a reputation as greedy or selfish simply by entertaining people lavishly at wedding or a funeral), it is also true that people expect, admire, and envy the conspicuously ostentatious aspects of these ceremonies. This is not only, as Pierce (2016) has pointed out, because such displays demonstrate a man's financial (and therefore social and political) capacities, but also because most ordinary Nigerians want a lot of money and the things it can buy. Even as Nigerians are critical of what the obsession with money has done to their society, few would not also admit that they love money.

Finally, in my explication of conspicuous redistribution I have concentrated mainly on large public ceremonies like weddings, funerals, and title-taking ceremonies because they are the most striking and therefore the most evocative examples. But, as I have shown in previous chapters, in smaller ways these same undercurrents play out in more everyday interactions as well. When a man offers "kola" to welcome a visitor to his house, for example, the kinds of food and drink he presents are received and evaluated with similar attention to the way that these commodities signal the social status of both the giver and the receiver. At the tennis clubs, or at any drinking establishment, buying and presenting beer (and snacks) to one's peers has a similar feel. Even a man entertaining his girlfriend is involved in a kind of conspicuous redistribution. These dynamics apply widely in the performance of masculinity. They are no doubt most salient in moments when the relationships between money, sociality, inequality, and morality are most obviously at stake.

Masculinity and Social Change

Money has become central to how men perform their expected roles in a wide range of important relationships—from lover, husband, and father to friend, patron, and politician. Yet as one of the men I quoted earlier in the book noted astutely, in Nigeria "money is God and money is the devil." Money occupies this polyvalent and contradictory position in Nigerian social life because it stands for and contributes to wider transformations in the economy, politics, and everyday social life—changes that Nigerians both welcome and lament. Behind the discourses—both public and private—that are critical of how men spend their money, particularly in the conduct of social relationships, is a high level of popular discontent and a profound ambivalence about many aspects of social change in Nigeria.

In this section I briefly retrace the intersection of money and sociality—what I have purposely called money and intimacy—across the range of domains and positions along the life course illustrated in the previous chapters. But here I do so with an eye toward using the complex geometry of money and intimacy in the performance of manhood to reflect more directly on the nature and consequences of recent social changes in Nigeria.

Before proceeding, it might be instructive to revisit briefly the reason I chose to foreground the term intimacy. As I explained in the introduction, I see intimacy as an aspect or subset of the larger category of sociality. I believe it would have been perfectly possible to present most of the material and develop the main arguments in this book if sociality replaced intimacy in the vast majority of instances I have used the term. But, to me at least, sociality is too broad to describe what I have been interested in as men use money to navigate their most important social relationships. Terms like "face-to-face sociality" or "intimate sociality" would come much closer to doing the job. Indeed, readers will have noted that I have often used intimacy and sociality as synonyms. I have done that consciously, though when I have done so the kind of sociality I am describing has mostly been intimate and face-to-face (as opposed to the more anonymous interactions that characterize many aspects of urban, industrialized, bureaucratic social life).

The concept of intimacy is most readily associated with romantic, personal, or family life, but it is applicable to many kinds of face-to-face social relations in which the personalistic aspect of the tie is paramount, and wherein trust is elemental (Geschiere 2013). In Nigeria, such trust-imbued personal relationships are central to business and politics as well as to romance and family. Thinking about this more personalistic form of sociality as intimacy has allowed me to explore the paradoxes men face when intimate social relationships must be maintained by spending money. The problem, as I hope I have illustrated amply, is that in Nigeria money stands for, or at least raises the specter of, the intimacy's opposites: deception, fraud, and self-serving greed, as well as alienating levels of inequality.

The notion of intimacy turns out to be helpful, I think, in understanding the relationship between masculinity and social change, though not in a simple way. On the one hand, in the spheres of sexuality, romance, marriage, and fatherhood, it is fair to say there has been a rise in expectations of intimacy—the idea being that in such relationships things like emotional commitment, communication, and trust are more explicitly expected and valued than in previous generations. Yet as I have also tried to show, men in modern Nigeria need to spend money to perform adequately as lovers, husbands, and fathers, even (and one might argue especially) with the rise of these new expectations. But as I have repeatedly illustrated, the specter of money threatens the very premise of intimacy, as it introduces the possibility of a range of other more sinister motives that people commonly see or suspect in contemporary Nigeria, and with which they associate money. In these closest domains of men's personal lives, money is required for intimacy but also threatens it.

On the other hand, in the realms of economics and politics, the role and fate of intimacy (in the sense of explicitly face-to-face, or intimate, sociality) has been different. Rather than recent changes bringing a rise in expectations for intimacy, in many ways the modern state and market would seem to demand less intimacy. In the political sphere, the state is meant to be more bureaucratic and less personalistic. In economic life, the market is meant to reward objective worth or achievement rather than personal connections. Of course in contemporary Nigeria, as in many places, these transformations toward less personalistic economics and politics are incomplete and often highly resisted. Much of economic and political life still depends on intimate social ties. Nigerians simultaneously work energetically to make sure this continues to be so and lament the consequences of persistent favoritism, patronage politics, and corruption. The relationship of money to these changing ideas about intimacy in political and economic life is complex. Money both stands for the demise of face-to-face sociality and is central to the enduring importance of those very ties.

When individual men navigate this fraught terrain to try to be good men they are not, for the most part, imagining themselves as actors shaping the future of economic, social, and political life in Nigeria. But by briefly retracing some of the central aspects of how manhood is performed at the intersection of money and intimacy across the life course, it is possible to show how the geometry of masculinity, money, intimacy is integral to the dynamics of social life and social change more generally in contemporary Nigeria.

Becoming a Man: Learning to Love Money and Women

In the first ethnographic chapter about becoming a man, I showed how secondary schools (and, for a more select, elite population, universities) served as central arenas in which boys and young men learned to understand the paramount importance of money for manhood. In school, the class and consumption-based foundations for the successful performance of masculinity become evident not only, for example, in the way one's peers scrutinize whether one's shoes are "original," "China," "tokunbo," or "local," but also in how possibilities for sex and romance with girls and young women depend on having money, or at least maintaining appearances. While schools contribute to cultivating desires for money and consumption, it is also easy to observe there the emergence of ambivalence about the effects of money on intimacy.

Even as schoolboys and university men aspire to have the money and fashionable commodities to attract members of the opposite sex, they also resent the fact that wealthier competitors have an advantage over them, and they regularly condemn the idea that some women make sex and love available to the highest bidder. The awareness that wealthier men—whether they are elite students who supposedly dominate university campus cults, older "sugar daddies" who lure women with material things, or even professors who "sexualize" grades—can convert money into intimacy is not only threatening, it is also seen as a sign of social and moral crisis associated with troubling inequalities. While formal education is widely touted and still largely perceived as the most desirable pathway to a successful life as a man, young men in school (and university) come to realize that money as the measure of a man leaves many men short in the pursuit of intimacy with women.

It is not only in the realm of romance that money is problematic for boys trying to become men. Countless young Nigerians drop out of school precisely because they and their families do not have enough money to continue. Further, even many who complete secondary school (and university) are left struggling to find jobs in a context of high unemployment. To find money, those who cannot continue in school often seek economic opportunity through becoming an apprentice to a businessman. Indeed, for more than a decade now I have been hearing stories about young men who purposely drop of school to pursue business because the promise of money there is better than getting an education and looking for an elusive job after graduation. But for apprentices looking to become businessmen, money almost always becomes the object of contentiousness, manifesting in disputes about compensation and capital.

I want to emphasize, however, that not all of what boys and young men learn about the geometry of masculinity, money, and intimacy is negative. Although money and intimate sociality often sit in uneasy tension in contemporary Nigeria, as the example of Bonafice (the former apprentice who succeeded on his own) suggests, young men who wish to be successful also learn that money's most important value is in the way it facilitates social, economic, and political relations. As boys grow into men they learn that sharing money as well as consuming it is critical to morally acceptable masculinity and its associated forms of face-to-face sociality.

But in Nigeria's political economy, most young men find it very difficult to earn enough money to be good men. Like the youth Marc Sommers (2012) writes about in Rwanda, many young men in Nigeria see themselves as "stuck" in a kind of perpetual adolescence. Ultimately, achieving adulthood requires marrying and having children, and for that a man needs wealth.

Provider Love and Expensive Intimacies

In chapter 2, I explored the dynamics of money and intimacy in courtship, marriage, and fatherhood. One of the most striking social changes in the last few decades in southeastern Nigeria has been the rise of romantic love as a relationship ideal for marriage. Nowadays, most young men choose their own spouses and one criterion is being in love. In this world of choice marriage a man must convince a woman to marry him. He does this, in part, by proving his love. But as I have shown, love and money are deeply intertwined in Igbo courtships. A significant part of demonstrating love depends on spending money. While the expectation that a man must spend to show his love is shared by both men and women, so too are suspicions about motives created when love requires money.

Already in courtship men are preforming what has been described in the literature as "provider love" (Hunter 2010; Bhana and Pattman 2011). A man's capacity to be a good husband and a good father is measured, in large part, by his ability to cater for his wife and children financially. Whether a man has the money to spend during courtship is almost like a test of whether he will have the wherewithal in marriage. While a man's financial performance as a measure of successful provider love extends across courtship and marriage, it is during courtship that women are able to insist on and most effectively enforce his performance of romantic love. Patriarchal gender dynamics are slowly eroding across the board in southeastern Nigeria, but they remain much more entrenched in marriage than in courtship. If a man has enough money to provide for his wife and children, he feels entitled to many masculine privileges that he is less likely to assert when still wooing a potential wife.

But having enough money to take care of one's family is a huge challenge for most men. Indeed, even accruing the wealth to marry is a formidable task. Men are marrying later, in part because the financial burden of getting married is so daunting. Not only is it increasingly up to individual men to raise a significant portion of their bridewealth payments, the costs of marriage ceremonies themselves—both traditional and Christian weddings—have spiraled out of control. These performances of conspicuous redistribution mirror wider trends in which cultivating and cementing the social relationships for successful manhood requires huge expenditures on these public spectacles.

Fatherhood has also changed such that men are more directly responsible for the costs of raising their children and they are also sometimes more involved in the intimate aspects of parental caregiving. Whereas taking care of children used to be spread more widely across kin networks, with urbanization, lower fertility, and household nucleation, parents themselves are more singularly responsible for childrearing. Further, women's growing participation in the labor force and the gradual (if fitful, incomplete, and often resisted) spread of globally circulating ideas and practices one might describe as feminist have drawn men into new fatherhood practices. But the primary metric for judging a man's capacity as a father remains rooted in spending money, with provider love marked, above all, by a man's capacity to pay his children's school fees.

Making Money

As I described in chapter 3, the demands for money put great pressure on men to find work or engage in business that generates enough
wealth. In southeastern Nigeria, one of the most striking changes over
the past two generations has been the demise of farming as a viable
male livelihood strategy, not only because farming is more precarious
due to population growth and land scarcity, but also primarily because
most men have ambitions for money and lifestyles well above what is
possible through traditional farming.

Urban life beckons new generations of men. But migration to the
city is no guarantee of a better life. Many urban-based men struggle
to find jobs or establish businesses that enable them to flourish in the
ways they wish. The precariousness of their finances regularly rears its
head, often in the form of crisis. Common causes of financial crises
include deadlines for annual (lump-sum) rent payments, yearly school
fees, health emergencies, and the death of a parent. Many men incur
debts to meet up with these challenges and hard work is no guarantee
of financial security.

Even as men move to cities in large numbers, the continued importance of their kin and community in their rural places of origin looms
large in the performance of masculinity. Ties to village communities
illuminate the significant role that money plays in enabling proper sociality. Igbo migrant men are compelled to return home regularly to
see parents and visit kin, especially at Christmas. They feel obligated
to participate in and contribute to village-based social ceremonies and
development projects. Perhaps most importantly (and certainly most
expensively), every man is expected to (and nearly all desire to) build
a house in the village. Probably only the failure to marry or childless-
ness weigh on an Igbo man more than the lack of a village house. Like
so many of the ways that men spend money, building a house in one's
community of origin is above all a social act, symbolic of continued
loyalty to and belonging among one's kin and community. Indeed,
many men barely use these houses at all, yet they often suffer great
hardships to build them.

For the few men who become wealthy, the social work of money is
equally (if not even more strongly) apparent. The widely recognized
phrase "big money, big trouble" stands for the intense pressure rich
men experience to spend their money in order solidify social ties, both
among fellow elites and among the larger population of people who

might be considered their clients in Nigeria's vast networks of patron-clientelism. While such obligations can be quite burdensome, it is important to note—though hopefully obvious—that poor men would happily switch places with the rich and take on the "big trouble" that comes with big money.

In the dynamics that characterize social relations between the rich and the poor—between patrons and clients—suspicions about the source of a wealthy man's money always loom in the background. No doubt the realities in Nigeria of fraud, deceit, corruption, exploitation, and other mechanisms for accruing ill-gotten riches engender many of these rumors about the basis of men's wealth. But such questions about the legitimacy of wealth and its associated inequalities also serve to pressure the rich into spending some of their wealth on others, pushing conspicuous consumption in the direction of conspicuous redistribution.

Male Peer Groups—the King in Every Man

The durability of relatively gender-segregated social life in southeastern Nigeria means that for most men much of the performance of masculinity takes place in all-male (or at least male-dominated) social settings. In chapter 4, I focused on how the intertwining of money and intimacy unfolds in men's relationships with each other. Using the tennis clubs in Owerri and Umuahia at which I have spent so much time over the last twenty-five years as examples, I showed the ways that men's status among their male peers is measured in relation to how much money they have, how they spend it, and with regard to whether their motives are perceived as appropriately social as opposed to selfishly aggrandizing.

At the tennis clubs, as throughout society in southeastern Nigeria, men are obsessed with receiving appropriate recognition and respect. The elaborate formalities that characterize addressing the club or distributing beer—reproduced similarly not only in most public events and ceremonies in society more generally, but also in daily occurrences such as the presentation of kola nuts to household visitors—seem designed to assure that each man is accorded his due. While wealth and political power shape status hierarchies among men, one of the things that the guys in the clubs most appreciated about membership was that everyone in the club could expect to be a "celebrity" in his own right. Of course the tension between the idea that there is a king in every man and the reality that "money makes a man" played out even in the club.

As in so many other aspects of the performance of masculinity, men's behavior and their peers' evaluation of their behavior reflected the complex and sometimes contradictory geometry of money, inequality, and sociality. Having and spending lots of money was socially rewarded, but how sincere a man's generosity was perceived to be figured heavily in moral assessments of his conduct. The distinction between conspicuous consumption and conspicuous redistribution featured prominently. And while "conspicuous" almost always seems to be celebrated in the performance of masculinity in Nigeria, my time at the club showed me that men also take into account someone's "size" (i.e., economic capacity) when judging how he spends and shares money. Further, men sometimes shielded their closest friends from economic embarrassment by lending them money privately, or keeping quiet about a man's money problems about which all were, in fact, aware.

It is hard to overstate the importance of male peer groups in masculine social life in southeastern Nigeria, or exaggerate the centrality of money in how men navigate their relationships with each other. Indeed, as I also showed in the chapter, even men's heterosexual behavior—particularly married men's extramarital relationships—must be understood, in part, as a performance for their male peers. Among other things, these relationships provide men yet another arena to show off their money and their masculinity to their fellow men.

Men Behaving Badly

As demonstrated in chapter 5, even bad men—men who are violent or criminal in their behavior—can be usefully analyzed and understood in terms of the familiar dynamics of money and sociality that manifest themselves in the performance of masculinity more generally. Desires and needs for money are behind much of the behavior of criminals, as well as the bad behavior of otherwise good men. The degree to which even thieves, fraudsters, and drug dealers can rehabilitate their social standing (or not), depending on how they behave with their ill-gotten wealth, attests to the social underpinnings of money's importance for the performance of competent masculinity.

Many men who are not criminals are nonetheless violent, especially in their relationships with women. Although it is my observation that most men in southeastern Nigeria do not beat their wives, society's relative tolerance for intimate partner violence and the failure to even acknowledge marital rape as a conceptual possibility confirm the continued power of patriarchy in gender relations. While domestic violence is a manifestation of patriarchy, male dominance is enforced (and violence enabled) by more implicit and nonviolent mechanisms, some of which are being challenged in a changing society. Indeed, to the extent that men justify both unfettered sexual access to their wives and the prerogative to slap disrespectful wives and children (as some men do), it is often in the guise of defending tradition (reflected in narratives about bridewealth and masculine authority).

As the examples of the drug smuggler who returned to Nigeria after a long prison sentence in the United States and the 419er who failed in his bid to become governor suggest, the fate of a criminal in Nigerian society depends a lot on how much money he has and how he spends it. Although the drug smuggler's conduct was the subject of some continued behind-the-back criticism, by and large he was able to rehabilitate his life and reputation by using his money to solidify kin, community, and business ties in Nigeria. In contrast, though people abided the notorious 419er when he spent money to show off his wealth, mostly he was viewed with derision and his bid to become governor failed miserably—not, it seemed, because of the criminal way he made is money, but because of the socially problematic ways that he flaunted it.

The fact that criminals with money can secure a legitimate social standing if they spend it appropriately in society should not obscure the reality that criminals without money—many of whom engage in crime precisely because it is so difficult to earn honestly the money they need—are judged very differently than the rich. As my interviews with the Bakassi Boy in Aba and the area boys in Lagos illustrated, for many poorer men, their lives brush up on (or become fully) criminal partly because they have few other options. While not excusing their behavior, it is worth remembering that most of them share similar aspirations with other men, yet without money their pathways to successful manhood appear—and often are—blocked.

Aging and Dying

In chapter 6, I examined the lives of older men and the ways that navigating money and social relations are pivotal to the performance of masculinity in both aging and death. As the examples in the chapter suggest, many older men complain that the younger generation's obsession with money has had negative consequences for Nigeria, including diminishing the respect for seniority. While some of this discontent can be chalked up to the typical grumbling of the elderly about the young, men insisted—and seemed right in asserting—that preoccupations with wealth and social class appeared to lessen the respect for age and seniority.

But old age still signifies something important in southeastern Nigeria. Further, many (indeed, in my experience, most) of the children of elderly men (and women) seemed deeply committed to taking care of their parents. Old men's narratives about their children's filial piety revealed complex tensions between money and intimacy. On the one hand, men were proud when their children made good money and spent it on their care. Many older men talked frequently about the things their children provided for them—and complained about the things they did not. On the other hand, the fact that the pursuit of money commonly entailed outmigration meant that the elderly were increasingly likely to be alone in the village, or at least had very few children nearby. Many men lamented not only the lack of time spent in the company of their children and grandchildren, but also the long-term fate of the community with so many youth occupied elsewhere.

The processes and cycles of circular migration—the ways migrants move back and forth between destinations and their rural places of origin—figure centrally in the lives of older men. Many men who were rural-to-urban migrants return home to their villages to retire, finally living in the houses that for most of their lives had been little more than symbolic structures signaling belonging. But as I showed, older return-migrants face many challenges when they retire "at home," not least how they manage their relations with kin and community neighbors. Those relations are judged in large measure by how return-migrants spend their money, especially if they are perceived to have significant amounts. Of course, as the case of Joseph the watchman at the sports club in Umuahia reminds us, many men who migrate in search of better lives never find the money they hope for, and more than a few men work until they die, never fulfilling dreams for retirement in the village.

But even men like Joseph who die in town are buried at home. As I show in the final sections of the chapter, burials in southeastern Nigeria are quintessential rituals of conspicuous redistribution. A man's burial is the ultimate opportunity for his kin—especially his sons—not only to celebrate his lifelong performance of masculinity, but also to show off their social connections through spending money on a "befitting" burial. Kinship ties, rural-urban relations, and patron-client networks are all at stake and on full display in the final ritual to mark the end of a man's life.

A Crisis of Masculinity?

With all the difficulties that plague contemporary Nigeria—corruption, crime, insecurity, and long-simmering and sometimes explosive regional conflicts—and given the fact that men, not women, are the primary actors perpetuating these problems, it is tempting to conclude that Nigeria is suffering a crisis of masculinity. The idea that social problems in Nigeria, and in Africa in general, are the result of such a crisis has gained currency in the media and in certain sectors of the donor and development communities. The concept of a crisis of masculinity has been received more skeptically in academic scholarship (Walker 2005; Morrell 2002, 2005, 2006). Rather than accept or dismiss the notion entirely, I think it is more productive to examine how it captures something about the current situation in Nigeria, but also what it misses and misdiagnoses.

On the one hand, it is true that almost all of the tribulations about which Nigerians feel most aggrieved are—at least proximally—the

12 Like these young men repairing the author's car, the vast majority of Nigerian men aim and struggle to be good men.

result of men's actions, many of them undertaken specifically to fulfill desires and expectations related to manhood. Whether it is elites who collude to rig elections and loot the state, unemployed youths who become area boys, campus cultists who rape female students, men who beat their wives, or "money bags" who flaunt their wealth to intimidate others, I think it is indisputable that men behave in the ways that they do, in large measure, because they are responding to shared aspirations, expectations, and frustrations regarding the performance of masculinity. As so many of the men I have described in this book attested in the own words, Nigerians are complicit in reproducing the very social problems they simultaneously lament. Men's narratives about the tyranny of money in social and political life, as well as their own participation in the same activities they decry—whether it is seeking corrupt contracts from the government, capitulating to the arms-race-like costs associated with rituals such as weddings and funerals, or using their money to tempt young, single women to become their extramarital sexual partners—all of these demonstrate both men's complicity and their self-conscious critiques of these same behaviors.

On the other hand, the lives and stories of the men in this book, and of the larger population of Nigerian men who I have known over twenty-five years, suggest something more complicated than either pure greed associated with the tyranny of money or a straightforward crisis of masculinity. Where I depart from much of the public discourse about a crisis of masculinity in Africa is in the way that it constructs masculinity as pathology and blames men and manhood for the political and economic problems to which men are responding. The distinction I am making between acknowledging men's complicity in Nigeria's problems and simply blaming men is subtle but important.

One obvious shortcoming of a crisis-of-masculinity explanation for Nigeria's ailments is the extent to which it blames Nigerian men for circumstances shaped by the country's position in the global economy. Poverty and inequality, as well as the desires for consumption that fuel many everyday aspirations in Nigeria, cannot be explained in purely local terms. Much could be said about both the contemporary and the historical global underpinnings of Nigeria's difficulties. But that is beyond the scope of this book.

The evidence I have presented suggests that a crisis-of-masculinity trope also misses and misrepresents important realities on the ground in Nigeria itself. Most significantly, the performance of masculinity is undertaken with primarily and profoundly social motivations. As the men I have portrayed demonstrated over and over again, nearly every masculine act is geared to achieve a social goal, whether it is exhibiting the capacity to provide as a husband or a father, fulfilling one's role as a patron, or bolstering one's reputation among peers.

I focused on the relationship between money and intimacy—and money and sociality more generally—not only because this dynamic animates so much of the performance of masculinity, but also because it is central to the concrete challenges that men face. Money is such a potent force and highly charged symbol precisely because it is simultaneously both antithetical to and absolutely necessary for the social relationships that Nigerians most value—money is both God and the devil all at once. As God, money is the very means for survival, but also the essential prerequisite to enable a man to fulfill his most important social duties. As the devil, it represents the threats to a moral economy associated with face-to-face sociality in which sharing, caring, reciprocity, and collective interests and belonging are highly prized. Money is often perceived to replace these prized qualities with individualism, greed, and unacceptable levels of inequality. Ultimately, as the men depicted in this book illustrate, competent masculinity in Nigeria is evaluated based not simply on whether a man has money (though having it is a huge advantage), but on how he uses it socially. To the extent that men and masculinity should be the target of interventions to improve everyday life in Nigeria, such efforts will only be successful if they begin with the recognition that most men are preoccupied above all else with trying to be good men.

Acknowledgments

The Igbo people with whom I work in southeastern Nigeria have a saying that "a debt never dies." My debts to those who have enabled me to write this book cannot be adequately repaid with the words I offer here. I am not settling what I owe, just acknowledging it.

None of the research grants that have enabled me to conduct fieldwork in Nigeria explicitly supported the study of masculinity. Each project was ostensibly about something else, but all of them involved men. Over time, I realized that I had collected a large corpus of material about masculinity, which became the basis for this book. My work has been supported by awards from the National Institutes of Health (3 P30 HD28251-10S1; 1 R01 41724-01A1; P30 AI042853; 1 R01 HD057792-01A2), the National Science Foundation (BCS-0075764), the Wenner-Gren Foundation for Anthropological Research (6636), and the Pentecostal and Charismatic Research Initiative, through the Center for Religion and Civic Culture at the University of Southern California, funded by the John Templeton Foundation (Grant #13893, Subcontract #143426). To all of these institutions I am most grateful.

Parts of this book draw on material I have published elsewhere. While nothing is reproduced in its entirety or exactly as it appeared previously, I want to acknowledge the pieces I have drawn on and thank the publishers for permission to incorporate this material. The section on fatherhood in chapter 2 is adapted from my book chapter "Fatherhood, Companionate Marriage, and the Contradictions of Masculinity in Nigeria," which appeared in

Globalized Fatherhood, edited by Marcia Inhorn, Wendy Chavkin, and José-Alberto Navarro, in 2014. I thank Berghahn Books for permission to use a portion of that chapter. The brief section on intimate partner violence in chapter 5 draws from my book chapter "Modern Marriage, Masculinity, and Intimate Partner Violence in Nigeria," which was published in *Marital Rape: Consent, Marriage, and Social Change in Global Context*, edited by Kersti Yllo and M. Gabriela Torres, in 2016. I thank Oxford University Press for permission to use a portion of that chapter. The second half of chapter 6, about Igbo burials, is adapted from my article "Burials and Belonging in Nigeria: Rural-Urban Relations and Social Inequality in a Contemporary African Ritual," published in *American Anthropologist* (106 [3]: 569–79) in 2004. I am grateful to John Wiley & Sons for permission to use that article.

While I was writing and thinking about this book, I presented papers at a number of different venues where I received valuable feedback and suggestions. In particular, I thank Jennifer Cole and Kate McHarry for inviting me to present a paper in October 2014 at the Red Lion Seminar in Chicago, jointly sponsored by the African Studies programs at the University of Chicago and Northwestern University. That paper became the first draft of the introduction to this book. The questions, criticisms, and suggestions I received there, from Jennifer and Kate, as well as from Caroline Bledsoe, William Murphy, Emily Osborn, Rachel Riedl, Erin Moore, and others, proved invaluable. I also gave papers about which I received constructive feedback that I used in writing this book at the University of Maryland, where in particular I thank Sangeetha Madhavan; at the University of Florida, where I thank Sean Adams, Brenda Chalfin, Susan deFrance, Abraham Goldman, and Luise White; at the University of Cape Town, where I thank Chris Colvin and Alison Swartz; at Boston University, where I thank Joanna Davidson and Parker Shipton; and at South Asia University, where I thank Diya Mehra.

I continue to feel indebted to a wonderful group of scholars I worked with on a project we called "Love, Marriage, and HIV." At our meetings—and in our publications from the study—we frequently discussed men and masculinity in our different field sites. I benefited tremendously from that collaborative work. Its influence on this book is probably even more than I realize. The members of the group are Jennifer Hirsch, Constance Nathanson, Shanti Parikh, Harriet Phinney, and Holly Wardlow.

I am extraordinarily fortunate to have a position at Brown University, where both my faculty colleagues and the university administration have been immensely supportive. In the Department of Anthropology, I thank all my colleagues, including Sarah Besky, Rebecca Carter, Paja Faudree, Lina Fruzzetti, Matthew Gutmann, Sherine Hamdy, Stephen Houston, David Kertzer, Jessaca Leinaweaver, Catherine Lutz, Katherine Mason, Robert Preucel, Patricia Rubertone, Andrew Scherer, William Simmons, Bhrigupati Singh, Peter Van Dommelen, Parker Van Valkenburgh, and Kay Warren. During the time I was writing this book I was either department chair or on sabbatical between two terms as chair. My experience as chair has given me new appreciation for the importance of good leadership and competent administrative support at the highest levels of the university. As dean of the faculty, Kevin McLaughlin has been especially effective and encouraging, and his associate deans reflect and reproduce the welcome competence and uncommon normalcy that characterize the Office of the Dean of the Faculty at Brown. In addition to Kevin, I thank Janet Blume, Joel Revill, and Anne Windham.

My graduate students over the years have helped keep me from lagging too far behind in the discipline. I suspect most of them don't realize just how important their intellectual vitality is to faculty mentors like me. I have thanked all those who have already graduated in previous acknowledgments. Here I mention my current students, including Whitney Arey, Emily Avera, Chelsea Cormier-McSwiggin, Hannah Marshall, Mohamed Yunus Rafiq, Stephanie Savell, Derek Sheridan, Katharine (Marsh) Stockland, Katherine Thompson, Megan Turnbull, and Marcus Walton. In addition, as fellow Nigerianists, my former students Kathryn Rhine and Stacey Vanderhurst continue to inspire. Two amazing undergraduates worked with me as research assistants on this project. To Lily Gordon and Chimezie Udozorh I am most grateful. I also want to say a big thank you to our outstanding Anthropology Department staff—Mariesa Fischer, Matilde Andrade, and Marjorie Sugrue. Without them we would be in trouble.

Writing this book made me reflect on all my years in Nigeria, including the first three years I lived in Owerri, when I worked for the US NGO Africare. I realize that none of my longer journey would have been possible without the initial support of the late Bishop John T. Walker, C. Payne Locus, Joseph Kennedy, and Alan Alemian. I also owe a huge debt to my Nigerian colleagues at Africare in Owerri, most especially Chibuzo Oriuwa, but also Regina Obiagwu, Nnenna Ukwoma, and many others. They first made Nigeria feel like home to me.

Many other people in Nigeria deserve to be acknowledged and thanked because, more than anyone else, they made this book possible.

Nigerian academic colleagues located in other settings around the continent include, among others, Alex Ezeh, Chimaraoke Izugbara, Blessing Mberu, and Clifford Odimegwu. In Nigeria, many scholars have helped and influenced me, including Pat Ngwu, Oka Obono, Akachi Odoemene, Ogwo E. Ogwo, Chidi Ugwu, and Morenike Ukpong. As I have noted elsewhere, I worked with superb research assistants in Nigeria over the past two decades, including Chidozie Amuzie, Ugochukwu Anozie, Frank Ehuru, Jane Ibeaja, Enyinna Iheancho, Elizabeth Oduwai Uhuegbu, and the late Chinkata Nwachukwu. I also want to thank Benjamin Mbakwem. Despite the fact that we have lost touch in recent years, I remain grateful for all the help and insights he provided me in the past. I hope we can someday work together again.

I owe much to many others as well. In Ubakala, they include Jemmaimah Agoha, Eze Raphael Mbagwu, the late Chief Israel Iroabuchi, Prince Udo Ogbuehi, Chief and Lolo Ufomba Ihenacho, and the late Okwuchukwu Amuzie. In Owerri, I want to thank especially James Anukam, Bishop M. N. Nkemakolam, S. K. Okpi, and Ukay Wachuku for what are now lifelong friendships. In Umuahia, friends are too many to name, but I want recognize especially C. C. Anyalebechi, Emeka Emeh, Dr. James Ifediora, Kalu Ire Kalu, Goddy Nwogu, Ike Obgokiri, Ferguson Onuoha, and Lawrence Ukattah. To them and all my other friends at both Owerri Sports Club and Umuahia Sports Club, I say again, "*Ahhheee* Club!" In many ways, all those hours in your company served as the inspiration for this book.

I am deeply grateful to the many other men who shared with me parts of their life stories, whose identities are concealed in the book with pseudonyms. I hope the book does at least small justice to their lives, struggles, and courage. I cannot thank them by name, but they know who they are.

At the University of Chicago Press I thank David Brent, Priya Nelson, and Dylan Montanari for shepherding my book throughout. As David retires after such a long and towering career, I feel particularly lucky to have had a second book at Chicago come to fruition while he was still at the helm. I am also sincerely grateful to two anonymous reviewers for careful, thoughtful, and constructively critical readers' reports. The book is—I hope—better because I tried to respond to their suggestions. Of course it goes without saying (but I still feel obliged to say it) that any shortcomings are solely my responsibility.

While I was finishing this book three men I cared about deeply died: my friend, Igwe Aja-Nwachukwu; my uncle, Lyle G. Hall; and my brother-in-law, Christian Agoha. I miss them.

The hardest part is to say an appropriate thank you to Ada Agoha Smith, who was my wife for more than twenty-four years. I will not try to do more here than acknowledge how much she and her family have meant to me and given me over all these years. This book—and so much more—would not have been possible without Ada and her family.

I have much else to be grateful for, including my mother and Don, my sister Story and her partner Cheryl, my brother Derek and his wife Sonia, my niece and nephews, and all of the amazing Jordan family and our special place, The Preserve. My daughter Kimmy, who is growing up so fast and probably wants me to write Kim or Kimberly, is the apple of my eye. I am so lucky to have her. Finally, there is Eleanor. Everything about her makes me smile. She makes me glad that being a man is much longer than a one-day job.

Notes

1. I am grateful to Robert Morrell for introducing me to Remy's chapter.
2. Fears of armed robbery occupy a prominent place in the Nigerian popular imagination, particularly among elites, sometimes disproportionate to its prevalence (Marenin 1987; Alemika and Chukwuma 2005; Fourchard 2006).
3. For very prominent people, a burial may be delayed for up to a year or more. One close friend of mine, whose father had been a federal government minister (with six wives and thirty-eight living children), spent over a year working with his siblings, his community, and many other organizations, including the federal government, to arrange a befitting burial.
4. While the hometown associations in Nigerian cities typically cover the greater share of the cost of transporting a member "home" for burial, for the associations overseas members' contributions tend to be more symbolic, as the costs of flying a corpse to Nigeria can be many thousands of dollars. I have no data on the proportion of Igbo migrants who die overseas that are buried at home in Nigeria, but I know that this practice is common, despite the cost.
5. I have never witnessed an ambulance used in Igboland for any other purpose than to carry the dead.
6. In families in which decision makers belong to increasingly popular Pentecostal churches, night vigils and other phases of the burial ceremony may not include any alcoholic beverages but attention to social status in the sharing of entertainment is still important.
7. Despite the common practice of burying the dead on Saturdays to enable maximum urban participation, one way families with lesser means try to live up to expectations for

how much entertainment they must provide is by scheduling a burial on a weekday, thereby enabling them to cater for fewer people.

8. One sometimes hears murmurs in the audience when the orations depict levels of magnanimity wildly different from people's memories.

9. While women are depicted mostly as good daughters, wives, and mothers, they are also frequently remembered as patrons in their own right. Locating woman in the webs of patronage that characterize Igbo and other African societies is sadly understudied. My observations suggest that Igbo women's roles as patrons are partly obscured by male rhetoric that attributes such public action to men.

References

Adamchak, Donald. 1989. "Population Aging in Sub-Saharan Africa: The Effects of Development on the Elderly." *Population and Environment* 10 (3): 162–76.

Adebanwi, Wale. 2005. "The Carpenter's Revolt: Youth, Violence and the Reinvention of Culture in Nigeria." *Journal of Modern African Studies* 43 (3): 339–65.

Adebanwi, Wale, and Ebenezer Obadare. 2011. "When Corruption Fights Back: Democracy and Elite Interest in Nigeria's Anti-Corruption War." *Journal of Modern African Studies* 49 (2): 185–213.

Adeboye, Olufunke. 2007. "The Changing Conception of Elderhood in Ibadan, 1830–2000." *Nordic Journal of African Studies* 16 (2): 261–78.

Adepoju, Aderanti. 2003. "Migration in West Africa." *Development* 46 (3): 37–41.

Afigbo, Adiele. 1972. *The Warrant Chiefs: Indirect Rule in Southeastern Nigeria, 1891–1929*. London: Longman.

Agulanna, Christopher. 2011. "Ezigbo Mmadu: An Exploration of the Igbo Concept of a Good Person." *Journal of Pan African Studies* 4 (5): 139–62.

Ahearn, Laura. 2001. *Invitations to Love: Literacy, Love Letters, and Social Change in Nepal*. Ann Arbor: University of Michigan Press.

Aihie, Ose. 2009. "Prevalence of Domestic Violence in Nigeria: Implications for Counseling." *Edo Journal of Counseling* 2 (1): 1–8.

Ajayi, I., Haastrup Ekundayo, and F. Osalusi. 2010. "Menace of Cultism in Nigerian Tertiary Institutions: The Way Out." *Anthropologist* 12 (3): 155–60.

Alber, Erdmute. 2004. "Grandparents as Foster-Parents: Transformations in Foster Relations between Grandparents and Grandchildren in Northern Benin." *Africa* 74 (1): 28–46.

Alemika, Etannibi. 1988. "Policing and Perceptions of Police in Nigeria." *Police Studies* 11(4): 161–76.

Alemika, Etannibi, and Innocent Chukwuma. 2005. "Criminal Victimization and Fear of Crime in Lagos Metropolis, Nigeria." Lagos, Nigeria: CLEEN Foundation Monograph Series, No. 1.

Amadiume, Ifi. 1987. *Male Daughters, Female Husbands: Gender and Sex in an African Society.* New York: Palgrave Macmillan.

Ansa-Ansare, Kwaku. 2003. "Marital Rape in Ghana: A Solution in Search of a Problem." *Africa Legal Aid Quarterly* 3:15–23.

Ashforth, Adam. 2005. *Witchcraft, Violence, and Democracy in South Africa.* Chicago: University of Chicago Press.

Baiyewu, O., A. F. Bella, J. D. Adeyemi, B. A. Ikuesan, E. A. Bamgboye, and R. O. Jegede. 1996. "Attitude to Aging among Different Groups in Nigeria." *International Journal of Aging & Human Development* 44 (4): 283–92.

Baker, Bruce. 2002. "When the Bakassi Boys Came: Eastern Nigeria Confronts Vigilantism." *Journal of Contemporary African Studies* 20 (2): 223–44.

Barber, Karin. 1982. "Popular Reactions to the Petro-Naira." *Journal of Modern African Studies* 20 (3): 431–50.

———. 1995. "Money, Self-Realization and the Person in Yoruba Texts." In *Money Matters: Instability, Values and Social Payments in the Modern History of West African Communities,* edited by Jane Guyer, 205–24. Portsmouth, NH: Heinemann.

Bayart, Jean-François, Stephen Ellis, and Béatrice Hibou. 1999. *The Criminalization of the State in Africa.* Oxford: International African Institute.

Bearman, Peter. 1997. "Generalized Exchange." *American Journal of Sociology* 102 (5): 1383–1415.

Beasley, Christine. 2008. "Rethinking Hegemonic Masculinity in a Globalizing World." *Men and Masculinities* 11 (1): 86–103.

Berry, Sara. 1985. *Fathers Work for Their Sons: Accumulation, Mobility, and Class Formation in an Extended Yorùbá Community.* Berkeley: University of California Press.

———. 1989. "Social Institutions and Access to Resources." *Africa* 59 (1): 41–55.

Bhana, Deevia, and Rob Pattman. 2011. "Girls Want Money, Boys Want Virgins: The Materiality of Love amongst South African Township Youth in the Context of HIV and AIDS." *Culture, Health & Sexuality* 13 (8): 961–72.

Bird, Sharon. 1996. "Welcome to the Men's Club: Homosociality and the Maintenance of Hegemonic Masculinity." *Gender & Society* 10 (2): 120–32.

Bledsoe, Caroline. 1980. *Women and Marriage in Kpelle Society.* Stanford: Stanford University Press.

———. 1993. "The Politics of Polygyny in Mende Education and Child Fosterage Transactions." In *Sex and Gender Hierarchies,* edited by Barbara Miller, 170–92. Cambridge: Cambridge University Press.

Bledsoe, Caroline, and Gilles Pison, eds. 1994. *Nuptiality in Sub-Saharan Africa: Contemporary Anthropological and Demographic Perspectives*. Oxford: Clarendon Press.

Bloch, Maurice, and Jonathan Parry, eds. 1989. *Money and the Morality of Exchange*. Cambridge: Cambridge University Press.

Bohannan, Paul. 1959. "The Impact of Money on an African Subsistence Economy." *Journal of Economic History* 19 (4): 491–503.

Brouard, Pierre, and Mary Crewe. 2012. "Sweetening the Deal? Sugar Daddies, Sugar Mummies, Sugar Babies and HIV in Contemporary South Africa." *Agenda* 26 (4): 48–56.

Castle, Sarah. 1996. "The Current and Intergenerational Impact of Child Fostering on Children's Nutritional Status in Rural Mali." *Human Organization* 55 (2): 193–205.

Cherlin, Andrew. 2009. *Marriage, Divorce, Remarriage*. Cambridge: Harvard University Press.

———. 2010. *The Marriage-Go-Round: The State of Marriage and the Family in America Today*. New York: Random House.

Chien, Vincent. 2015. "'Keep Them at Arm's Length': Relationships between Homosociality and Power in Anthills of the Savannah." *Proceedings of the National Conference on Undergraduate Research*. Asheville: University of North Carolina.

Chika, Sylvia. 2011. "Legalization of Marital Rape in Nigeria: A Gross Violation of Women's Health and Reproductive Rights." *Journal of Social Welfare and Family Law* 33 (1): 39–46.

Chukwuezi, Barth. 2001. "Through Thick and Thin: Igbo Rural-Urban Circularity, Identity and Investment." *Journal of Contemporary African Studies* 19 (1): 55–66.

Clarno, A. J., and Toyin Falola. 1998. "Patriarchy, Patronage, and Power: Corruption in Nigeria." In *Corruption and the Crisis of Institutional Reforms in Africa*, edited by John Mbaku, 167–92. New York: Edwin Mellen Press.

Coe, Cati. 2005. *Dilemmas of Culture in African Schools: Youth, Nationalism, and the Transformation of Knowledge*. Chicago: University of Chicago Press.

Cole, Jennifer. 2004. "Fresh Contact in Tamatave, Madagascar: Sex, Money, and Intergenerational Transformation." *American Ethnologist* 31 (4): 573–88.

———. 2009. "Love, Money, and Economies of Intimacy in Tamatave, Madagascar." In *Love in Africa*, edited by Jennifer Cole and Lynn Thomas, 109–34. Chicago: University of Chicago Press.

———. 2010. *Sex and Salvation: Imagining the Future in Madagascar*. Chicago: University of Chicago Press.

Cole, Jennifer, and Lynn M. Thomas, eds. 2009. *Love in Africa*. Chicago: University of Chicago Press.

Collier, Jane. 1997. *From Duty to Desire: Remaking Families in a Spanish Village*. Princeton, NJ: Princeton University Press.

Comaroff, John. 1980. *The Meaning of Marriage Payments*. New York: Academic Press

Comaroff, Jean, and John L. Comaroff. 1999 "Occult Economies and the Violence of Abstraction: Notes from the South African Postcolony." *American Ethnologist* 26 (2): 279–303.

Connell, R. W. 1995. *Masculinities*. Berkeley: University of California Press.

Constable, Nicole. 2009. "The Commodification of Intimacy: Marriage, Sex, and Reproductive Labor." *Annual Review of Anthropology* 38:49–64.

Coontz, Stephanie. 2004. "The World Historical Transformation of Marriage." *Journal of Marriage and Family* 66 (4): 974–79.

———. 2006. *Marriage, a History: How Love Conquered Marriage*. New York: Viking.

Cornwall, Andrea. 2002. "Spending Power: Love, Money, and the Reconfiguration of Gender Relations in Ado-Odo, Southwestern Nigeria." *American Ethnologist* 29 (4): 963–80.

———. 2003. "To Be a Man Is More than a Day's Work: Shifting Ideals of Masculinity in Ado-Obo, Southwestern Nigeria." In *Men and Masculinities in Modern Africa*, edited by Lisa A. Lindsay and Stephan Miescher, 230–48. Portsmouth: Heinemann.

Coursey, D. G., and Cecilia K. Coursey. 1971. "The New Yam Festivals of West Africa." *Anthropos* 66 (3–4): 444–84.

Dada, Adekunle. 2004. "Prosperity Gospel in Nigerian Context: A Medium of Social Transformation or an Impetus for Delusion?" *ORITA: Ibadan Journal of Religious Studies* 36 (1–2): 95–107.

Daloz, Jean-Pascal. 2003. "'Big Men' in Sub-Saharan Africa: How Elites Accumulate Positions and Resources." *International Studies in Sociology and Social Anthropology* 2 (1): 271–85.

Darkwa, O. K., and F. N. M. Mazibuko. 2002. "Population Aging and Its Impact on Elderly Welfare in Africa." *International Journal of Aging and Human Development* 54 (2): 107–23.

D'Azevedo, Warren. 1962. "Common Principles of Variant Kinship Structures among the Gola of Western Liberia." *American Anthropologist* 64 (3): 504–20.

Dhillon, Navtej, and Tarik Yousef, eds. 2009. *Generation in Waiting: The Unfulfilled Promise of Young People in the Middle East*. Washington, DC: Brookings Institution Press.

Diamond, Larry. 2008. "The Rule of Law Versus the Big Man." *Journal of Democracy* 19 (2): 138–49.

Di Leonardo, Micaela, ed. 1991. *Gender at the Crossroads of Knowledge: Feminist Anthropology in the Postmodern Era*. Berkeley: University of California Press.

Dilger, Hansjörg. 2003. "Sexuality, AIDS, and the Lures of Modernity: Reflexivity and Morality among Young People in Rural Tanzania." *Medical Anthropology* 22 (1): 23–52.

Duru, Mary. 1983. "Continuity in the Midst of Change: Underlying Themes in Igbo Culture." *Anthropological Quarterly* 56 (1): 1–9.

Dyson, Tim. 2010. *Population and Development: The Demographic Transition*. London: Zed Books.

Ebeogu, Afam. 1993. "Onomastics and the Igbo Tradition of Politics." *African Languages and Cultures* 6 (2): 133–46.

Eguavoen, Irit. 2008. "Killer Cults on Campus: Secrets, Security and Services Among Nigerian Students." *Sociologus* 58 (1): 1–25.

Ekeh, Peter. 1975. "Colonialism and the Two Publics in Africa: A Theoretical Statement." *Comparative Studies in Society and History* 17 (1): 91–112.

Ekpenyong, Stephen. 1989. "Social Inequalities, Collusion, and Armed Robbery in Nigerian Cities." *British Journal of Criminology* 29 (1): 21–34.

Ellis, Stephen. 2009. "West Africa's International Drug Trade." *African Affairs* 108 (431): 171–96.

———. 2011. "'Campus Cults' in Nigeria: The Development of an Anti-Social Movement." In *Movers and Shakers: Social Movements in Africa*, edited by Stephen Ellis and Ineke van Kessel, 221–36. Leiden: Brill.

———. 2016. *This Present Darkness: A History of Nigerian Organized Crime*. London: Hurst.

Esere, Mary, Adeyemi Idowu, and Irene Durosaro. 2009. "Causes and Consequences of Intimate Partner Rape and Violence: Experiences of Victims in Lagos, Nigeria." *Journal of AIDS and HIV Research* 1 (1): 1–7.

Falola, Toyin. 1995. "Money and Informal Credit Institutions in Colonial Western Nigeria." In *Money Matters: Instability, Values and Social Payments in the Modern History of West African Communities*, edited by Jane Guyer, 162–87. Portsmouth, NH: Heinemann.

Fawole, Olufunmilayo, Adedibu Aderonmu, and Adeniran Fawole. 2005. "Intimate Partner Abuse: Wife Beating among Civil Servants in Ibadan, Nigeria." *African Journal of Reproductive Health* 9 (2): 54–64.

Fenstermaker, Sarah, and Candace West, eds. 2002. *Doing Gender, Doing Difference: Inequality, Power, and Institutional Change*. New York: Routledge.

Flood, Michael. 2008. "Men, Sex, and Homosociality: How Bonds between Men Shape Their Sexual Relations with Women." *Men and Masculinities* 10 (3): 339–59.

Fortes, Meyer. 1978. "Parenthood, Marriage and Fertility in West Africa." *Journal of Development Studies* 14 (4): 121–48.

Foucault, Michel. 1978. *The History of Sexuality, Volume 1: An Introduction*. Translated by R. Hurley. New York: Vintage.

Fourchard, Laurent. 2006. "Lagos and the Invention of Juvenile Delinquency in Nigeria, 1920–60." *Journal of African History* 47 (1): 115–37.

Geschiere, Peter. 1997. *The Modernity of Witchcraft: Politics and the Occult in Postcolonial Africa*. Charlottesville, VA: University of Virginia Press.

———. 2013. *Witchcraft, Intimacy, and Trust: Africa in Comparison*. Chicago: University of Chicago Press.

Geschiere, Peter, and Josef Gugler. 1998. "Introduction: The Urban-Rural Connection: Changing Issues of Belonging and Identification." *Africa* 68 (3): 309–19.

Giddens, Anthony. 1992. *The Transformation of Intimacy: Sexuality, Love and Intimacy in Modern Societies*. Cambridge: Polity.

Gilbert, Emily. 2005. "Common Cents: Situating Money in Time and Place." *Economy and Society* 34 (3): 357–88.

Goffman, Erving. 1959. *The Presentation of Self in Everyday Life*. New York: Anchor Books.

Goody, Jack, and Stanley Tambiah. 1973. *Bridewealth and Dowry*. Cambridge: Cambridge University Press.

Gore, Charles, and David Pratten. 2003. "The Politics of Plunder: The Rhetorics of Order and Disorder in Southern Nigeria." *African Affairs* 102 (407): 211–40.

Green, Margaret. 1964. *Ibo Village Affairs*. New York: Routledge.

Green, Margaret, and Ann Biddlecom. 2000. "Absent and Problematic Men: Demographic Accounts of Male Reproductive Roles." *Population and Development Review* 26 (1): 81–115.

Groes-Green, Christian. 2012. "Philogynous Masculinities: Contextualizing Alternative Manhood in Mozambique." *Men and Masculinities* 15 (2): 91–111.

Gugler, Josef. 1991. "Life in a Dual System Revisited: Urban-Rural Ties in Enugu, Nigeria, 1961–87." *World Development* 19 (5): 399–409.

———. 2002. "The Son of the Hawk Does Not Remain Abroad: The Urban–Rural Connection in Africa." *African Studies Review* 45 (1): 21–41.

Gutmann, Matthew. 1996. *The Meanings of Macho: Being a Man in Mexico City*. Berkeley: University of California Press.

———. 1997. "Trafficking in Men: The Anthropology of Masculinity." *Annual Review of Anthropology* 26:385–409.

Guyer, Jane. 1993. "Wealth in People and Self-Realization in Equatorial Africa." *Man* 28 (2): 243–65.

———. 1995a. "Wealth in People, Wealth in Things—Introduction." *Journal of African History* 36 (1): 83–90.

———, ed. 1995b. *Money Matters: Instability, Values and Social Payments in the Modern History of West African Communities*. Portsmouth, NH: Heinemann.

———. 2004. *Marginal Gains: Monetary Transactions in Atlantic Africa*. Chicago: University of Chicago Press.

Harneit-Sievers, Axel. 1998. "Igbo 'Traditional Rulers': Chieftaincy and the State in Southeastern Nigeria." *Africa Spectrum* 3 (1): 57–79.

———. 2006. *Constructions of Belonging: Igbo Communities and the Nigerian State in the Twentieth Century*. Rochester: University of Rochester Press.

Harnischfeger, Johannes. 2003. "The Bakassi Boys: Fighting Crime in Nigeria." *Journal of Modern African Studies* 41 (1): 23–49.

Harrison, Abigail. 2008. "Hidden Love: Sexual Ideologies and Relationship Ideals among Rural South African Adolescents in the Context of HIV/AIDS." *Culture, Health & Sexuality* 10 (2): 175–89.

Haynes, Jonathan. 2006. "Political Critique in Nigerian Video Films." *African Affairs* 105 (421): 511–33.

Henderson, Richard. 1972. *The King in Every Man: Evolutionary Trends in Onitsha Ibo Society and Culture*. New Haven, CT: Yale University Press.

Henderson, Richard, and Helen Henderson. 1966. *An Outline of Traditional Onitsha Ibo Socialization*. Ibadan, Nigeria: Institute of Education, University of Ibadan.

Hills, Alice. 2008. "The Dialectic of Police Reform in Nigeria." *Journal of Modern African Studies* 46 (2): 215–34.

Hirsch, Jennifer. 2003. *A Courtship after Marriage: Sexuality and Love in Mexican Transnational Families*. Berkeley: University of California Press.

Hirsch, Jennifer S., and Holly Wardlow, eds. 2006. *Modern Loves: The Anthropology of Romantic Courtship and Companionate Marriage*. Ann Arbor: University of Michigan Press.

Hirsch, Jennifer S., Holly Wardlow, Daniel Jordan Smith, Harriet Phinney, Shanti Parikh, and Constance Nathanson. 2009. *The Secret: Love, Marriage, and HIV*. Nashville: Vanderbilt University Press.

Hodzic, Saida. 2009. "Unsettling Power: Domestic Violence, Gender Politics, and Struggles Over Sovereignty in Ghana." *Ethnos* 74 (3): 331–60.

Honwana, Alcinda. 2012. *The Time of Youth: Work, Social Change, and Politics in Africa*. Washington, DC: Kumarian Press.

———. 2013. *Youth, Waithood and Protest Movements in Africa*. International African Institute.

Hosegood, Victoria, Nuala McGrath, and Tom Moultrie. 2009. "Dispensing with Marriage: Marital and Partnership Trends in Rural KwaZulu-Natal, South Africa 2000–2006." *Demographic Research* 20 (13): 279–312.

Hunter, Mark. 2002. "The Materiality of Everyday Sex: Thinking beyond 'Prostitution.'" *African Studies* 61 (1): 99–120.

———. 2004. "Masculinities, Multiple-Sexual-Partners, and AIDS: The Making and Unmaking of Isoka in KwaZulu-Natal." *Transformation: Critical Perspectives on Southern Africa* 54 (1): 123–53.

———. 2005. "Cultural Politics and Masculinities: Multiple-Partners in Historical Perspective in KwaZulu-Natal." *Culture, Health & Sexuality* 7 (4): 389–403.

———. 2010. *Love in the Time of AIDS: Inequality, Gender, and Rights in South Africa*. Bloomington: Indiana University Press.

Igbinovia, Patrick. 2003. "The Criminal in All of Us: Whose Ox Have We Not Taken?" *Benin City: University of Benin*.

Inhorn, Marcia C., Tine Tjornhoj-Thomson, Helene Goldberg, and Maruska la Cour Mosegaard, eds. 2009. *Reconceiving the Second Sex: Men, Masculinity, and Reproduction*. New York: Berghahn Books.

Isiugo-Abanihe, Uche. 1985. "Child Fosterage in West Africa." *Population and Development Review* 11 (1): 53–73.

———. 1994. "Consequences of Bridewealth Changes on Nuptiality Patterns among the Ibo of Nigeria." In *Nuptiality in Sub-Saharan Africa: Contemporary Anthropological and Demographic Perspectives*, edited by Caroline Bledsoe and Giles Pison, 74–91. Oxford, UK: Clarendon Press.

———. 1995 "Bridewealth, Marriage and Fertility in the East-Central States of Nigeria." *Genus* 51 (3–4): 151–78.

Izugbara, Chimaraoke. 2001. "Tasting the Forbidden Fruit: The Social Context of Debut Sexual Encounters among Young Persons in a Rural Nigerian Community." *African Anthropologist* 8 (1): 96–107.

———. 2004a. "Notions of Sex, Sexuality and Relationships among Adolescent Boys in Rural Southeastern Nigeria." *Sex Education* 4 (1): 63–79.

———. 2004b. "Patriarchal Ideology and Discourses of Sexuality in Nigeria." Presented at Understanding Human Sexuality Seminar Series 2, December 2, Lagos, Nigeria.

———. 2005. "The Socio-Cultural Context of Adolescents' Notions of Sex and Sexuality in Rural South-Eastern Nigeria." *Sexualities* 8 (5): 600–617.

———. 2008. "Masculinity Scripts and Abstinence-Related Beliefs of Rural Nigerian Male Youth." *Journal of Sex Research* 45 (3): 262–76.

Joseph, Richard. 1981. "Democratization under Military Tutelage: Crisis and Consensus in the Nigerian 1979 Elections." *Comparative Politics* 14 (1): 75–100.

———. 1987. *Democracy and Prebendal Politics in Nigeria*. Cambridge: Cambridge University Press.

Kandiyoti, Deniz. 1988. "Bargaining with Patriarchy." *Gender & Society* 2 (3): 274–90.

Kelly, John. 1992. "Fiji Indians and 'Commoditization of Labor.'" *American Ethnologist* 19 (1): 97–120.

King, Sharon. 2008. "Introduction, Special Issue on Aging and Social Change in Africa." *Journal of Cross-Cultural Gerontology* 23 (2): 107–10.

Kolawole, O. D., and V. O. Okorie. 2008. "New Yam Festival amongst the Igbo People of South-Eastern Nigeria as a Strategy for Agricultural Extension Communication." In *Culture and Society in Nigeria: Traditions, Gender Relations and Political Economy*, vol. 1, edited by Akin Alao and Tunde Babawale, 363–80. Lagos: Centre for Black and African Arts and Civilization.

Korieh, Chima J. 2007. "Yam is King! But Cassava is the Mother of All Crops: Farming, Culture, and Identity in Igbo Agrarian Economy." *Dialectical Anthropology* 31 (1–3): 221–32.

Lambo, Lesley. 2005. "Why Men Hit: Deconstructing Men's Narratives of Conjugal Violence and the Cultural Construction of Masculinity in Nigeria." PhD diss., Concordia University.

Lawuyi, Olatunde. 1991. "The Social Marketing of Elites: The Advertised Self in Obituaries and Congratulations in Some Nigerian Dailies." *Africa* 61 (2): 247–63.

Leclerc-Madlala, Suzanne. 2003. "Transactional Sex and the Pursuit of Modernity." *Social Dynamics* 29 (2): 213–33.

Lentz, Carola. 1994. "Home, Death and Leadership: Discourses of an Educated Elite from North-Western Ghana." *Social Anthropology* 2 (2): 149–69.

Lévi-Strauss, Claude. 1969. *The Elementary Structures of Kinship*. Boston: Beacon Press.

Lindsay, Lisa. 2003. "Money, Marriage, and Masculinity on the Colonial Nigerian Railway." In *Men and Masculinities in Modern Africa,* edited by Lisa Lindsay and Stephan Miescher, 138–55. Portsmouth: Heinemann.

Lindsay, Lisa, and Stephan Miescher. 2003a. "Introduction: Men and Masculinities in Modern African History." In *Men and Masculinities in Modern Africa,* edited by Lisa Lindsay and Stephan Miescher, 1–30. Portsmouth: Heinemann.

———, eds. 2003b. *Men and Masculinities in Modern Africa.* Portsmouth: Heinemann.

Luke, Nancy. 2005. "Confronting the 'Sugar Daddy' Stereotype: Age and Economic Asymmetries and Risky Sexual Behavior in Urban Kenya." *International Family Planning Perspectives* 31 (1): 6–14.

Majekodunmi, Aderonke, and Kehinde Adejuwon. 2012. "Globalization and African Political Economy: The Nigerian Experience." *International Journal of Academic Research in Business and Social Sciences* 2 (8): 189–205.

Makoni, Sinfree. 2008. "Aging in Africa: A Critical Review." *Journal of Cross-Cultural Gerontology* 23 (2): 199–209.

Mann, Kristin. 1985. *Marrying Well: Marriage, Status and Social Change among the Educated Elite in Colonial Lagos.* Cambridge: Cambridge University Press.

Marenin, Otwin. 1987. "The Anini Saga: Armed Robbery and the Reproduction of Ideology in Nigeria." *Journal of Modern African Studies* 25 (2): 259–81.

Marshall, Ruth. 2009. *Political Spiritualities: The Pentecostal Revolution in Nigeria.* Chicago: University of Chicago Press.

Marx, Karl. 2012 [1844]. *Economic and Philosophic Manuscripts of 1844.* Courier Dover Publications.

Masquelier, Adeline. 2004. "How is a Girl to Marry Without a Bed? Weddings, Wealth, and Women's Value in an Islamic Town of Niger." In *Situating Globality: African Agency in the Appropriation of Global Culture,* edited by William van Binsbergen, Rijk A. van Dijk, and Jan-Bart Gewald, 220–56. Leiden: Brill.

———. 2005. "The Scorpion's Sting: Youth, Marriage and the Struggle for Social Maturity in Niger." *Journal of the Royal Anthropological Institute* 11 (1): 59–83.

Maurer, Bill. 2006. "The Anthropology of Money." *Annual Review Anthropology* 35:15–36.

Mberu, Blessing. 2005. "Who Leaves and Who Stays? Rural Out-Migration in Nigeria." *Journal of Population Research* 22 (2): 141–61.

McCall, John. 2002. "Madness, Money, and Movies: Watching a Nigerian Popular Video with the Guidance of a Native Doctor." *Africa Today* 49 (3): 79–94.

Meagher, Kate. 2006. "Social Capital, Social Liabilities, and Political Capital: Social Networks and Informal Manufacturing in Nigeria." *African Affairs* 105 (421): 553–82.

———. 2007. "Hijacking Civil Society: The Inside Story of the Bakassi Boys Vigilante Group of South-Eastern Nigeria." *Journal of Modern African Studies* 45 (1): 89–115.

———. 2009. "The Informalization of Belonging: Igbo Informal Enterprise and National Cohesion from Below." *Africa Development* 34 (1): 31–45.

———. 2010. *Identity Economics: Social Networks and the Informal Economy in Nigeria*. Suffolk: James Currey.

———. 2014. "Smuggling Ideologies: From Criminalization to Hybrid Governance in African Clandestine Economies." *African Affairs* 113 (453): 497–517.

Meek, Charles. 1950. *Law and Authority in a Nigerian Tribe*. Oxford: Oxford University Press.

Melvin, Agunbiade. 2013. "Dating Practices and Patterns of Disclosure among In-School Adolescents in Oyo State, Nigeria." *Africa Development* 37 (3): 19–39.

Merry, Sally Engle. 2006. *Human Rights and Gender Violence: Translating International Law Into Social Justice*. Chicago: University of Chicago Press.

Meyer, Birgit. 1998. "The Power of Money: Politics, Occult Forces, and Pentecostalism in Ghana." *African Studies Review* 41 (3): 15–37.

———. 2004. "Christianity in Africa: From African Independent to Pentecostal-Charismatic Churches." *Annual Review of Anthropology* 33:447–74.

Miescher, Stephan. 2005. *Making Men in Ghana*. Bloomington: Indiana University Press.

Mojola, Sanyu. 2014a. *Love, Money, and HIV: Becoming a Modern African Woman in the Age of AIDS*. Berkeley: University of California Press.

———. 2014b. "Providing Women, Kept Men: Doing Masculinity in the Wake of the African HIV/AIDS Pandemic." *Signs* 39 (2): 341–63.

Momoh, Abubakar. 2000. "Youth Culture and Area Boys in Lagos." In *Identity Transformation and Identity Politics under Structural Adjustment in Nigeria*, edited by Attahiru Jega, 181–203. Uppsala: Nordiska Afrikainstitutet.

———. 2003. "The Political Dimension of Urban Youth Crisis: The Case of the Area Boys in Lagos." In *Security, Crime and Segregation in West African Cities since the 19th Century*, edited by Laurent Fourchard and Isaac Albert, 183–200. Paris: Karthala.

Moore, Henrietta L., and Todd Sanders, eds. 2001. *Magical Interpretations, Material Realities: Modernity, Witchcraft and the Occult in Postcolonial Africa*. London: Routledge.

Morrell, Robert. 1998. "Of Boys and Men: Masculinity and Gender in Southern African Studies." *Journal of Southern African Studies* 24 (4): 605–30.

———, ed. 2001a. *Changing Men in Southern Africa*. London: Zed Books.

———. 2001b. "The Times of Change: Men and Masculinity in South Africa." In *Changing Men in Southern Africa*, edited by Robert Morrell, 3–40. London: Zed Books.

———. 2002. "Men, Movements, and Gender Transformation in South Africa." *Journal of Men's Studies* 10 (3): 309–27.

———. 2005. "Youth, Fathers and Masculinity in South Africa Today." *Agenda* 30 (8): 84–87.

———. 2006. "Fathers, Fatherhood and Masculinity in South Africa." In *Baba: Men and Fatherhood in South Africa*, edited by Linda Richter and Robert Morrell, 13–25. Cape Town: Human Sciences Research Council Press.

Nabalamba, Alice, and Mulle Chikoko. 2011. *Aging Population Challenges in Africa*. African Development Bank.

National Bureau of Statistics. 2014. *Statistical Report on Women and Men in Nigeria, 2013*. Abuja, Nigeria.

Ngwudike, Benjamin, and Tabitha Otieno. 2012. "The Care of Aged Parents by the Igbo of Nigeria and the Gusii of Kenya." In *National Social Science Proceedings*, 176–84. Albuquerque Professional Development Conference, 2012.

Nigerian Telecommunications Commission. 2016. Industry Statistics: Subscriber Data. http://www.ncc.gov.ng/index.php?option=com_content&view=article&id=125&Itemid=73.

Njaka, Elechukwu. 1974. *Igbo Political Culture*. Evanston, IL: Northwestern University Press.

Nwagbara, Eucharia. 2007. "The Igbo of Southeast Nigeria: The Same Yesterday, Today and Tomorrow?" *Dialectical Anthropology* 31 (1–3): 99–110.

Nwaubani, Adaobi Tricia. 2009. *I Do Not Come to You by Chance*. New York: Hyperion.

Nwoye, Chinwe. 2011. "Igbo Cultural and Religious Worldview: An Insider's Perspective." *International Journal of Sociology and Anthropology* 3 (9): 304–17.

Nyerges, A. Endre. 1992. "The Ecology of Wealth-in-People: Agriculture, Settlement, and Society on the Perpetual Frontier." *American Anthropologist* 94 (4): 860–81.

Obadare, Ebenezer. 2009. "The Uses of Ridicule: Humour, 'Infrapolitics' and Civil Society in Nigeria." *African Affairs* 108 (431): 241–61.

———. 2016. *Humor, Silence, and Civil Society in Nigeria*. Rochester: University of Rochester Press.

Obiechina, Emmanuel. 1973. *An African Popular Literature: A Study of Onitsha Market Pamphlets*. Cambridge: Cambridge University Press.

Obono, Oka. 2003. "Cultural Diversity and Population Policy in Nigeria." *Population and Development Review* 29 (1): 103–11.

Ogbu, John. 1978. "African Bridewealth and Women's Status." *American Ethnologist* 5 (2): 241–62.

Ogbuagu, Stella. 1989. "The Changing Perception of Death and Burial: A Look at Nigerian Obituaries." *Anthropologica* 31:85–101.

Oha, Obododimma. 2009. "Praise Names and Power De/constructions in Contemporary Igbo Chiefship." *Culture, Language and Representation* 7 (7): 101–16.

Okemgbo, Christian, Adekunbi Omideyi, and Clifford Odimegwu. 2002. "Prevalence, Patterns and Correlates of Domestic Violence in Selected Igbo Communities of Imo State, Nigeria." *African Journal of Reproductive Health* 6 (2): 101–14.

Okome, Onookome. 2007. "Nollywood: Spectatorship, Audience and the Sites of Consumption." *Postcolonial Text* 3 (2): 1–21.

Okonkwo, C. O. 2003. "Zero Tolerance to Violence Against Women: The Way Forward." In *A Cry for Justice: The Truth about Sexual Violence Against Women in Nigeria*. Enugu, Nigeria: Women's Aid Collective.

Olawoye, Janice, Femi Omololu, Yinka Aderinto, Iyabode Adeyefa, Debo Adeyemo, and Babatunde Osotimehin. 2004. "Social Construction of Manhood in Nigeria: Implications for Male Responsibility in Reproductive Health." *African Population Studies* 19 (2): 1–20.

Olivier de Sardan, Jean-Pierre. 1999. "A Moral Economy of Corruption?" *Journal of Modern African Studies* 37 (1): 25–52.

Olutayo, Olanrewaju. 1999. "The Igbo Entrepreneur in the Political Economy of Nigeria." *African Study Monographs* 20 (3): 147–74.

Omitoogun, Wuyi. 1994. "The Area Boys of Lagos: A Study of Organized Street Violence." In *Urban Management and Urban Violence in Africa*, edited by Isaac Albert, Jinmi Adisa, Tunde Agbola, and G. Herault, 2:201–8. Ibadan, Nigeria: IFRA.

Omoruyi, Joan. 1988. "Nigerian Funeral Programs: An Unexplored Source of Information." *Africa* 58 (4): 466–69.

Onokala, Uchechi, and Adeleke Banwo. 2015. "Informal Sector in Nigeria through the Lens of Apprenticeship, Education and Unemployment." *American Advanced Research in Management* 1 (1): 13–22.

Onwumechili, Cyril Agodi. 2000. "Ìgbo énwé ezè: The Ìgbo Have No Kings." Àhịajíọkụ́ Lecture. Owerri: Ministry of Information, Culture, Youth and Sports.

Onyejekwe, Chineze. 2008. "Nigeria: The Dominance of Rape." *Journal of International Women's Studies* 10 (1): 48–61.

Onyima, Blessing. 2015. "Marriage Ceremony: The Clash between Traditional Marriage Rites and Western Marriage." *Journal of Religion and Human Relations* 1 (6): 171–80.

Oppong, Christine. 2006. "Familial Roles and Social Transformations: Older Men and Women in Sub-Saharan Africa." *Research on Aging* 28 (6): 654–68.

Oriji, John. 1981. "Oracular Trade, Okonko Secret Society and Evolution of Decentralised Authority among the Ngwa-Igbo of Southeastern Nigeria." *Ikenga: Journal of African Studies* 5 (1): 35–52.

Osotimehin, Babatunde. 1999. *Male Responsibility in Reproductive Health: Marriage, Husbandhood, and Fatherhood in Nigeria*. Ibadan, Nigeria: Social Sciences and Reproductive Health Research Network, University College Hospital.

Ottenberg, Simon. 1959. "Ibo Receptivity to Change." *Continuity and Change in African Cultures*, edited by William Bascom and Melville Herskovits, 205–23. Chicago: University of Chicago Press.

———. 1968. *Double Descent in an African Society: The Afikpo Village-Group.* Seattle: University of Washington Press.

———. 1971. *Leadership and Authority in an African Society: The Afikpo Village-Group.* Seattle: University of Washington Press.

———. 1982. "Boys' Secret Societies at Afikpo." In *African Religious Groups and Beliefs: Papers in Honor of William R. Bascom*, edited by Simon Ottenberg, 170–83. Berkeley: Folklore Institute.

———. 1988. "Oedipus, Gender and Social Solidarity: A Case Study of Male Childhood and Initiation." *Ethos* 16 (3): 326–52.

———. 1989. *Boyhood Rituals in an African Society.* Seattle: University of Washington Press.

———. 2005. *Farmers and Townspeople in a Changing Nigeria: Abakaliki During Colonial Times (1905–1960).* Ibadan, Nigeria: Spectrum Books.

Ouzgane, Lahoucine, and Robert Morrell, eds. 2005. *African Masculinities: Men in Africa from the Late Nineteenth Century to the Present.* New York: Palgrave Macmillan.

Oyediran, Kolawole, and Uche Isiugo-Abanihe. 2005. "Perceptions of Nigerian Women on Domestic Violence: Evidence from 2003 Nigeria Demographic and Health Survey." *African Journal of Reproductive Health* 9 (2): 38–53.

Oyěwùmí, Oyèrónkẹ́. 1997. *The Invention of Women: Making an African Sense of Western Gender Discourses.* Minneapolis: University of Minnesota Press.

Parikh, Shanti. 2005. "From Auntie to Disco: The Bifurcation of Risk and Pleasure in Sex Education in Uganda." In *Sex in Development: Science, Sexuality and Morality in Global Perspective*, edited by Vincanne Adams and Stacy Pigg, 125–58. Durham, NC: Duke University Press.

———. 2007. "The Political Economy of Marriage and HIV: The ABC Approach, 'Safe' Infidelity, and Managing Moral Risk in Uganda." *American Journal of Public Health* 97 (7): 1198–207.

———. 2012. "'They Arrested Me for Loving a Schoolgirl': Ethnography, HIV, and a Feminist Assessment of the Age of Consent Law as a Gender-Based Structural Intervention in Uganda." *Social Science & Medicine* 74 (11): 1774–1782.

———. 2016. *Regulating Romance: Youth Love Letters, Moral Anxiety, and Intervention in Uganda's Time of AIDS.* Nashville, TN: Vanderbilt University Press.

Peterson, Kristin. 2014. *Speculative Markets: Drug Circuits and Derivative Life in Nigeria.* Durham, NC: Duke University Press.

Pierce, Steven. 2016. *Moral Economies of Corruption: State Formation and Political Culture in Nigeria.* Durham, NC: Duke University Press.

Pierotti, Rachael. 2013. "Increasing Rejection of Intimate Partner Violence: Evidence of Global Cultural Diffusion." *American Sociological Review* 78(2): 240–65.

Polanyi, Karl. 2001 [1944]. *The Great Transformation: The Political And Economic Origins of Our Time*. Boston: Beacon Press.

Preston-Whyte, Eleanor. 1993. "Women Who Are Not Married: Fertility, 'Illegitimacy,' and the Nature of Households and Domestic Groups among Single African Women in Durban." *South African Journal of Sociology* 24 (3): 63–71.

Rebhun, Linda-Anne. 2002. *The Heart Is Unknown Country: Love in the Changing Economy of Northeast Brazil*. Stanford: Stanford University Press.

Remy, John. 1990. "Patriarchy and Fratriarchy as Forms of Androcracy." In *Men, Masculinities and Social Theory*, edited by Jeff Hearn and David Morgan, 43–54. London: Unwin Hyman.

Richter, Linda, and Robert Morrell, eds. 2006. *Baba: Men and Fatherhood in South Africa*. Cape Town: HSRC Press.

Rotimi, Adewale. 2005. "Violence in the Citadel: The Menace of Secret Cults in the Nigerian Universities." *Nordic Journal of African Studies* 14 (1): 79–98.

Routley, Laura. 2016. *Negotiating Corruption: NGOs, Governance and Hybridity in West Africa*. London: Routledge.

Serra, Renata. 2009. "Child Fostering in Africa: When Labor and Schooling Motives May Coexist." *Journal of Development Economics* 88 (1): 157–70.

Setel, Philip. 1996. "AIDS as a Paradox of Manhood and Development in Kilimanjaro, Tanzania." *Social Science & Medicine* 43 (8): 1169–1178.

———. 1999. *A Plague of Paradoxes: AIDS, Culture, and Demography in Northern Tanzania*. Chicago: University of Chicago Press.

Shelton, Austin. 1972. "The Aged and Eldership among the Igbo." In *Aging and Modernization*, edited by Donald Cowgill and Lowell Holmes, 31–49. New York: Appleton-Century-Crofts.

Shija, Terhemba. 2016. "Tragedy and Its Cathartic Effect in Tiv Praise Poetry: A Reflection on Misery and Death in the Praise Poetry of Obadiah Kehemen Orkor." *Nile Journal of English Studies* 1 (1): 67–77.

Shu'ara, Jamila. 2010. "Higher Education Statistics—Nigerian Experience in Data Collection." Paper presented at the UNESCO Institute of Statistics Workshop on Education Statistics in Anglophone Countries, Windhoek, 17th–21st October 2010.

Silverstein, Stella. 1984. "Igbo Kinship and Modern Entrepreneurial Organization: The Transportation and Spare Parts Business." *Studies in Third World Societies* 28:191–209.

Simmel, Georg. 1990 [1907]. *The Philosophy of Money*. London: Routledge.

Simpson, Anthony. 2009. *From Boys to Men in the Shadow of AIDS: Masculinities and HIV Risk in Zambia*. New York: Palgrave Macmillan.

Singerman, Diane. 2011. "The Negotiation of Waithood: The Political Economy of Delayed Marriage in Egypt." In *Arab Youth: Social Mobilisation in Times of Risk*, edited by Samir Khalaf and Roseanne Khalaf, 67–78. London: Saqi Books.

Smah, Sam. 2001. "Perception and Control of Secret Cult and Gang-Induced Difficulties for Quality Living and Learning in Nigerian Universities: The

Case Study of Universities in the Middle Belt Zone." Center for Development Studies, University of Jos, Nigeria.

Smith, Daniel Jordan. 1999. "Having People: Fertility, Family and Modernity in Igbo-Speaking Nigeria." PhD diss., Emory University.

———. 2000. "'These Girls Today Na War-O': Premarital Sexuality and Modern Identity in Southeastern Nigeria." *Africa Today* 47 (3): 99–120.

———. 2001a. "Kinship and Corruption in Contemporary Nigeria." *Ethnos* 66 (3): 344–64.

———. 2001b. "Romance, Parenthood and Gender in Modern African Society." *Ethnology* 40 (2): 129–51.

———. 2001c. "Ritual Killing, 419, and Fast Wealth: Inequality and the Popular Imagination in Southeastern Nigeria." *American Ethnologist* 28 (4): 803–26.

———. 2002. "'Man No Be Wood': Gender and Extramarital Sex in Southeastern Nigeria." *Ahfad Journal* 19 (2): 4–23.

———. 2003. "Imaging HIV/AIDS: Morality and Perceptions of Personal Risk in Nigeria." *Medical Anthropology* 22 (4): 343–72.

———. 2004a. "Contradictions in Nigeria's Fertility Transition: The Burdens and Benefits of Having People." *Population and Development Review* 30 (2): 221–38.

———. 2004b. "Youth, Sin and Sex in Nigeria: Christianity and HIV/AIDS-Related Beliefs and Behaviour among Rural-Urban Migrants." *Culture, Health & Sexuality* 6 (5): 25–37.

———. 2004c. "The Bakassi Boys: Vigilantism, Violence, and Political Imagination in Nigeria." *Cultural Anthropology* 19 (3): 429–55.

———. 2006. "Love and the Risk of HIV: Courtship, Marriage and Infidelity in Southeastern Nigeria." In *Modern Loves: The Anthropology of Romantic Courtship and Companionate Marriage*, edited by Jennifer Hirsch and Holly Wardlow, 137–53. Ann Arbor: University of Michigan Press.

———. 2007a. *A Culture of Corruption: Everyday Deception and Popular Discontent in Nigeria*. Princeton: Princeton University Press.

———. 2007b. "Modern Marriage, Men's Extramarital Sex, and HIV Risk in Southeastern Nigeria." *American Journal of Public Health* 97 (6): 997–1005.

———. 2008. "Intimacy, Infidelity, and Masculinity in Southeastern Nigeria." In *Intimacies: Love and Sex across Cultures*, edited by William Jankowiak, 224–44. New York: Columbia University Press.

———. 2009. "Managing Men, Marriage, and Modern Love: Women's Perspectives on Intimacy and Male Infidelity in Southeastern Nigeria." In *Love in Africa*, edited by Jennifer Cole and Lynn Thomas, 157–80. Chicago: University of Chicago Press.

———. 2011. "Stretched and Strained But Not Broken: Kinship in Contemporary Nigeria." In *Frontiers of Globalization: Kinship and Family Structures in Africa*, edited by Ana Marta Gonzalez, Laurie DeRose and Florence Oloo, 31–69. Trenton, NJ: Africa World Press.

———. 2014a. *AIDS Doesn't Show Its Face: Inequality, Morality, and Social Change in Nigeria*. Chicago: University of Chicago Press.

———. 2014b. "Fatherhood, Companionate Marriage, and the Contradictions of Masculinity in Nigeria." In *Globalized Fatherhood*, edited by Marcia Inhorn, Wendy Chavkin and José-Alberto Navarro, 315–35. New York: Berghahn Books.

Smock, Audrey. 1971. *Ibo Politics: The Role of Ethnic Unions in Eastern Nigeria*. Cambridge: Harvard University Press.

Sommers, Marc. 2012. *Stuck: Rwandan Youth and the Struggle for Adulthood*. Athens, GA: University of Georgia Press.

Spronk, Rachel. 2012. *Ambiguous Pleasures: Sexuality and Middle Class Self-Perceptions in Nairobi*. New York: Berghahn Books.

Stambach, Amy. 2013. *Lessons from Mount Kilimanjaro: Schooling, Community, and Gender in East Africa*. New York: Routledge.

Tambiah, Stanley. 1989. "Bridewealth and Dowry Revisited: The Position of Women in Sub-Saharan Africa and North India." *Current Anthropology* 30 (4): 413–27.

Tamuno, Tekena. 1972. "Patriotism and Statism in the Rivers State, Nigeria." *African Affairs* 71 (284): 264–81.

Taussig, Michael. 1980. *The Devil and Commodity Fetishism in South America*. Chapel Hill, NC: University of North Carolina Press.

Thornton, Arland. 2005. *Reading History Sideways: The Fallacy and Enduring Impact of the Developmental Paradigm on Family Life*. Chicago: University of Chicago Press.

Townsend, Nicholas. 2002. *The Package Deal: Marriage, Work, and Fatherhood in Men's Lives*. Philadelphia: Temple University Press.

Trager, Lillian, 2001. *Yoruba Hometowns: Community, Identity and Development in Nigeria*. Boulder, CO: Lynne Rienner.

Uchendu, Egodi. 2007. "Masculinity and Nigerian Youths." *Nordic Journal of African Studies* 16 (2): 279–97.

Uchendu, Victor C. 1964. "Kola Hospitality and Igbo Lineage Structure." *Man* 64:47–50.

———. 1965. *The Igbo of Southeast Nigeria*. New York: Holt, Rinehart and Winston.

Udvardy, Monica, and Maria Cattell. 1992. "Gender, Aging and Power in Sub-Saharan Africa: Challenges and Puzzles." *Journal of Cross-Cultural Gerontology* 7 (4): 275–88.

Ukaegbu, Alfred O. 1975. "Marriage and Fertility in East Central Nigeria: A Case Study of Ngwa Igbo Women." PhD diss., London School of Economics and Political Science (University of London).

Ukah, Asonzeh. 2008. "Roadside Pentecostalism: Religious Advertising in Nigeria and the Marketing of Charisma." *Critical Interventions* 2 (1–2): 125–41.

Ukeje, Charles. 2013. "Youths, Violence and the Collapse of Public Order in the Niger Delta of Nigeria." *Africa Development* 26 (1–2): 337–66.

Umoh, Dominic. 2013. "Prosperity Gospel and the Spirit of Capitalism: The Nigerian Story." *African Journal of Scientific Research* 12 (1): 654–67.

Van Allen, Judith. 1972. "'Sitting on a Man': Colonialism and the Lost Political Institutions of Igbo Women." *Canadian Journal of African Studies* 6 (2): 165–81.

Van Den Bersselaar, Dmitri. 2005. "Imagining Home: Migration and the Igbo Village in Colonial Nigeria." *Journal of African History* 46 (1): 51–73.

Van de Walle, Nicolas. 2007. "Meet the New Boss, Same as the Old Boss? The Evolution of Political Clientelism in Africa." In *Patrons, Clients and Policies: Patterns of Democratic Accountability and Political Competition*, edited by Herbert Kitschelt and Steven Wilkinson, 50–67. Cambridge: Cambridge University Press.

Walker, Liz. 2005. "Negotiating the Boundaries of Masculinity in Post-Apartheid South Africa." In *Men Behaving Differently*, edited by Graeme Reid and Liz Walker, 161–82. Cape Town: Double Story.

Watts, Michael. 2007. "Petro-Insurgency or Criminal Syndicate? Conflict and Violence in the Niger Delta." *Review of African Political Economy* 34 (114): 637–60.

White, Michael, Blessing Mberu, and Mark Collinson. 2008. "African Urbanization: Recent Trends and Implications." In *The New Global Frontier: Urbanization, Poverty and Environment in the 21st Century*, edited by George Martine, Gordon McGranahan, Mark Montgomery, and Rogelio Fernandez-Castilla, 301–16. London: Earthscan.

Whitehead, Ann. 1981. "'I'm Hungry Mum': The Politics of Domestic Budgeting." In *Of Marriage and the Market: Women's Subordination in International Perspective*, edited by Kate Young, Carol Wolkowitz and Roslyn McCullagh. London: CSE Books.

Whyte, Susan Reynolds, Erdmute Alber, and P. Wenzel Geissler. 2004. "Lifetimes Intertwined: African Grandparents and Grandchildren." *Africa* 74 (1): 1–5.

Whyte, Susan Reynolds, Erdmute Alber, and Sjaak van der Geest. 2008. "Generational Connections and Conflicts in Africa: An Introduction." In *Generations in Africa: Connections and Conflict*, edited by Erdmute Alber, Sjaak van der Geest and Susan Reynolds Whyte, 1–26. London: LIT Verlag.

Wolpe, Howard. 1974. *Urban Politics in Nigeria: A Study of Port Harcourt*. Berkeley: University of California Press.

Wyrod, Robert. 2008. "Between Women's Rights and Men's Authority: Masculinity and Shifting Discourses of Gender Difference in Urban Uganda." *Gender & Society* 22 (6): 799–823.

———. 2011. "Masculinity and the Persistence of AIDS Stigma." *Culture, Health & Sexuality* 13 (4): 443–56.

———. 2016. *AIDS and Masculinity in an African City: Privilege, Inequality, and Modern Manhood*. Berkeley: University of California Press.

Yan, Yunxiang. 2003. *Private Life under Socialism: Love, Intimacy, and Family Change in a Chinese Village, 1949–1999*. Stanford: Stanford University Press.

Zelizer, Viviana. 2005. *The Purchase of Intimacy*. Princeton: Princeton University Press.

Index